BRIDGE IS STILL AN EASY GAME

BRIDGE IS STILL AN EASY GAME

BY

PETER DONOVAN
and
IAIN MACLEOD

ASHFORD, BUCHAN & ENRIGHT
Southampton

First published in 1988 by Ashford Press Publishing.

This edition published in 1990 by Ashford, Buchan & Enright, an imprint of Martins Publishers Ltd, 1 Church Road, Shedfield, Hampshire SO3 2HW

British Library Cataloguing in Publication Data

Donovan, Peter
  Bridge is still an easy game.
  1. Contract Bridge – Manuals
  I. Title   II. Macleod, Iain
  III. Macleod, Iain. Bridge is an easy game
  795.41'5

  ISBN 1-85253-118-5   (Paperback)

Printed in Great Britain by Hartnolls Ltd, Bodmin, Cornwall

To the Barrels—and especially Peter, who demonstrates that there are world class performers among the ranks of casual and social players—and to Ann, who doesn't play bridge yet, but she might after reading this.

P.D.

CONTENTS

Iain Macleod was a member of the original Acol team that first captured the Gold Cup in 1937 and cut a swathe through all opposition in the pre-war years. He was rated one of the top experts in the country when he forsook Bridge for politics in 1948. A brilliant political career was cut short by his untimely death in 1970 when holding the office of Chancellor of the Exchequer.

Peter Donovan has been one of the mos prominent players and personalities of th Bridge world for many years, and his regu lar column in the *Daily Mail* has guide many players towards a greater enjoymer of the game. His views and ideas buil upon the Macleod classic, broadening th appeal of this established best-seller t every corner of the Bridge world.

FOREWORD

I am so pleased that Iain's book *Bridge is an Easy Game* is to be published again. It has not been available for about three years and recently many people have asked me where they can get a copy; these are experienced players, as well as beginners who want to learn tips from a former 'master'. Peter Donovan, a present day 'master', has up-dated the original book as well as adding much-valued advice of his own, and I am delighted that he has undertaken this task.

Iain could play a good game of Bridge by the age of nine, and it certainly stood him in good stead all his life. His memory was prodigious, he could read a page almost at a glance, and his power of concentration was remarkable—though often tiresome when, as his wife, I tried to attract his attention. These qualities, so useful at the Bridge table, helped him enormously when he was a senior minister in the government for many years. Many times he thanked his father, a doctor, for his early coaching.

As everyone knows, Bridge is a game of great skill. From auto-Bridge, family Bridge, club Bridge, tournament Bridge and perhaps international Bridge, it is enjoyed by millions of people. Long winter evenings seem much shorter if one can enjoy a rubber with friends! If a player is unable to leave his home he will be able to exercise his brain by asking a few friends to join him for a game.

As players will know, and would-be players will find out, Bridge is a game of many 'systems' and conventions. Iain and his friends were responsible for inventing the Acol system which I understand is still in use today.

My qualification for writing this foreword is nil. Iain sometimes threatened to teach me the game, but he soon realised that the price was late nights and cold dinners, and said that he preferred hot meals on time! However, I do remember with gratitude that our meagre coffers were sometimes replenished after a game of Bridge.

Peter Donovan is celebrating twenty-five years of writing a daily Bridge column for the *Daily Mail*; he has been asked by so many persuasive readers to put his advice in a more concise form that he had the clever idea of this book; luckily he writes in the same style as Iain—informative but easy to read. I am sure it will be a 'must' for every present and future Bridge player because he will prove that *Bridge is Still an Easy Game*.

I wish it great success.

Macleod of Borve

CHAPTER I

WHO SHOULD READ THE BOOK

WHEN my publisher asked how many first edition copies she should print, I answered unhesitatingly "Forty thousand—in hardback only—as a special edition." It seemed a reasonably conservative estimate that one in every hundred players would want to buy it, yet this figure was considered grossly excessive in the light of average sales of Bridge books, which rarely exceed 5,000. I was confronted by one of the most difficult marketing forecasts I've ever had to make—pitting my conviction about the massive demand for a book with simple, positive doctrines against the pessimism of the publishing world.

Friends around the country tell me that their copies of *Bridge is an Easy Game* disappeared mysteriously from their bookshelves ages ago, so for starters, we'll need a few hundred, perhaps a few thousand replacement copies. Then, there are the thousands of disciples of the Macleod doctrine who still model their game on his philosophies—this book will be a useful update on the sensible modifications to Acol which are now in popular use, especially for those who have taken up playing social duplicate—or even serious competition. The younger generation and those who have learnt Bridge in the last decade probably haven't heard of *Bridge is an Easy Game* and almost certainly haven't read it—they ought to, if only to find out how much their understanding differs from our Acol theory (putting it diplomatically)! That adds up to a 40,000 sell-out already, before touching on those who have been largely responsible for the inspiration of this book and to whom it is partly dedicated—my *Daily Mail* readers, my partners, and Bridge teachers everywhere.

For many years, I've received hundreds of requests for the newspaper articles to be published in book form; this goes a little bit further, for it gives the complete framework on which *Daily Mail* Bridge is based. The game has so many added

1

dimensions of fun and skill, to be enjoyed once one has reached a certain level of competence. So one of my greatest satisfactions has been in helping others to attain that competence—not without considerable frustration at times! During the past forty years, I've had over twelve hundred partners from over twenty-three countries; survivors of this ordeal must read this book—in case we play again!

For many years, I've been critical of the general approach to Bridge teaching—though not of the teachers themselves, who, by and large, give excellent value for money in terms of hours spent on the job. Every teacher I know makes a conscientious effort to make his or her students proficient to hold their own at the table. So why do beginners emerge at the end of tuition with pages of bidding sequences, but no understanding of the finesses, end-plays, suit preference signals, or even squeezes? By far the most important step in Bridge is becoming familiar with the count and play of the cards—both in attack and defence. Bidding is only the means to an end, and, of course, it's the greatest potential source of dispute and misunderstanding. It's the first phase of the game, but it shouldn't be the first phase of teaching—babies learn to walk before they learn to talk. Teaching time is best spent in demonstrating card logic, judgment and common-sense, but admittedly, this isn't always easy with so many tempting and tangible bidding theories to discuss at the same time.

This is where books play such a valuable role in teaching, the theory can be well learnt by students before they attend practical instruction, and in particular, this book sets out the simple and basic principles of Acol bidding in an emphatic and most readable manner. Even though I've said that bidding is of secondary importance to play, we have still had to devote more than twice as many chapters to the subject—which will save many hours of teaching time. Every beginner should read *Bridge is Still an Easy Game* and I hope that all teachers will find it a great boost to their efforts because it contains nothing which is logically controversial or at variance with their Acol doctrine.

CHAPTER II

HOW I DISCOVERED BRIDGE

As a small boy during the last War, I was allowed to play in the local weekly Whist Drives in our tiny North Yorkshire village hall. I vividly remember my frustration at holding five or six cards in the suits which had been trumps on the previous deal, and wishing that there might be some fairer way of determining what trumps should be. As my partner never seemed to hold many of the chosen trump suit either, we didn't do very well but I'm conscious of developing a system of card signals so that we learnt not to miss taking all our available tricks outside of trumps.

I was obsessive about cards, and would spend many hours in memorising deals, working out different lines of play—and above all, trying to find a means of selecting trumps other than by a cut of the cards. My poor maternal grandmother, who had to look after me during the holidays, loved to play Patience on her own, but she got little respite from being a guinea pig—and she got no sympathy for refusing to play with me on Sundays, because she was a Methodist.

By the age of ten, I'd cracked the problem of choosing which suit would be trumps, through the introduction of a bidding auction among the players. I thought I'd invented a new game. Then, one day, someone told me that my paternal grandmother in Sunderland played a lot of Whist with bidding—it was called auction Bridge. In the wilds of Yorkshire, and in the wartime blackout, it was understandable that I'd been kept in the dark about such a vital piece of information, although it was unpalatable to be told that this was a game for grown-ups, and not suitable for children!

I abandoned Whist and Pelmanism immediately, and even gave up fortifying our back garden against Hitler's invasion, all in the quest to watch this new game in action. Grandma's Bridge tea-parties were apparently highly rated on the social calendar in Sunderland, but, as I discovered many years later, this popularity had been seriously threatend by my arrival as a "kibitzer", I wanted the ladies to try using my system (I think it was Acol!), and it obviously didn't dawn on me that I was becoming insufferable, when Grandpa was told to take me for a walk to the toy shop—about two miles away. (I owned a very large collection of unused Dinky toys).

By the time I went to school in Malvern, I knew I could play Bridge efficiently, although I'd still not had an opportunity to do so. To my surprise and delight two of my contemporaries were interested in the game; they were both mathematicians and major scholars, so the odds in brain-power were stacked against me. We soon taught a few others to make up a four, and I've got fond memories of the many fun sessions we enjoyed. John and Brian were responsible for making me aware of the statistical elements of Bridge; they also convinced me that you don't have to be a statistician to be a good Bridge player!

In Sandhurst and the Army, I always seemed to find a reasonable Bridge school without much difficulty, and I came to realise that the game I once thought I had invented was considered to be one of the social attributes of any eligible bachelor before the War—together with golf, dancing and after-dinner speaking. The Army is a good training ground for keen gambling and, when I returned to civilian life and the bright lights of London, I was well-equipped to play profitably in the high-stake games at Crockfords and the Hamilton—household names, which sadly no longer exist for Bridge .

Whilst it's fun winning lots of money playing a game one loves, high-stake Bridge has never given me the full flavour of enjoyment, which this fascinating pastime has to offer. I've always preferred playing all night "for love" with a trio I liked, or competing for pride of place against other pairs in tournaments. My overwhelming satisfaction comes from being able to help younger and less experienced players to improve their game, and I was given the opportunity to do this when I joined the *Daily Mail* in 1960. Bridge for schools and evening classes, daily Acol tips for the fireside player, the start of a consensus on bidding theory in Britain—all became possible.

CHAPTER III

HOW YOU CAN DISCOVER BRIDGE

YOU can learn to play Bridge in less than six weeks—a shorter period than it would take you to learn a foreign language—and much more useful to you. The analogy with language is most appropriate, for the bidding phase of Bridge is nothing more than a dialogue between you and your partner to exchange information about the cards you hold. If you choose the wrong word in conversation, you'd be misunderstood; just so in Bridge when you choose the wrong bid to best describe your hand, you'll be misunderstood.

The bidding auction, which is used to determine the trump suit and the final contract, is made up of a series of bids between your side and the opponents. Your objective is to describe your hand as accurately as possible, at the same time as understanding the description your partner gives you of his hand, to reach your optimum final contract. This of course is when you have the values of the cards on your side; when the opponents have them, it's equally important to understand their bidding, so that you can later defend against them effectively. Sometimes both sides have values, and you start competing to win the auction; this is an exciting time when you particularly need to have good understanding and communications with your partner, and it also calls on one of the attributes you need to be a good player—sound judgment.

The various methods and styles of bidding are called systems (though I'd prefer to call them languages and dialects). The system popularly used in England—or the English language of bidding—is called Acol; it could equally have been called Virol, Schipol or Glucol, except that it was originally composed in Acol Road, North London. Acol is the natural common-sense approach to bidding based on logic. So, if you're logical, you'll have no problem in learning and understanding Acol quickly.

People keep saying that Bridge is a difficult game to learn—

and so it is, if you compare it with other games such as Snap or Knock-Out Whist. But we all know that to be proficient at anything one needs to have interest, aptitude and, above all, time to practise. If you've got those ingredients, the learning process will be simple, painless and absorbing. You may never be able to become a great player, but few players do become great, and, for the highest levels of achievement, you'll need considerable amounts of judgment, psychology, stamina, mental agility, statistical logic and experience. But you'll get by quite adequately and have a lot of fun with just an average amount of common-sense and a reasonable memory.

For those who haven't yet taken up the game, here's the best tip you'll ever get for easy learning. Before you even think of taking lessons or reading books (except, of course, finishing this one), sit and watch the game being played for as long as you can bear it (in Bridge parlance we call this "kibitzing"). Try to watch fairly good players, and try to watch with an enquiring mind. You'll discover first of all whether the game is going to interest you, and if it does, you'll find subconsciously that you've started to grasp the fundamentals much quicker than if someone was lecturing at you. If you kibitz for often and long enough you'll probably find that you don't need lessons, because you've taught yourself from the model, and all you need is practice—so cut in quick! Another benefit of this approach is that you'll also be starting to develop your own style from seeing what works and what doesn't. But remember, you need to have an enquiring mind to achieve the desired result. I had a student recently who had never seen Bridge played before; he kibitzed me during two and a half duplicate competitions (eight hours) after which his urge to play was irresistible, and he insisted on taking part in the following week's competition; he played, and finished with an above average score—admittedly he was a maths graduate.

Once you've got the flavour of the game—and like it—try to find three other players who are slightly better than you, or even much better, if they will be forbearing. Then play as much as you can over a concentrated period of time. You'll learn and improve much more if you play every day for a week than, say, once a week for two months. I know that this isn't practical for most people, but the object is to get the basics so well bedded-in that they become second nature to you (like the grammar of a

6

new language). After that, you can tuck them away in a cupboard to be brought out on a rainy day.

Whenever possible, try to get your indoctrination and practice playing rubber Bridge before you get lured into duplicate. This may prove difficult, because most Bridge clubs are now pre-occupied with competitions, and the temptation to start competing is considerable. Try to avoid this temptation by inviting friends home out of harm's way. I say this because it's important that you should feel uninhibited about making mistakes, experimenting, trial and error, developing your flair, gaining confidence, having post-mortems, etc. You can do all these things at rubber Bridge, whereas in duplicate competition you're under pressure to "do the right thing" on each hand to avoid having a bad score. You're unlikely to become a good player without a rubber Bridge foundation, and whenever I come across a successful tournament player who claims never to have played rubber Bridge, I tell him he would be even more successful if he had. It's the difference between being a free-range hen and a battery-hatched chick!

If you feel you are the sort of person who learns better from being taught rather than self-tuition, there are now a plethora of facilities available. First of all, most Evening Institutes in Britain have Bridge included in their curricula; they're nearly always over-subscribed, which gives some measure of the game's growing popularity. Secondly, some Bridge clubs run classes and often throw in a year's free membership as a bonus for attending. And thirdly, there are individual Bridge teachers dotted all over the place, who are more than happy to give individual or group tuition. When you decide that tuition will be a good idea, either from scratch, or after a bit of kibitzing, there are three points you must bear in mind (apart from the nominal cost):

(1) A good teacher doesn't have to be, and may not be a good player, and vice versa. If you can't find the perfect combination, opt for the good teacher.

(2) Courses are run for different levels of ability and experience: beginners, intermediate, advanced. Be sure the subject matter is relevant to your needs, or you'll be wasting your time—and money.

(3) Some teachers have themselves played little or no rubber Bridge and have been weaned on duplicate alone. There's a

distinct difference in the bidding theory and style between the two forms of Bridge, which is dealt with more fully later on. So check your tutor's pedigree—not literally, of course!

I'm sure that teachers would welcome situations where all their students arrived with a basic awareness of Bridge, its procedures, terminologies and objectives. So I stress again the importance of trying to learn the game as far as possible from watching others play. Perhaps the most important reason for doing this is to get the true perspective of bidding in relation to the game as a whole. In the 'classroom' the bidding element of Bridge occupies a vastly disproportionate amount of time to its importance in the early stages of learning to play the game—indeed, over half this book is devoted to bidding. This is understandable, and perhaps inevitable, for there are a myriad of sequences, permutations and conventions which can be discussed and easily illustrated for the many millions of possible distributions of the cards.

However, at the end of the day, there's little point in knowing how to reach the best contract if you don't know how to play the cards to make it. In many cases, the recommended contract for a beginner playing the hand would be at least one level lower than for an expert. Unnecessarily complex bidding theory has been the stumbling block and deterrent for many would-be "bridgeurs", although I have to admit that I've come across some who find the modern science of bidding so irresistibly fascinating that the rest of the game doesn't matter. My philosophy of bidding is that it should be as direct and simple as possible to achieve the optimum result. This philosophy is set out much more forcibly in the ensuing chapters, however, were I to allocate a hundred hours of tuition and practice on the three main elements of Bridge, my breakdown would be: declarer play, 40; defence, 40; bidding, 20.

There are many reasons why it's a good thing to learn Bridge, but, by far and away the most important is that it's the best antidote to loneliness which has ever been invented. Nearly everyone has some period of life when they're unexpectedly on their own without immediate and necessary occupation: most commonly this applies to us in old age, when a marriage partner dies or we can no longer pursue outdoor sports; but there are many other situations, such as protracted and demoralising unemployment, isolation from friends and family through hospitalisation, work assignment—or even prison, when two packs of cards and a knowledge of Bridge can make a world of difference to sanity, tolerance and contentment. On the happier side, the social benefits of Bridge have long been recognised—the traditional afternoon hen parties for wives while husbands are away, special interest cruises and holidays, and our expectation of living longer and retiring earlier.

Bridge is certainly a game which is easier to learn when one is young and the brain cells are still functioning actively; for there's a fair amount to remember and develop in order to become really proficient. Don't let this put you off just because you're the wrong side of forty; most of us "oldies" will admit that one reaches a peak of individual competence after sufficient practice, and then remains static until the decline sets in with the fading memory. Many people have played several times a week for donkey's years without getting any better; in these cases, the declining memory is usually compensated for by instinct and vast experience. If you happen to be one of those who wants to learn late in life, or when you feel you've lost the ability to grasp and retain new ideas, let me give you a word of caution—be careful whom you get to teach you and what you're taught. You require the absolute basics, with no frills, for several months. For some, this book will help you decide whether Bridge is for you; if you can understand and identify with the following chapters, you're halfway there!

Britain has been slow in recognising the therapeutic and recreational merit of Bridge, although schools have certainly relaxed their disapproving attitude towards card games in the classroom. Since we started our *Daily Mail* National Schools' Competition over twenty years ago, there's been a steady growth of School Bridge Clubs, and many cases where it has been taught as a subject in the Sixth Form after exams. This is still no comparison with the Swedish system, where magistrates give probationary sentences to juvenile first offenders, provided they join either a Tennis or Bridge Club—no wonder we can't win the Davis Cup!

CHAPTER IV

ABOUT THE MASTERPIECE

IAIN Macleod and I were contemporaries for a short time on the *Daily Mail* in the early 'sixties, although unfortunately I never played with or against him. When I read his book I recall that it was the first one with which I was in total accord—and that record still stands. Not surprisingly therefore, I've been preaching our joint maxims every day in the *Daily Mail* for nearly a quarter of a century. But obviously not enough players read the *Daily Mail*, for I come across widespread abortions of the basic play and bidding principles every time I visit a local or national event.

The theme of my first book inevitably had to concentrate on emphasising that Bridge is not a difficult game to play—indeed, it's easy when one can understand and follow the principles, rather than merely learn a few conventions and bidding sequences parrot fashion. Iain had already written *Bridge is an Easy Game* thirty years ago, so why should I try to re-invent the wheel? His book was hailed instantly as a classic, and Somerset Maugham even put it on his shortlist of Books of the Year. A prominent literary critic wrote at the time: "This book is a classic; it's eminently readable and could become the standard textbook for the future."

Iain was one of the pioneers of the Acol system so there can be no question about his credentials or qualifications on its theory. The fact that he was able to write about it in such a compelling and entertaining manner makes his work a masterpiece and the classic of Bridge literature. Tens of thousands of players used it as their "bible" during the 'sixties and 'seventies, and it should have been adopted as a standard textbook for Bridge. After all these years have elapsed, it's still the most powerful and effective guide to learning how to play Bridge properly which has ever been written in Britain. Alas, the original has long been out of print, so I've re-produced the text, completely unabridged, in the following chapters. All the principles and philosophies which you'll read about bidding and playing correctly will never change, and one of the great strengths of Iain's text is that he explains the logic of why you should not make certain bids and plays. This is in keeping with my own basic philosophy, that it's not always possible to make the best bid or play, but it's quite easy to avoid making the wrong one. If both players in a partnership adopt this philosophy, they'll usually win!

Card-play techniques at Bridge remain universally standard, but there are several different methods of bidding the cards, which fall under two main headings: artificial and natural. The artificial method is strictly for the "scientist", who enjoys spending hours memorising complex sequences with his partner in a quest to achieve the ultimate precision in describing his cards— and perhaps, also, to bamboozle his opponents. Such a method has no Bridge merit outside of competitions; even then, it's extremely vulnerable to sabotage by competent opponents, and requires much more practice with a regular partner.

For the "artists", "sportsmen", "socialites" and "rabbits" who make up over 90 per cent of the Bridge-playing world, a natural method is the sensible option. Of the natural methods, Acol is generally acknowledged to be the best. Dozens of books have been written on the subject by different authors, a variety of new theories and philosophies have been expressed over the years. If you've read any of these, you'd be excused for wondering just what to believe—for there's a wide divergence of opinion among the "experts"—and they're probably all right; for one of the strengths of Acol is its flexibility, which makes it easily adaptable to individual styles and preferences. However, the Acol system has stood the test of time for over fifty years with very little modification. What change there has been is largely the result of the "scientists" adapting it to their needs for the modern tournament game. I'm not even going to mention some of the dreadful practices which have emerged under the name of Acol in recent years. Suffice to say that bidding systems aren't like ladies' hemlines—they don't have to be altered each year to keep pace with fashion trends. That doesn't mean that systems can't be modified for improvement, but the acid test for a change is that it should have unequivocal Bridge merit for the game as a whole.

In the later chapters, I'll introduce a few ideas which meet this criterion; they're a development of Macleod's theories, though not specifically covered by him in detail.

CHAPTER V

BRIDGE CONVENTIONS

THE Portland Club, the M.C.C. of Bridge, play no conventions at all. If everyone else would agree to do the same, Bridge no doubt would be more fun. It isn't of the slightest importance but there are after all about one million million million million million different ways in which fifty-two cards can be dealt, and it is asking rather a lot to expect two players to reach reasonable contracts without at least some understanding of what their bids are to mean. In any case, even if you started with no conventions you would sooner or later attach different meanings to the bids. When Colonel X bids one No Trump you will discover it means something quite different from Mrs. Z's bid, and you will reply accordingly. Contract Bridge is little more than fifty years old, and in that time millions of words have been written on Bridge systems and Bridge conventions. And yet little new has been discovered since 1936, and while Contract lasts I doubt if there will be any dramatic change. Dozens of conventions have been invented, tested in play and discarded. In Culbertson's heyday in the early 'thirties each year brought a new version of the Culbertson system, for exactly the same reason as Christian Dior brings out yearly or twice yearly his new fashions. Culbertson and Dior are both salesmen and their wares have to be new to sell. There are still new systems and new conventions brought out every year, but bidding remains more or less as it was when by 1936 the Four Aces in America and the Acol players here had finished grafting their ideas on to the Approach Forcing foundation. I am not, therefore, going to try and teach you a new system of bidding. I am trying to teach you Bridge.

I shall use the framework of what is called the Acol system. Partly because it is the system I helped to build: partly because it is the system that most expert players in this country use. It is less of a system than an approach to Bridge. It is infinitely flexible, and a hopeless system for the unimaginative. It looks deceptively easy. It isn't as easy to master as you may think. But it can be very rewarding.

HOW ACOL WAS BORN

Somewhere in Hampstead is an Acol Road. Somewhere in that road used to be, perhaps still is, an Acol Bridge Club. I have never been there. But it was there, nearly twenty years ago that Jack Marx and the late S.J. Simon began to talk over their Bridge theories. Bridge in this country was still dominated by one or two West End Clubs. Bidding was in its infancy, and the British teams were regularly massacred by American sides. American bidding, guided by the Culbertsons, was much more scientific than our casual and direct methods. Yet if you look back now to the published hands of those early matches, you will find over and over again (even from the Americans) bidding which looks inconceivable to the eyes of today.

Look, for example, at this hand from the 1933 match Culbertson's American team against England:

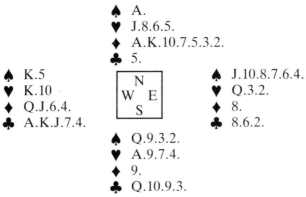

Bidding:

West (Culbertson)	North (Beasley)	East (Lightner)	South (Sir Guy Domville)
1♣	2♦	—	2NT
—	3NT	—	—
Dble	4♦	—	4NT
Dble	—	—	—

14

West	North	East	South
(Morris)	(Mrs. Culbertson)	(Tabbush)	(Gottlieb)
1♣	Dble	—	—

In Room 1 Ely Culbertson opened his fourth best Club, then covered the Nine of Diamonds and finally in response to some obscure signal from Lightner threw his King of Spades. Sir Guy landed his incredible contract, but you might care to work out what happens to it if the King of Clubs is opened and a Spade follows. In the other room a bad double and a bad pass and poor defence gave West his contract.

The real criticism of this bidding is that it is hopelessly illogical. Logic is the first thing to learn in good Bridge.

Marx and Simon saw then that the Culbertson system was far superior to the English methods. They saw too, that the Culbertson system was imperfect: far too wide a range for the bidding at the level of one: the game forcing two bid sound in principle but wasteful in its application: the No Trump bidding was hopelessly rigid: too many bids were used to achieve the simplest results. So gradually their ideas developed and began to make headway. In the years 1932-5 two notable teams were pre-eminent in duplicate bridge in this country. One captained by Harry Ingram, whose chief lieutenant was S. E. Hughes, devastated their opponents with their psychic bidding. The other— the first outstanding team in this country—captained by Richard Lederer included another player of the highest class in Kosky. The Ingram team played a One Club system, the Lederer side the Lederer Two Clubs which fought a long losing battle later with Acol. Both systems were inexact and only the brilliance of the players brought tournament success. For the 1935-6 season Simon and Marx joined forces with Harrison Gray, then, as were they, almost unknown. I had come down from Cambridge in the summer of 1935 and in October gone to work in the City. I met Jack Marx and played in a duplicate pairs with him. So I became the fourth member. Acol was still only a series of ideas unproven in play, unwritten in any Bridge journal. We hammered out our theories in endless sessions night after night into the small hours. Thousands of scraps of paper were smothered with scrawled Bridge hands. The next year we won the main trophy at every Bridge Congress, and all the national team-of-four events for which we entered. We won the Gold Cup—Bridge's Blue Riband, but our most important victory was in the Brighton Invitation Teams of Four. Incidentally, we nearly weren't invited at all to take part in this event which was played early in the season. The entry of eight teams was perhaps the strongest there has ever been in an English tournament. Colonel Beasley's team represented the old school, Lederer and Ingram were the leaders at the moment, Dodds and Konstam and ourselves were newcomers. We won by an overwhelming margin. Acol had arrived.

SINCE 1936

Afterwards, we never again played a full season as a team. We still entered various events and usually we won. In differing combinations, we continued to win more than our share of teams-of-four, pairs, and individual tournaments. But we could no longer count on victory. Not because we were playing any worse, but because our tremendous bidding margin of superiority had narrowed. In 1936, as the first team to discover and apply modern bidding principles, we had no competition. Later we had to work for our victories. Before the war, Acol was still limited to London and a few provincial disciples, mostly in Yorkshire. But already by 1939 more than half the players in the Invitation Masters Individual were Acol players. That our ideas did not spread faster was our own fault, for a combination of laziness and shortsightedness prevented us from publishing our system. Terence Reese, perhaps the clearest analyst in Bridge, joined our circle after the first triumphant year and with Cohen wrote a book on the Acol system. None of the original team ever wrote on Acol although we have all been Bridge journalists and S. J. Simon has written excellent and entertaining books on Bridge.

The war, of course, scattered Bridge players and ended Bridge. But by 1947 Harrison Gray's name was back on the Gold Cup as captain of a team based on his winning pre-war side with Boris Schapiro and Neil Furse added. From then Acol has retained its mastery. For three years running, at Copenhagen in 1948, at Paris in 1949, at Brighton in 1950, Great Britain won the European Championship. Each year Harrison Gray had been captain. For the first year, until his sudden death took one of the finest and certainly the most colourful player from Bridge, S. J. Simon was in the team. In 1950 Jack Marx came out of post-war retirement to partner Gray. I was selected for the Copenhagen team, but politics were claiming all my time and I had to decline. I have not played tournament Bridge since. All these teams either played Acol or a system closely cousin to it. In 1949 Acol had its greatest triumph. A Crockford's Club team played Acol in a 100-board match against the American Champions and won easily by 2,960 points. We had come a long way since 1936. In that time in England Acol teams had probably won more important tournaments than all other sytems put together.

The same Americans, beaten unquestionably on bidding technique in 1949 were in the winning team of the World Championship at Bermuda in 1950. Unfortunately Terence Reese, Boris Schapiro and Adam Meredith, certainly three out of the best five players in this country, did not go to Bermuda. Perhaps a future match will show where the supremacy lies. If Britain plays her best Acol players I do not doubt the result.

I am not seeking to persuade you to change your system. If your own suits you and it brings results that satisfy you, then by all means stick to it. The Bridge principles I shall try and teach you hold good whatever system you play. I have printed at Appendix "A" a summary of the Acol system. If the story of how a system conceived in a 3*d.*-a-hundred game in Hampstead, evolved by trial and error and scrap-paper arguments, and finally tested in match play modernized Contract Bridge and became the accepted "master" system in this country intrigues you, then read the summary. If the summary appeals to you, learn it and play it. One word of warning. Don't try to play Acol on the strength of having read the summary. It isn't a system you can learn by rote. Wait till you—and your partner—have read this book, and then try. Perhaps I'll fail to show you what the Acol approach to Bridge means. You will know when you have read.

Acol then will colour this book. But only this chapter is really about Acol. The book is about Bridge.

CHAPTER VI

THE OPENING SUIT BID OF ONE

THIS is the foundation of Bridge. Very rarely is it possible later to retrieve the consequences of a thoroughly bad opening bid. Partner is always entitled to assume when you open with one of a suit:

(a) That your hand is not good enough for a bid of two.

(b) That it is too good to pass.

(c) That the suit you name will normally be your best suit.

(d) That your hand is not one that should be opened with a pre-emptive (or-shut out) bid.

If your bid ignores any one of these criteria it may prove disastrous. The first thing to decide is the upper and lower limits of the bid: where the decision to open with a bid of one shades into the decision on one hand to bid two, on the other to pass. These limits cannot be precisely defined, and the deciding factor must always be one of personal judgment. A dozen influences may sway you: the state of the rubber or the match: the calibre of your partner and opponents: who is to play the hand. Many systems pretend to be able to count winners or losers at suit contracts and present formulae for each hand and situation. They are of little value to the player who has passed the beginners' stage. Remember then, when you read these chapters on bidding, that one can only be dogmatic about clear-cut situations. In the border country you must judge. As your judgment develops, so will your strength as a player. Remember too, that in good Bridge there is no such thing as "never" or "always". To every rule exceptions can be found, and yet I will use the words frequently. Until you become, if you are not there already, the best player in your circle or, if you play duplicate, until you begin consistently to win tournaments, take them literally. Later read them as "practically never" or "almost always" and begin to allow yourself liberties with your bidding. Finally, you will reach the stage when assessing a hand is automatic to you. When you need neither worry nor calculate nor read Bridge books. If you reach that stage, you will be a master player. There are only about twenty in the whole of Britain. But there are thousands of good players, and that standard at least is well within your grasp.

THE UPPER AND LOWER LIMIT

The upper limit presents no difficulty. Any hand on which you must force to game cannot be opened with a bid of one. Your bid is Two Clubs (Acol) or Two of your suit (Culbertson). If you play a Two-Club system you have also the opening bids of Two Diamonds or Two of a major suit. This is the best rule. If there is a probable game, even if partner cannot reply to a bid of one, then you must open with a stronger bid. For example you dare not open with One Spade on:

♠ A.K.Q.x.x.x.
♥ Q.J.x.x.x.
♦ none.
♣ K.Q.

Any of these "useless" dummys will probably produce a game:

(a)	(b)	(c)
♠ x.x.x.	♠ J.x.	♠ x.
♥ K.x.	♥ 10.x.x.x.	♥ K.x.x.x.
♦ x.x.x.x.	♦ x.x.x.	♦ x.x.x.x.x.x.
♣ x.x.x.x.	♣ x.x.x.x.	♣ x.x.x.

But partner would surely pass all these hands. It follows, therefore, that your hand is too good. It is not your honour strength, but your potential playing strength that makes your hand too strong. Apply the same principle to this hand—far stronger in high cards:

(d)   ♠ A.K.x.x.
       ♥ A.K.x.
       ♦ A.x.x.
       ♣ x.x.x.

19

Five quick tricks! And yet not a chance of a game unless partner can respond to your opening bid. To have a reasonable chance of 3 N–T you need something like this in dummy:

(e)   ♠   Q.x.x.
        ♥   x.x.x.
        ♦   J.10.9.x.
        ♣   K.Q.x.

Even so your chances are not very bright, and with this hand — or even a worse one — partner will clearly not pass your opening bid. So a one bid it is.

The more difficult problems concern the lower limit. Here you have to take a decision that will affect the whole of your bidding. Are you going to open "light"? The average hand contains, of course, one Ace, one King and so on. To open the bidding, which contracts to make at least seven tricks out of thirteen, you should be above average — say an extra King. Hence the two and a half trick shibboleth which has done more than anything else to encourage bad bidding and bad Bridge. If you have been accustomed to assess your hands on such a basis whether you use honour tricks or quick tricks, then abandon it now. Reject it, even if you are a beginner. For a method based on it will never never (and this time I mean "never") make you anything but a rabbit. The reason, of course, is exactly the same as led us to open one Spade on:

(f)   ♠   A.K.x.x.
        ♥   A.K.x.
        ♦   x.x.x.
        ♣   A.x.x.

but reject:

(g)   ♠   A.K.Q.x.x.x.
        ♥   Q.J.x.x.x.
        ♦   none
        ♣   K.Q.

as too good even though it is weaker in high cards. If then we utterly reject any exact minimum standard for our opening bid it does not follow that we cannot offer guidance which will cover about 90 per cent. of the hands on which a problem arises. Let us use the Milton Work count, not to influence our decisions – although we'll use it later for No Trump bidding – but to describe the hands. The count is:

Ace 4
King 3
Queen 2
Jack 1

Here then, remembering what I have said about "never", are the rules:

(1) Never pass a hand with fourteen points.
(2) Always bid on thirteen, unless your hand is 4–3–3–3 and you are vulnerable. A pass here is optional.
(3) Always bid on twelve if you have a fair five-card suit.
(4) Always bid on eleven and usually on ten if you have one six-card or two five-card suits.
(5) Never bid on less than ten unless your hand is a freak.

Soon you will be able to discard these "rules" which are no more than a guide until you begin to reach the first class. One more rule and this one applies whatever your standard:

(6) When in doubt, bid.

The tendency for masters is to open lighter and lighter. This is partly on the principle that attack is the best form of defence, and partly because to bid on the first round is both cheaper and safer than to bid on the second. Of course if your high card strength has been shaded, your playing strength must compensate. Very rarely do expert players open lightly without the protection of a six-card suit. The light opening bid is particularly practised by English experts, and has proved a most powerful weapon against the more rigid systems played by European teams. For example, in the 1950 European Championship, these hands were all opened by the English team where their opposite numbers in the other room passed. Each of the hands had an excellent result for England:

(h) ♠ A.x.x.x.x.(Leslie Dodds: 1 ♠)
♥ 10.x.
♦ x.
♣ A.Q.x.x.x.

21

(i)   ♠ A.Q.x.x.
     ♥ 10.x.x.x.x.(Gardener: 1 ♥)
     ♦ A.J.x.
     ♣ x.

(j)   ♠ K.x.x.x.x.x.(Kenneth Konstam: 1 ♠)
     ♥ A.10.x.x
     ♦ none.
     ♣ Q.x.x.

(k)   ♠ Q.x.x.
     ♥ none.
     ♦ A.Q.x.x.
     ♣ Q.x.x.x.x.x.(Harrison Gray: 1♣)

(l)   ♠ A.J.10.x.x.x.(Gardener: 1 ♠)
     ♥ Q.x.x.
     ♦ Q.
     ♣ J.x.x

The first two hands show the good players normal shading of the usual requirements. The last three illustrate the protection and power of the six-card suit. Not all these bids qualify under the rules I have given you, and yet no expert player should hesitate to make them. Some Acol experts would quarrel with Dodds' bid of One Spade, arguing that One Club is preferable. So it is, if you can guarantee that the opponents will not bid. As it is the pre-emptive nature of the Spade suit may shut out an overbid by an opponent in a red suit.

These rules, then, will tell you, if you need telling, when to bid. What to bid is rather easier.

WHAT TO BID

First of all, let's slay a couple of dragons: the prepared Club bid, and the reverse. For both of these bids in certain very rare circumstances there is a case to be made. Unfortunately those who use them persist in bidding them on hands which are utterly unsuitable. Nearly all Bridge players would be better players if they never used either.

The prepared Club (sometimes but much more rarely the

Diamond suit is used) is a bid of a three-card minor suit. It is a lineal descendant of the early discredited One Club systems. The theory is that on hands which have no safe re-bid and are unsuitable for a bid of one No Trump, you should open one Club so that partner can respond at the one level and you can find an early fit. It follows that the higher you put your requirements for No Trumps the more you will have to fall back on the prepared Club. If, therefore, you are playing the weak non-vulnerable No Trump (thirteen to fifteen points) you need never non-vulnerable use a prepared Club bid at all. The prepared Club is normally used only on the 4–3–3–3 distribution. Your hand can then either open with a No Trump bid — assuming you don't like your four-card suit — or you should pass. Ely Culbertson in his latest *Contract Bridge Complete* gives a bid of one Diamond as correct in any position on:

(*m*) ♠ A.x.x.x.
♥ K.J.x.
♦ A.J.x.
♣ J.x.x.

but non-vulnerable this is an ideal Acol No Trump bid. It is because Culbertson insists on rigid No Trump requirements not because he likes the bid of one Diamond, that such an absurd bid has to be recommended.

When vulnerable it is dangerous to have a No Trump minimum under sixteen points. We have decided that no hand with fourteen points can be passed. Therefore in this small range of hands fourteen to sixteen points, vulnerable, and with no biddable suit you are sometimes correct to open the prepared Club. For example on:

(*n*) ♠ A.K.x.
♥ x.x.x.x.
♦ K.x.x.
♣ A.x.x.

I would, vulnerable, bid one Club. But you must be clear that it is only to be used as a last resource. Hunt for any other bid first: scale your four-card suit requirements as low as you feel you dare: try and make a No Trump out of it if you can. Only if all these fail open with a prepared bid. Its disadvantages are manifest:

(1) You are not bidding your longest suit. So partner can never know if he dare sacrifice against an opponent's bid, say of four Spades. Disaster may follow five Clubs if you have J.x.x.

(2) If you have to defend against a No Trump contract your partner will probably lead Clubs, and this may well be fatal. Countless times a light three No Trump bid has got home because the partner of the Club bidder has opened the suit.

(3) If you make a habit of the prepared Club bid partner never knows whether you have the suit or not.

(4) The bid of one Club is the easiest of all for your opponents to overbid.

Harrison Gray and other leading Bridge journalists have stamped for years on the prepared Club bid. It is a hardy weed and it still survives. An example of the harm it can do may help to convince you. The hand comes from rubber bridge.

Score: Love All.

```
                        ♠ x.x.
                        ♥ x.x.x.
                        ♦ Q.x.x.x.x.
                        ♣ J.x.x.

    ♠ A.Q.10.          ┌─────────┐          ♠ K.J.x.x.
    ♥ J.10.9.x.        │    N    │          ♥ K.x.x.x.
    ♦ K.x.             │  W   E  │          ♦ x.x.
    ♣ A.10.x.x.        │    S    │          ♣ K.9.x.
                       └─────────┘
                        ♠ x.x.x.x.
                        ♥ A.Q.
                        ♦ A.J.x.x.
                        ♣ Q.x.x.
```

The bidding was:

N	E	S	W
—	—	1♣	1NT
—	3NT	—	—
—			

24

North opened a Club and West made game. Four Spades, four Clubs and one Diamond. No other lead except a Club allows this game to be made. The normal lead of a Diamond defeats the contract by two tricks. So does a Heart lead with a Diamond switch. It isn't North's fault. On the bidding a Club lead may be the only one to defeat the bid. The trouble is the prepared Club. The hand can be bid either as a Diamond or as one No Trump. In neither case would it come to any harm in a contract of two Diamonds doubled. The maximum loss is 100 points and the contract can be made if the opponents lead Clubs. In any case E-W can make three Hearts—and indeed four if again Clubs are led.

REVERSE BIDDING

The second dragon is the theory of reverse bidding. Here again a grain of sense has been built into a mountain of nonsense. If the bidding goes:

N	E	S	W
1♥	—	2♦	—
2♠			

the two Spade bid is a "reverse". If South wants to give preference back to Hearts he has to contract for an extra trick. On the other hand, if North had opened with one Spade and on the second round bid two Hearts, South could put the contract back to Spades without increasing the bid. It follows, therefore, that the first holding is potentially the stronger of the two. Obviously if South's hand is:

(o) ♠ J.x.
     ♥ x.x.x.
     ♦ A.Q.10.x.x.
     ♣ Q.x.x.

North prefers to play in Hearts rather than Spades, and he announces that he is prepared to accept a contract at a higher level. Reversing then, incidentally, shows a strong hand, but it is not the object of the reverse to show such a hand. The reverse primarily shows, or ought to show, the shape and not the strength of the holding. Unfortunately this simple principle has become so distorted that there are players who bid their shorter suit first not in accordance with the principle of preparedness (that is to say selecting your opening bid with an eye on your possible rebids) which has a proper function to perform in bidding, but simply in order that a later reverse may proclaim strength. As with the prepared Club there is one fatal flaw. Your partner never knows which of your suits is the longest and which the strongest. One of the classic examples of a reverse bidding tragedy comes from the 1946 England and Wales match. The hand has been quoted many times—Simon uses it in his brilliant posthumous *Design for Bidding*—but it is well worth repeating This was the hand:

♠ A.J.9.x.
♥ A.10.x.x.x.
♦ A.x.x.
♣ x.

♠ 10.		♠ Q.x.x.x.x.
♥ J.x.x.	N	♥ x.x.
♦ J.x.x.	W E	♦ x.x.
♣ A.x.x.x.x.x.	S	♣ K.Q.J.x.

♠ K.x.x.
♥ K.Q.9.
♦ K.Q.10.x.x.
♣ 10.x.

In Room 1 Welsh players were N–S. Harrison Gray and I were West and East. The bidding went at game all with West dealing:

W	N	E	S
—	1♠	—	2♦
—	2♥	—	3♠
—	4♠	—	—

I led the King of Clubs and the ridiculous contract went four down.

Unfortunately in the other room we failed to reap the full benefit of this catastrophe. Our other pair were modern scientific bidders and this small school also consider one Spade is the correct opening bid. So the bidding went:

W	N	E	S
—	1♠	—	2♦
—	2♥	—	3♣
—	3♦	—	4♦
—	5♦	—	—
—			

Six Hearts or six Diamonds of course are cold. England gained 1,020 points and should have gained 1,830. This hand is not a question of a player making a mistake: all players do that. Nor of failing to follow the system played; again, sometimes we all do that. For both the Welsh approach forcers and the English scientists, although for different reasons, one Spade is the correct opening bid. If they held the hands tomorrow, the opening bid would be the same. For the Welsh pair to open with one Heart would mean that they might have to reverse—and they are not strong enough on the system for that. The English scientists have to bid one Spade because otherwise—on their system—they can never bid the suit. And both of them ignore the overwhelming disadvantage that partner does not know from the first bid, and may never know at all, which of your suits is the best. No possible consideration can make up for this loss, and the lack of understanding and confidence that must follow.

So then having cleared out some of the weeds, let's look again at what to bid. Remember that one of the assumptions partner is still entitled to make is that "the suit you name is normally your best suit." Your "best" suit means your longest and if you have two of equal length, then the higher ranking. Straight away then at least 95 per cent. of the hands are solved—one of your best suit is the answer. Only the doubtful cases remain. When you propose to depart from this rule remember that doing so involves deceiving your partner—at least for one round, perhaps for the whole hand.

Before we consider the odd 5 per cent. of hands, let's tidy up one or two points on which you may be doubtful.

(1) If you have a chioce between two five-card or six-card suits, bid the higher ranking.

(2) With two four-card suits bid normally the higher ranking.

(3) With three four-card suits bid the suit ranking under the singleton, e.g.:

27

(p)	♠ A.Q.x.x.	(q)	♠ A.Q.x.x.	(r)	♠ A.Q.x.x.
	♥ A.J.x.x.		♥ x.		♥ A.J.x.x.
	♦ x.		♦ A.J.x.x.		♦ K.Q.x.x.
	♣ K.Q.x.x.		♣ K.Q.x.x.		♣ x.
	(1 ♣)		(1 ♦)		(1 ♠)

Notice that there is never a problem when the suits are adjacent: the higher ranking is almost invariably bid. You may make an exception to each of these three rules if the suit you would normally select is extremely weak. For example:

Rule 1:	(s)	♠ x.	
		♥ x.x.x.x.x.	
		♦ A.x.	
		♣ A.K.Q.10.x.	bid 1 ♣.
But on—(t)		♠ x.	
		♥ Q.10.x.x.x.	
		♦ K.x.	
		♣ A.K.Q.10.x.	bid 1 ♥.
Rule 2:	(u)	♠ x.x.x.x.	
		♥ A.K.Q.J.	
		♦ x.x.x.	
		♣ A.K.	bid 1 ♥.
But on—(v)		♠ J.10.x.x.	
		♥ A.K.Q.x.	
		♦ x.x.x.	
		♣ A.K.	bid 1 ♠.
Rule 3:	(w)	♠ x.x.x.x.	
		♥ A.K.Q.x.	
		♦ A.K.x.x.	
		♣ x.	bid 1 ♥.

It is fair to tell you that as far as Rule 1 is concerned, I am, in one case, in a minority among Acol players. Most Acol experts believe that a hand with five Spades and five Clubs should open one Club. There are obvious advantages here if the bidding goes slowly enough for you to rebid Spades. Indeed the stronger the hand the sounder the case for the Club bid. I am not convinced. I prefer, I always do, the natural bid of one Spade. Compare hand (h). But I may well be wrong.

For the rest we have to consider what Culbertson calls the

28

Principle of Preparedness. Shortly expressed this means that when you are in doubt about the correct bid, you should look one round ahead, and select the bid which will best facilitate the bidding over your partner's response. If you hold:

(x) ♠ A.K.x.x.
     ♥ x.x.x.
     ♦ x.x.
     ♣ A.K.x.x.

and open one Spade, you have an impossible rebid if partner responds with two Diamonds. You are not strong enough for two No Trumps, and you can hardly either rebid your four-card Spade suit or bid Clubs at the level of three. So you avoid your problem by opening one Club. Over a red suit response you can now bid one Spade. The bid of one Club would be wrong though on:

(y) ♠ A.K.x.x.
     ♥ K.x.x.
     ♦ x.x.
     ♣ A.K.x.x.

because you could now rebid two No Trumps if the bidding goes 1♠—2♦—. Only use this device then when your normal bid leaves you with an unsatisfactory rebid over partner's probable response.

Ely Culbertson—and indeed many English experts—consider that the question of preparedness should sometimes induce you to bid a four-card suit before a five-card one. See, for example, the bidding given in the hand from the England v. Wales match in this chapter. I believe you should only so distort your holding on the very rarest occasions. Culbertson, for example, says on:

(z) ♠ A.K.x.x.
     ♥ A.x.x.x.x.
     ♦ x.x.
     ♣ x.x.

you should bid one Spade, because otherwise you cannot show this suit if partner bids two Clubs or two Diamonds to your opening Heart bid. I would bid one Heart. I admit that I may never be able to show Spades (over two Clubs or two Diamonds

I have to rebid two Hearts), and this is a disadvantage. It is, however, unlikely that your partner has a four-card Spade suit, because he did not bid it over one Heart. On the other hand, Culbertson may find himself playing in Spades rather than in hearts, if partner has x.x.x. in each and gives preference, as he would, to the first bid suit. This too is a disadvantage. Culbertson, in fact, thinks it is so important to bid both suits that he is prepared to deceive his partner: I think it is so important to tell the truth to my partner that I will take my chance of not being able to bid Spades. You must weigh these two opinions and take your choice. If, however, my hand is:

(a2)   ♠   A.Q.J.10.
       ♥   K.x.x.x.x.
       ♦   K.x.
       ♣   x.x.

then I would open one Spade, because I cannot afford to suppress the suit.

No set of rules can be infallible, and however elaborate the instructions there will still be a number of hands on which you are thrown back on your own judgment. Apply here, and to every bidding problem, one golden rule. If in doubt always make the most natural bid.

BIDDABLE SUITS

Any five-card suit is biddable. A four-card suit should normally be not worse than J.10.9.x. but it isn't difficult to construct hands on which you have to open on 10.x.x.x. or even x.x.x.x. Often, though, you have to consider whether your suit is not only biddable, but re-biddable. These are the normal rules:

(1) Any six-card suit is re-biddable.
(2) Five-card suits should be at least K.J.x.x.x.
(3) No four-card suit is re-biddable.

Once again—and for the last time—there are, of course, exceptions: especially to (3). Sometimes you just have to rebid a good four-card suit—say A.K.J.10. Don't make a habit of it though.

CHAPTER VII

NO TRUMP BIDDING

IT isn't at all inconsistent to suggest that you bid No Trumps on a point count which we have scornfully rejected for suit bids. The reason is clear. In No Trump bidding there is no ruffing element, your distribution is normally balanced, and your singletons and doubletons are liabilities and not assets. We use again the 4–3–2–1 count with the addition (sometimes) of half a point for each ten.

I can't tell you whether you should or should not count tens. I don't know how good you are. Frequently in this book you will read "rules" solemnly set out for you—and then the cheerful assurance that as you get better you can ignore them. Let's put it in parable form. If you start playing golf you will probably sooner or later take a golf lesson. You will be given basic instruction. You will point the chin behind the ball, you will keep your left arm poker straight, you will glue your head down and glare at the ball. You may or may not hit it as well. These rules are sound. But Henry Cotton or Bobby Locke or Sam Snead don't have to mutter a series of incantations to themselves before they drive off. They know their feet are placed right and their swing is in the grove. And in exactly the same way Harrison Gray or Terence Reese or Kenneth Konstam don't have to add up on their fingers to see if they can bid. They know what the hand is worth. They've seen thousands like it before. It isn't that they ignore basic principles, but that they use them without thinking. So with you. Start by learning the basic rules. Secondly—to continue the golf metaphor—remember Ted Ray's immortal advice to a pupil who said he was doing everything correctly but couldn't get sufficient length: "Hit it a b— sight harder mate." Finally, because they have become automatic, forget the rules.

Now back to No Trump bidding. It takes 25–26 points between the two hands to make three No Trumps. Apart from the actual cards you hold whether you will make game depends on how good a dummy player you are and how good the defence will be. Good that is, in relation to your particular circle. If you are one of the best players in Barchester then—in Barchester— count tens and get into those close game contracts in No Trumps. But if you play for Barchester against London, don't count them. You'll be up against a tight and accurate defence. It follows also that you should or should not count tens—again in Barchester—depending on whether you or a weak partner will play the hand. Don't tell him, of course, that you are doing this: he might be offended. Anyway, for this chapter we count them.

The first decision to make is whether we play a strong or a light No Trump. In other words whether we want to bid No Trumps as often or as rarely as possible. I have no doubts. Bridge has come a long way since Culbertson in the mid-thirties fixed the No Trump requirements so rigidly that the bid virtually disappeared from play. In fact, provided you have a narrow range between the maximum and the minimum, the No Trump bid is much more informative than the suit bid of one. More-over, the bid which outranks all suit bids has great obstructive value. It follows that I want to make the bid as often as possible, and it follows again that the requirements must be as low as possible. But not below the safety margin. With balanced hands we agreed in suit bids that we would normally pass under thirteen points. So that—or perhaps twelve and a half—becomes our minimum. If we have a range beyond two points the accuracy disappears and partner cannot pin-point his responses. So our upper limit becomes fourteen and a half, or an absolute maximum of fifteen. Non-vulnerable only. For if we open on thirteen points, are doubled and make, say, four tricks, when partner has nothing, what have we lost? Five hundred points against a probable game or rubber. But vulnerable the price goes up to eight hundred, and that is too much especially if our opponents are not vulnerable. So we must put up the requirements. We cannot afford an expectation of defeat of more than two tricks, and this means a full three points extra. So vulnerable we need 16–18.

There used to be a theory that No Trumps should be bid on a 4-3-3-3 shape or sometimes on 4-4-3-2, and another theory which went with it that you could not have a four-card major suit. Both are completely out of date. If we want to make the bid as often as we can we must not be too insistent on distribution. A five-card minor suit is an asset to a No Trump. As far as the major suit is concerned it is, of course, important to make sure that the No Trump bid does not lose the chance of a better major suit game, especially on a 4–4 trump distribution. The answer is not to give up bidding No Trumps when you have a four-card major, but to find a foolproof method of finding the major suit fit. This method, invented by Jack Marx and rediscovered years later in the States by Sam Stayman, is described below and is an essential part of Acol. Don't be mesmerized by any old-fashioned yardsticks like "a stopper in each suit", or "at least six honour cards". All lone honours, except Aces, need help from your partner to be a sure trick and your J.x.x. becomes a stopper opposite Q.x. or 10.x.x.x., and it is manifestly absurd to consider the quantity rather than the quality of your honours.

These, then, are sound opening bids of No Trump non-vulnerable: add a King to make them typical of vulnerable No Trumps:

(a)	(b)	(c)	(d)
♠ A.x.x.	♠ J.x.x.	♠ Q.x.x.	♠ A.10.x.x.
♥ A.x.x.	♥ K.x.	♥ K.Q.x.x.	♥ A.x.x.
♦ A.J.x.	♦ K.x.x.	♦ A.x.x.x.	♦ K.x.x.
♣ J.x.x.x.	♣ A.K.x.x.x.	♣ Q.x.	♣ J.10.x.

but these are not good enough:

(e)	(f)
♠ A.x.x.	♠ K.Q.x.
♥ A.x.x.	♥ K.x.x.x.
♦ A.x.x.	♦ Q.10.x.
♣ x.x.x.x.	♣ J.x.x.

and these are too good:

(g)	(h)
♠ A.x.x.	♠ K.Q.x.
♥ A.x.x.	♥ A.K.x.x.
♦ A.x.x.	♦ Q.J.x.
♣ A.x.x.x.	♣ Q.x.x.

and should be opened one Club and one Heart respectively, non-vulnerable: vulnerable of course they qualify.

It is very simple for partner to work out the chances of game from the knowledge that 25-26 points are needed. With balanced hands the normal responses are:

Non-vulnerable—Bid two No Trump on ten and a half.
Bid three No Trump on twelve.
Vulnerable—Bid two No Trump on seven and a half.
Bid three No Trump on nine.

The opening bidder raises two No Trump to three on fourteen non-vulnerable and seventeen vulnerable. If you work it out you will see that the worst that can happen if both sides are minimum is to bid a game with twenty-four and a half points or to miss one with twenty-five. The margin of error is half a point, and, of course, no system is accurate enough to eliminate error. Distribution may well make a total of twenty-two or less enough, where the same rock wrecks a contract with twenty-eight. These requirements can often be shaded considerably if a long minor suit is held. Vulnerable, for example, you can afford to raise one No Trump to three on:

(i)   ♠ x.x.
        ♥ J.x.x.
        ♦ x.x.
        ♣ A.Q.x.x.x.x.

You should on no account bid the Clubs. In these days of short suit leads the suit may even be opened if you don't bid them.

This is the conventional bid referred to. It is absolutely forcing for one round and calls for the opener to bid a four-card major suit. If he has—unlikely of course—two four-card majors he bids Spades first, and Hearts on the next round. If he has no four-card major he bids (at least in the variation I prefer) two Diamonds to show a minimum and two No Trumps to show a maximum No Trump. Probably it is best only to use the bid when there is a real chance of game, i.e. when two clubs equals

2½ Spades or Hearts. But there are, of course, semi-psychic possibilities, and even the full-blown type of psychic shown below in hand (w). Some examples should make it clear. All non-vulnerable:

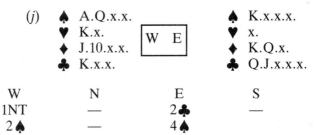

(j)

	♠ A.Q.x.x.		♠ K.x.x.x.
	♥ K.x.	W E	♥ x.
	♦ J.10.x.x.		♦ K.Q.x.
	♣ K.x.x.		♣ Q.J.x.x.x.

W	N	E	S
1NT	—	2♣	—
2♠	—	4♠	

Three No Trumps is surely defeated on a Heart lead. If West had responded two Hearts or two Diamonds, East of course bids two No Trumps. Two No Trumps East raises to three.

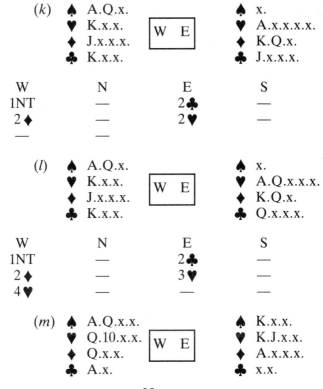

(k)

	♠ A.Q.x.		♠ x.
	♥ K.x.x.	W E	♥ A.x.x.x.x.
	♦ J.x.x.x.		♦ K.Q.x.
	♣ K.x.x.		♣ J.x.x.x.

W	N	E	S
1NT	—	2♣	—
2♦	—	2♥	—
—	—		

(l)

	♠ A.Q.x.		♠ x.
	♥ K.x.x.	W E	♥ A.Q.x.x.x.
	♦ J.x.x.x.		♦ K.Q.x.
	♣ K.x.x.		♣ Q.x.x.x.

W	N	E	S
1NT	—	2♣	—
2♦	—	3♥	—
4♥	—	—	

(m)

	♠ A.Q.x.x.		♠ K.x.x.
	♥ Q.10.x.x.	W E	♥ K.J.x.x.
	♦ Q.x.x.		♦ A.x.x.x.
	♣ A.x.		♣ x.x.

35

W	N	E	S
1NT	—	2♣	—
2♠	—	2NT	—
3♥	—	4♥	—
—	—	—	

Certain logical inferences are worth making a special note of:
  (1) If East still bids a major suit even when West has denied a four-card major, East's suit must be at least five cards. See hand (*k*).
  (2) If East, after a response of two Diamonds, bids only two No Trumps that usually will be the end of the bidding.

OTHER RESPONSES AT THE LEVEL OF TWO

The responses of two Diamonds, two Hearts or two Spades to a bid of one No Trump should almost invariably be passed. Exceptionally with a maximum point count, with a good fit, and with four trumps you may raise two of a major suit to three. No more. Partner's hand can be very weak indeed, say:

(*n*)　♠ Q.x.x.x.x.x.
　　　♥ x.x.
　　　♦ x.x.x.
　　　♣ x.x.

If he is as good as:

(*o*)　♠ Q.x.x.x.x
　　　♥ x.
　　　♦ K.Q.x.x.
　　　♣ J.x.x.

he should try two Clubs first. There is just a chance that partner might bid two Spades.

By using the Two Club response conventionally we have, of course, lost the use of it as a natural bid. This isn't of any real importance and in any case you can, if you wish, recover it by making the sequence:

W	N	E	S
1NT	—	2♣	—
2 anything	—	3♣	—

a hand to be passed: something like:

(p)   ♠   x.x.
         ♥   x.x.x.
         ♦   x.x.
         ♣   Q.J.x.x.x.x.

This bidding can also mean:

(q)   ♠   J.x.x.x.
         ♥   x.
         ♦   x.x.
         ♣   K.x.x.x.x.x.

Here once you fail to get a Spade response, three Clubs is perhaps the best spot. In theory—especially if the opener has shown a minimum of two Diamonds—the opponents can double you. In practice it is full of danger as for example, hand (q) will probably land his contract.

FORCING TAKE OUTS IN A SUIT

For obvious reasons these are rare. If your strength is in the majors the bid of two Clubs is usually best, followed if necessary by a jump. If you have minor suit strength, you should normally conceal it and raise to three No Trumps. But there are, of course, exceptions and I would force on these hands over a non-vulnerable No Trump:

(r)	(s)	(t)
♠ x.	♠ x.	♠ K.Q.x.
♥ A.K.J.x.x.x.	♥ x.	♥ x.
♦ K.Q.x.x.	♦ K.J.x.x.x.x.	♦ A.K.Q
♣ x.x	♣ A.Q.x.x.x.	♣ Q.x.x.x.x.x.
(3♥)	(3♦)	(3♣)

Note, by the way, as a good example of the value of shape that the point count of hand (s) which may be a lay down slam is not, in a balanced hand, even enough to raise an Acol No Trump to two.

Two No Trumps:

The requirements for an opening two No Trumps can be baldly stated—vulnerable or non-vulnerable 20–22. There is now no difference between the requirements because the risk of an opening two No Trump being doubled and left in for penalties is negligible. Partner obviously raises to three No Trumps on four-five points, again perhaps less if a long minor suit is held, e.g.:

(*u*) ♠ x.x.
♥ x.x.
♦ K.x.x.x.x.x.
♣ x.x.x.

Any response over two No Trumps is game forcing. Three Spades or three Hearts normally offer the opening bidder the choice of game in three No Trumps or that suit. If in doubt, the No Trump bidder should support to four of the major suit. Three Diamonds is rather a special case: it cannot be an invitation to three No Trumps nor can it be an invitation to a major suit game. It suggests five or perhaps six Diamonds. Partner must be very careful not to respond three No Trumps if his hand fits. The hand might be:

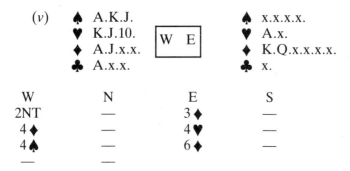

(*v*) ♠ A.K.J.   ♠ x.x.x.x.
♥ K.J.10.   ♥ A.x.
♦ A.J.x.x.   ♦ K.Q.x.x.x.x.
♣ A.x.x.   ♣ x.

W	N	E	S
2NT	—	3♦	—
4♦	—	4♥	—
4♠	—	6♦	—
—	—		

The three Club response over two No Trumps was invented by the Baron system. If it muddles you to have a slightly different sequence to remember, then play it exactly the same as the Two Club response to one No Trump. But the rather better way is for the opening bidder to respond by bidding his lowest four-card suit, and three No Trumps if his suit is Clubs. The Three

Club bidder then knows the shape and strength of the two hands, and should be able to pin-point the best contract. The strength of the three Club bid varies a great deal. There is one on record by Adam Meredith on:

(w) ♠ x.x.x.x.
♥ x.x.x.x.
♦ x.x.x.x.
♣ x.

Partner replied three Diamonds and Meredith passed. The gamble is, of course, against the opener having a four-card Club suit, but at least Meredith knows two No Trumps is going to be a hopeless contract and he may well try and do better.

Three No Trumps:
    The opening bid of three No Trumps is an Acol speciality. It is also an interesting example of the logic that is Acol. It seems illogical to open three No Trumps, which if "genuine", must mean that the opener holds a Two Club bid. But as he has not bid two Clubs he cannot have the requirements and so the bid is a phoney one. It can then only mean a long solid minor suit—not a major, of course, which would be opened either two or four—and some bits outside. Examples:

(x)	(y)
♠ Q.	♠ Q.x.
♥ J.x.x.	♥ Q.x.
♦ A.K.Q.J.x.x.x.	♦ K.x.
♣ A.x.	♣ A.K.Q.x.x.x.x.

It needs, of course, a few bits from partner to make game, but not many. One or two Queens and Jacks in the right place will do. The great rule for partner is not to disturb the bid into four of a major suit, say on:

(z) ♠ A.J.x.x.x.x.
♥ 10.x.x.x.
♦ x.
♣ x.x.

on which a bid of four Spades over an opening two No Trump would be correct. Any bid, then, over the Acol three No Trump becomes a slam try, and must guarantee the holding of enough high cards for a contract in five at least of the opener's long suit. Such a hand as:

$$(a2) \quad \spadesuit \text{ A.10.x.x.}$$
$$\heartsuit \text{ A.Q.x.x.}$$
$$\diamondsuit \text{ x.x.}$$
$$\clubsuit \text{ K.J.x.}$$

is worth an invitation to four No Trumps over which a strong opener like hand (*x*) should bid six Diamonds.

The Slam Zone:

Slams in No Trumps should rarely, except in match point duplicate, be attempted. The balanced nature of the hands makes it hard to garner the long card trick needed. Aces and Kings after all can only take eight of them. There are forty-two Milton Work points in a hand if we count tens. Put your slam zone at thirty-four if there is no five-card suit, thirty-three if there is. With more freakish holdings the point count is unreliable. If you can count thirty-four points even if partner had a minimum, bid six No Trumps as long as you are confident that two Aces aren't missing. If you count thirty-four with an average No Trumps, bid four No Trumps. Partner with a maximum can rebid to six. Avoid from both sides the bid of five No Trumps. The margin for error isn't adequate. Examples over a vulnerable No Trumps respond:

(b2)	(c2)	(d2)
♠ K.x.x.	♠ K.x.x.	♠ K.J.x.
♥ A.Q.x.	♥ A.Q.x.	♥ A.Q.x.
♦ K.J.x.x.	♦ K.Q.x.x.	♦ K.Q.10.x.
♣ Q.x.x.	♣ Q.J.x.	♣ Q.J.x.
(3NT)	(4NT)	(6NT)

Most slams, even after an opening bid in No Trumps, are still played in a suit. The route to these is usually via a forcing bid and subsequent cue-bidding. Their handling does not differ from normal slam bidding.

CHAPTER VIII

FORCING BIDS AND SLAM BIDDING

IN this country before Acol was developed, Richard Lederer's Two Club system began to oust the Culbertson Strong Two, at least in tournament play. The Strong Two retains its popularity in family Bridge, and is played by a tiny minority of tournament players. The Lederer Two Club had only a short life and the Two Club played now is usually Acol or a variant of it. In America until recently, the Strong Two held the field. American experts now tend to play the Two Club and a Weak Two for the other suits. You must select which method you prefer. I describe all three in the chapter, but I have no doubt that the Acol Two bid, together with the Two Clubs is the best solution to the problem of the big hands. It is true, of course, that the Two Club bid is wholly conventional and does not guarantee a club suit. On principle I dislike artificiality in bidding, but the bid has the double advantage of freeing the other bids of Two of a suit for specialized use, and coping with the rockcrusher hands which do not qualify for a Strong Two opening.

STRONG TWO

Whether you elect to play this system or not, you should study its requirements for you will meet it frequently. Any bid of Two of a suit is game forcing, unless, of course, a suitable double can be made. As it contracts for game even if partner's hand is blank, it should itself be not more—with reasonable breaks— than one trick short of making game. The Honour trick count is used:

A.K.	2
A.Q.	1½
A.,K.Q.,K.J.10.	1
K.x.,Q.J.x.	½

Two "plus values" (for example Q.x.x.) can be counted as ½ honour trick. If your suit is only four or five cards long your honour trick strength should be 5½—6. This can, of course, be shaded as your distribution improves down to perhaps 4½ on a semi-freak two suiter. The accepted check if you are in doubt is that you should have more honour tricks than losers. e.g.:

(a) ♠ A.K.Q.x.x.
♥ A.Q.x.
♦ x.
♣ A.K.x.x.

as 5½ honour tricks and 5 plus losers. It is a minimum Two Spade opening. If you exchange the King for the Queen of Clubs it fails to qualify. You will find this check simple and accurate.

These are examples of Two Bids:

(b) ♠ A.K.J.10.x.   ♠ x.   ♠ K.Q.J.10.
♥ A.K.Q.x.   ♥ A.K.Q.x.x.x. ♥ K.Q.J.10.9.
♦ A.x.x.   ♦ A.K.Q.x.x.x.   ♦ A.Q.J.10.
♣ x.   ♣ none.   ♣ none.

Because a Culbertson bid of one of a suit can be so very strong, Strong Two bidders are less ready to shade their requirements than Two Club players. For example, the most recent Gold Book says that:

(c) ♠ A.K.10.x.x.
♥ A.K.x.x.x.
♦ x.
♣ A.x.

is not a Two bid. Certainly I wouldn't care to risk bidding only one on such a hand. Any sort of a fit in either major suit will make a game.

The main responses to the Strong Two can be tabulated:
Negative: 2NT shows 0—1 Honour Tricks. If as much as 1 Honour Trick is held the bid denies a biddable suit.
Positive: 3NT shows 1½ Honour Tricks and no suit.
Suit bid at the same level: shows 1 Honour Trick with a five-card suit, or ½ Honour Trick with a six-card suit.

Except for one sequence—2♣–2♦–2NT discussed later—the bid is game forcing. Naturally as in the Strong Two a penalty double can be made if it is attractive enough. Normally the hand should have at least five high card tricks, and though this is a check rather than a rule, it should rarely be disregarded. In one case the opener may have to shade his highcard strength and that is where Clubs is the best suit; his partner should be able to recognize and allow for the situation. There is one tip to remember. If you are in any doubt at all whether the hand is worth a Two Club opening—it isn't. Strong one or two suiters should usually be opened with Two of a suit. Be very careful about opening Two Clubs unless you have at least two primary controls, and tread warily with a worthless doubleton. For example, neither:

(d)	♠	K.Q.J.
	♥	A.Q.
	♦	A.Q.J.10.x.x.
	♣	K.x.
nor	♠	A.x.
	♥	A.K.Q.10.9.
	♦	A.K.J.x.
	♣	x.x.

should be opened as Two Clubs. The first I would open as Two Diamonds or (with some partners) Two No Trumps. The reason for avoiding the Two Club bid is that partner, with, say, Two Aces and the King of Diamonds will surely "bull" you into a Grand Slam. On the second I prefer the slight risk of being left in with One Heart to launching into a game force with that horrible x.x. in Clubs.

The negative response to the Acol Two Club bid is Two Diamonds. This denies any of the following holdings.

An Ace and a King.

K.Q. and two Kings

Two K.Q.s.

Four Kings.

You are *not* allowed to add up plus values to make up these requirements. At first sight it is strange that the Acol system—always on the side of flexibility—should make such precise demands for its responses, while the Culbertson system, usually far more rigid is here the more flexible of the two. I think the reason a sound one. Of course it is rare for partner to have a positive response to an Acol Two Clubs, but if he has the final contract is shown almost at once. The real value, however, is a negative one. If partner does bid Two Diamonds he denies any of the requirements shown and however strongly he may bid later, all his bids are still subject to his first announcement that he has none of the required holdings. An Acol player can then bid freely after his first denial, where a Culbertson player whose "positive" response was perhaps only K.J.x.x.x.x. in another suit is bound to back-pedal. There is one relaxation of the Acol rules you should allow yourself. One K.Q. and one King will do for a positive response if either heads a six or a strong five-card suit. Take hand fifty-six in the 1949 Crockfords' v. U.S.A. match:

(e) ♠ K.Q.J.x.x.   ♠ A.10.x.
     ♥ K.9.x. | W E | ♥ A.Q.
     ♦ 10.   ♦ A.K.Q.J.9.8.
     ♣ 9.x.x.x.   ♣ A.J.

The bidding by Terence Reese (West) and Boris Schapiro (East) could scarcely be simpler:

E	S	W	N
2♣	—	2♠	—
7NT			

Notice, however, that Reese's positive response is the one exception I suggest. It is very difficult to "catch up" on these hands if Two Diamonds is bid first.

Unlike the Strong Two, therefore, the negative response can conceal a good hand, e.g.:

(f) ♠ A.x.x.x.x.
     ♥ J.x.
     ♦ Q.x.x.
     ♣ J.x.x.

You should never cheat on this type of hand and give a positive response; some at least of those plus values will be useless. If you have a positive response and a useful suit, bid it normally.

$$(g) \quad \spadesuit \quad \text{A.x.x.}$$
$$\heartsuit \quad \text{x.x.x.}$$
$$\diamondsuit \quad \text{K.J.x.x.x.x.}$$
$$\clubsuit \quad \text{x.}$$

Bid Three Diamonds. With no biddable suit, but the necessary high card strength bid 2NT.

There is one type of hand which is a nightmare for Strong Two players. Something like:

$$(h) \quad \spadesuit \quad \text{A.Q.x.}$$
$$\heartsuit \quad \text{A.K.x.}$$
$$\diamondsuit \quad \text{A.J.x.x.}$$
$$\clubsuit \quad \text{A.J.10.}$$

Too weak for a Two bid (and if they do open Two their partner responding Two No Trump will be declarer with the "wrong" hand) they must either risk a bid of one being passed, or gamble Three No Trumps and go down if partner has nothing. Acol has a simple answer. Partner can pass the sequence:

but will keep it open on about three points, say a Queen and a Jack. He might even shade this a trifle if he has a suit, say, of Q.10.x.x.x. The requirements are a balanced hand of 22½–24. Holdings 25–26 the rebid over Two Diamonds should be Three No Trumps:

$$(i) \quad \spadesuit \quad \text{A.J.x.}$$
$$\heartsuit \quad \text{A.K.10.}$$
$$\diamondsuit \quad \text{A.Q.J.}$$
$$\clubsuit \quad \text{A.Q.10.x.}$$

A balanced hand with a higher count than 26 should bid its best suit as a normal game force. Partner from his close knowledge of your point holding can, of course, easily calculate if the combined count is in the slam zone and raise accordingly. With a balanced holding of about eight points he should bid four No Trumps over three and with nine a direct six No Trumps.

I'm sure you play a special Slam convention, probably Blackwood, and I'm sure you'd play much better Bridge if you didn't. There's something about Blackwood that goes to Bridge players' heads—even goodish ones. The early rounds of bidding are hustled through so that the magic formula can be uttered. I remember well one hand in rubber Bridge playing against two such players. An opening Two Club bid got a positive response and the next bid inevitably was the Blackwood. They had all the Aces! On to the Five No Trump. They had all the Kings! And then—at the six level—they began to wonder what to play it in. Seven No Trumps was finally selected and four down doubled was the result. There are hands, of course, on which Blackwood is perfect. The sort of hands where only Aces matter. I never seem to hold them. In its place it's a perfectly good convention. Charles Goren described it once as a "sand wedge" and added, "but you don't want to use a sand wedge at every hole". If you use Blackwood or the 4/5 No Trump you should not employ them on more than 20 per cent. of all hands bid into the slam zone. Bid most of your slams either by the bludgeon of direct methods, or the rapier of cue-bidding. Read this warning again and then read on.

BLACKWOOD

Its greatest merit (and danger) is its extreme simplicity. The Four No Trump bid gives no guarantee of strength and partner must respond:

Five Clubs   —   Holding No Ace, or Four Aces.
Five Diamonds —   Holding One Ace.

and so on up to Spades showing three Aces. Voids do not count as Aces and cannot be shown. Afterwards a bid of Five No Trumps asks for Kings and the same routine is followed. If you are playing an Ace showing system in response to Two Clubs, then clearly the Four No Trumps bid is asking not for Aces (which are known) but for Kings. The Five No Trumps can then ask for Queens. There are dozens of variations and requirements, but I won't detail them. I know I'm prejudiced against the convention—so are nearly all the leading players in the country—but I hope you won't use it. Except, of course, against me.

4/5 NO TRUMP CONVENTION

This has largely been discarded in the States, but is played a great deal here. Its great advantage is that it can not only show the number of Aces held, but also which Aces they are. This is where it scores so heavily over Blackwood. If, for instance, you hold:

(*j*)   ♠   K.Q.J.x.x.x.
      ♥   A.K.Q.x.x.x.
      ♦   A.
      ♣   none.

it doesn't help at all to know that partner has one Ace. The important thing is to know if it is Spades or Clubs.

The conventional requirements for the strong hand are:
(1) Four No Trump shows either Three Aces or Two Aces and the King of a suit bid.
(2) Five No Trump (preceded by Four No Trump)—Four Aces.
(3) Five No Trumps (when not preceded by Four No Trump)—Three Aces and the King of a suit bid.

The newer Culbertson version of (3) is the Grand Slam Force ordering partner to bid Seven if holding two out of the top three honours:

e.g. if you hold   (*k*)   ♠   Q.x.x.x.x.
                     ♥   A.K.Q.x.x.x.
                     ♦   A.x.
                     ♣   none.

If partner opens One Spade and this variation is played a direct Five No Trumps could be bid. Partner with:

(*l*)   ♠   A.K.x.x.x.
      ♥   x.x.
      ♦   x.x.
      ♣   K.Q.x.x.

should bid Seven Spades, but with the "stronger" holding of:

(m) ♠ A.10.x.x.x.
    ♥ x.
    ♦ K.Q.x.
    ♣ A.K.J.x.

only six. I prefer the earlier version, but there is little in it. Responses to Four No Trumps are as follows:

(i) If holding Two Aces or One Ace and ALL the Kings of suits bid—five No Trumps.

(ii) Responder may (not must), if not holding the requirements for the Five No Trump response either:
    (a) Sign off in the lowest suit bid.
    (b) Cue bid an Ace or a void. If he holds both the void should first be shown, if the safety level permits.
    (c) Encourage by bidding a suit (usually the agreed but not the sign off suit) at the five level instead of signing off.
    (d) Bid a direct slam.

I agree that it sounds difficult, and it will take some study to master it. But it is well worth it. Before we illustrate each of the five possible responses let's make two notes. First, throughout when I use the term "bid suit" that means a suit bid as a genuine suit—it does not include cue-bids or overbids in the opponent's suit. Secondly the phrase I used "may not must" in discussing the four responses grouped above is in contradiction of Culbertson. Acol players take the view that partner shouldn't be forced to show an Ace just because he has one, or to sign off because he hasn't. Normally, of course, he will do so, but discretion should be left to him. He may, for example, have opened extremely lightly and be anxious to sign off even with an Ace. The Four No Trump bidder in any case can usually infer from his own holding that his partner must have at least one control and can judge future action in the light of his reluctance to show it.

Now for the examples. In each case you are South and the bidding has gone.

(n)	S	W	N	E
	1♥	—	3♣	—
	3♦	—	3♥	—
	4♥	—	4NT	—
	?			

(i) ♠ x.x.
♥ A.K.x.x.x.
♦ A.J.x.x.
♣ x.x.   —   Respond 5 NT.

(ii) ♠ x.x.
♥ K.Q.10.x.x.
♦ K.Q.x.x.x.
♣ x.   —   5♣ (Sign Off).

(iii) ♠ x.x.
♥ K.Q.J.x.x.
♦ A.x.x.x.x.
♣ x.   —   5♦ (Cue Bid).

(iv) ♠ A.x.
♥ K.J.x.x.x.
♦ K.x.x.x.x.
♣ x.   —   5♥.

The cue bid of Five Spades in this last hand would take you over the safety level of Five Hearts, and you are not quite good enough to commit the hand to a slam. As you have not signed off, the bid will be read as encouraging. If partner has the Ace of Hearts, as he almost surely has, he will be able to draw the obvious inference that you have the Spade control. Without an Ace you would probably sign off:

(v) ♠ x.
♥ A.K.J.x.x.x.
♦ K.x.x.x.x.
♣ x.   6♥.

Compare this with (iv). Those then are the two main slam conventions. For family Bridge and even small Club Bridge, Blackwood may well be best. For expert Bridge and tournament Bridge it is not nearly good enough. Let me pray in aid the late S. J. Simon: "The Culbertson Four-Five is an adult weapon, and the Blackwood merely a nice toy."

Acol harnesses this otherwise useless bid to cope with the hands where a player is interested only in the number of Aces, thereby incidentally adding one more to the many arguments against Blackwood. A typical hand would be:

$$(o) \quad \spadesuit \quad \text{K.Q.J.10.x.x.x.}$$
$$\heartsuit \quad \text{A.}$$
$$\diamondsuit \quad \text{A.K.Q.10.}$$
$$\clubsuit \quad \text{x.}$$

The responses are:

5♣—No Ace.

5♠, ♥ or ♦—Ace of the suit.

5NT—Two Aces.

6♣—Ace of Clubs.

THE WEAK TWO

If we are going to play the Two Club convention, we have to decide what to do with our other Two bids. The decision lies between the Weak Two and the Acol Two bid. S. J. Simon who discussed this problem exhaustively in *Design for Bidding* decided that the Weak Two should be played third in hand and Acol in the other three positions. I'm afraid that is too complicated a conclusion for me, and I'm certain it would lead to endless misunderstandings.

Study them both with your favourite partner and decide for yourself. I'm on the side of the Acols.

The Weak Two was born in the Cavendish Club of New York where there are more Life Masters to the square yard than anywhere else in the world. It was invented by Howard Schenken, perhaps the best player Contract Bridge has produced, and it is played by the American and World Champions. Clearly then it is worth the closest study.

It is a limit bid which is also designed to shut out or embarrass the opponents. Honour Trick strength is one and a half to two plus, nearly always with a six card suit. Typical bids are:

$$(p) \quad \spadesuit \quad \text{A.J.10.x.x.x.}$$
$$\heartsuit \quad \text{K.x.x.}$$
$$\diamondsuit \quad \text{x.x.}$$
$$\clubsuit \quad \text{x.x.}$$
$$(2\spadesuit)$$

or

(q) ♠ x.
       ♥ A.x.x.
       ♦ K.Q.10.x.x.x.
       ♣ x.x.x.
       (2♦)

It's worth noticing that an Acol player would open both these hands anyway with a bid of One. It follows that owing to our system of light opening bids there is less need for the Weak Two bid to cover these hands.

A response of Two No Trumps or any bid in a new suit is forcing for one round. If the responder raises the opener's suit, it is a quantitative bid only, and is usually designed to make it still more difficult for opponents to intervene. The great advantage of the Weak Two is that it robs the opponents of the vital early round of bidding. Certainly it gives opponents very difficult decisions. For example, over Two Spades the next bidder may as well toss a coin if he holds:

(r) ♠ x.x.
       ♥ A.Q.x.x.x.
       ♦ x.
       ♣ A.Q.x.x.x.

To bid or not to bid? Either may be disastrous. On balance I take the risk and bid Three Clubs, but I may get a horrible result. The only really effective answer to the Weak Two is the Weak Informatory Double, and this should be employed whenever possible, e.g. over Two Spades if you hold:

(s) ♠ x.
       ♥ K.10.x.x.
       ♦ A.x.x.
       ♣ A.Q.10.x.x.

don't bid Three Clubs. The Double is much more efficient, and it's important to show all round strength before the partner of the Weak Two opener has had a chance to speak. There's no doubt that the Weak Two has a strong psychological effect. Opponents are very apt to go too high just because they suspect they are being bullied out of something. The partner of the opener will surely do everything he can to add to the confusion by helping the barrage upwards. The system works best when the opponents hold the balance of cards, and, best of all, when played by strong players against weak.

Indeed, it's just because of this last point that I hesitate to recommend it. By all means, if you want to, play it in tournaments. That's fair enough. In friendly rubber Bridge I'm not so sure. Certainly a leading London Club banned it after due experiment. It aroused too much anger from the ordinary weak players to whom for twenty years a two bid has meant great strength. Invariably they either forgot it was a Weak bid and passed on good hands, or if they remembered went far too high against it. I know there was no good reason in logic for the ban, and yet I think it was sound policy. I'd keep the Weak Two, if you select it, for matches and tough no-quarter rubber Bridge. Like they play at the Cavendish.

THE ACOL TWO

The skeleton of these bids can be shown in a couple of lines. The Acol Two bid shows eight playing tricks, no particular honour strength and is forcing for one round: negative reply Two No Trumps. There's a good deal more to it than that, of course, and it is the principal distinctive contribution of the Acol system to Contract Bridge. It is an ideal weapon for dealing with all those hands that haunt the Strong Two player. The hands on their system too good for a one bid, not good enough for two. Hands like:

(t) ♠ A.Q.J.x.x.
      ♥ A.Q.x.x.x.x.
      ♦ x.
      ♣ none.

or

(u) ♠ A.
      ♥ K.Q.J.x.x.x.x.
      ♦ A.J.x.
      ♣ x.x.

There are many hands in this category on which game can easily be made, even if partner would pass to a bid of one. Remember though, not to place cards in your partner's hand. If you hold:

$$(v) \quad \spadesuit \quad \text{A.K.x.x.x.}$$
$$\heartsuit \quad \text{A.Q.x.x.x.x.}$$
$$\diamondsuit \quad \text{x.x.}$$
$$\clubsuit \quad \text{none.}$$

it is perfectly true that you may miss game if partner has, say the Queen of Spades and the Jack of Hearts. There are, however, dozens of other combinations he can hold in the minor suits which would be useless to you. So the bid is one Heart only.

You don't, of course, have to make a Two bid just because you have eight playing tricks. With the eight top Spades the bid is a pre-emptive Four Spades not Two. The essence of the Two bid is that you are very near to game, but prepared to stop out of it if partner has nothing, or if his "bits" don't fit. Nor should you open with a Two bid if there can be no game unless partner has a normal response to a bid of One.

The positive responses to a Two bid are absolutely at partner's discretion. There is no table to learn, no count to make. This may be a little difficult at first, but very soon you will find it beautifully simple. In general, if you have a hand on which you would make a suit reply to a bid of One, make the same response at the appropriate level, avoiding, however, ultra shaded suits. Remember, though, how strong his opening suit will be, and, if you possibly can, announce a fit at once. For example, over Two Diamonds bid Two Hearts on:

$$(w) \quad \spadesuit \quad \text{J.x.x.}$$
$$\heartsuit \quad \text{K.J.x.x.x.}$$
$$\diamondsuit \quad \text{J.x.}$$
$$\clubsuit \quad \text{K.x.x.}$$

but if the Diamonds and Clubs were reversed it is better to agree the suit at once with Three Diamonds. Trial bidding can then start at once.

Three No Trumps from you is a mild slam try on top cards, and the double raise in partner's suit shows good trump support and some interest in slams, but it denies either an Ace or a void. Obviously if you had such a control you would make a simple raise, and cue-bid later. There is one special bid common to all

Acol sequences which may be mentioned here. Where a forcing situation already exists a jump bid shows a solid suit, e.g. over Two Diamonds bid Three Hearts on:

(x) ♠ x.x.
    ♥ A.K.Q.J.x.x.x.
    ♦ x.x.
    ♣ x.x.

If you have bid a negative Two No Trumps and partner only rebids his suit, you can pass. Remember though, how little he wants for game: even three little trumps, and a singleton or a King outside should be enough. You can also—just—pass if he changes the suit, but only, of course, on the most hopeless misfit.

Here, as so often in bidding, you will find that the most natural bid is the best. That is, of course, the main theme of Acol and of this book—if you do not complicate it yourself Bridge really is an easy game.

Be swift then to proclaim a fit as soon as you reasonably can. Look more than once even at a pointless hand before you decide to pass. Sometimes on the other hand a hideous misfit is apparent almost from the opening bid. See for example Hand (y) (vi) below. Disaster can nearly always be avoided provided the opener listens to and appreciates his partner's responses. He's not just bidding because he likes the sound of his own voice. At least I hope he isn't.

I have illustrated all these points in the following hands, Study them carefully, and then read the text through again. It is easier than it looks.

TYPICAL SEQUENCES AFTER AN ACOL TWO BID

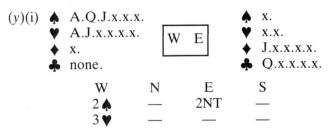

(y)(i) ♠ A.Q.J.x.x.x.   ♠ x.
       ♥ A.J.x.x.x.x.   W E   ♥ x.x.
       ♦ x.   ♦ J.x.x.x.x.
       ♣ none.   ♣ Q.x.x.x.x.

W	N	E	S
2♠	—	2NT	—
3♥	—	—	—

It is possible that West's Spades may be much stronger than

54

his Hearts and Three Spades a better contract. It is, however, safer to pass.

(ii)
	♠ A.Q.J.x.x.x.		♠ x.x.x.
	♥ A.K.Q.x.x.	W E	♥ x.
	♦ x.		♦ K.x.x.x.
	♣ x.		♣ J.x.x.x.x.

W	N	E	S
2♠	—	2NT	—
3♥	—	4♠	—
—	—		

You are too good for the mere preferences to Three Spades and must jump to game.

(iii)
	♠ none.		♠ J.x.x.
	♥ A.x.	W E	♥ K.J.x.x.x.
	♦ A.Q.J.x.x.x.		♦ K.x.x.
	♣ K.Q.10.x.x.		♣ J.x.

W	N	E	S
2♦	—	3♦	—
4♣	—	4♦	—
4♥	—	6♦	—
—	—		

After West's second Trial bid, East has a good enough fit to bid the slam. See hand (w).

(iv)
	♠ x.		♠ K.10.x.x.
	♥ A.K.Q.10.x.x.x.	W E	♥ J.x.x.x.
	♦ A.K.x.x.x.		♦ Q.x.
	♣ none.		♣ K.Q.x.

W	N	E	S
2♥	—	4♥	—
5♦	—	6♥	—

The key card is clearly the Diamond Queen.

(v)
	♠ A.		♠ x.x.
	♥ x.	W E	♥ A.K.Q.J.x.x.x.
	♦ A.K.Q.10.x.x.		♦ x.x.
	♣ A.Q.10.x.x.		♣ x.x.

W	N	E	S
2♦	—	3♥	—
7♥	—	—	— (See hand x.)

55

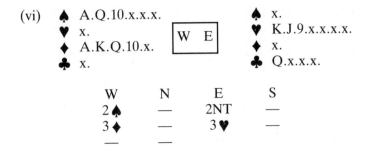

(vi)

	♠ A.Q.10.x.x.x.		♠ x.
	♥ x.		♥ K.J.9.x.x.x.x.
	♦ A.K.Q.10.x.	W E	♦ x.
	♣ x.		♣ Q.x.x.x.

W	N	E	S
2♠	—	2NT	—
3♦	—	3♥	—
—	—		

The one exception to the rule of natural responses. Best to discourage here and bid—if it can be done safely—on the next round. Partner cannot misread the situation.

CHAPTER IX

RESPONDING TO THE BID OF ONE OF
A SUIT

THERE are endless combinations and permutations possible
after the opening bid of one of a suit from a low part score to a
lay-down Grand Slam. No book can, or should try to legislate
for them all. It is far more important to understand the structure
of bidding and apply your knowledge to the situations that arise.
First of all, remember we have agreed to open light, and as our
Bridge improves, lighter still. So it follows we must be able to
stop easily, and a system that advocates light opening bids must
be studded with stop signals. Moreover, these stop signals must
be obeyed. One dare not bid one Spade, say, on:

(a)   ♠   K.J.x.x.x.x.
        ♥   x.
        ♦   A.x.x.x.
        ♣   J.x.

if partner holding a couple of Aces and a King is going to insist
on a game contract. Unless a forcing or an inferentially forcing
situation has been created either partner can always pass. We
must then have the minimum number of forcing situations. Take
the hand shown above. If partner bids two No Trumps that is not
forcing to game. He can bid game himself if he is good enough
without making me guess. So I reply three Spades. This bid is a
red light. The bidding must stop there. An expert partner with a
maximum two No Trump, plus a good Spade fit, plus his values
in top tricks, might sometimes bid four Spades. For the moment
it's an absolute sign off. It follows that if you—after the two No
Trump response—want to play in Four Spades, you bid it yourself. For example, if your Jack of Clubs was the King you are
just worth the game bid. This bid is perfectly safe because the

57

balanced nature of the two No Trump response guarantees some sort of tolerance for Spades.

Take again the other situation where you can be in doubt whether a forcing situation exists. 1S–3S. Is this forcing? Definitely no. Not in Acol. You are playing a natural system. The double raise of your partner's suit is better than the single raise, not as good as the triple. For example, if partner still has the original hand:

(a) ♠ K.J.x.x.x.x.
    ♥ x.
    ♦ A.x.x.x.
    ♣ J.x.

you raise to two Spades on:

(b) ♠ x.x.x.x.
    ♥ x.x.
    ♦ Q.x.x.x.
    ♣ K.Q.x.

to three Spades on:

(c) ♠ x.x.x.x.
    ♥ A.x
    ♦ Q.10.x.x.
    ♣ K.Q.x.

to four Spades on:

(d) ♠ Q.x.x.x.x.
    ♥ A.x.
    ♦ K.x.x.x.x.
    ♣ x.

Partner, with the hand shown, passes each of these bids. A trifle stronger, say with his trumps headed by K.Q., he raises three Spades to four. If he fears a Heart bid he may well raise 2S to 3S as a defensive measure. There can be no exact requirements for the different raises of partner's suit. One thing they should have in common is a minimum of four trumps. The point count for the simple raise has a normal minimum of around five and a half, but it can be shaded if necessary to nothing. See for instance Hand No. 2 in Acol in Action. If no particular bid is obvious, but you are too good to pass, give preference to the simple raise. This principle, the early agreement of the suit, runs right through Acol bidding. Here you can even on occasion cut the trump support from four to say Q.x.x. rather than bid a silly suit. Avoid, if you can, the simple raise on 4–3–3–3 shape: your hand has neither ruffling values, nor long card strength. For the double and triple raise I don't propose to offer any rules. I could invent some, but there would be so many exceptions, it would waste your time and mine. There is no theoretical difference between the majors and the minors in the raise of partner's suit. In practice, owing to the difficulty of taking eleven tricks, minor suit bidding always has one eye cocked at a three No Trump contract. Consequently, the double and triple raises in the minors are rarer bids. In a major suit the point count, for example, on the triple raise might only be four or five or even less. In some cases even zero. Sometimes the bid has to be made partly in hopes of making the contract, partly in hopes of shutting the opponents out. Bid what you think you can make. Don't, however, in your eagerness to make a game raise to four Spades on too good a hand. You may lose a Slam. If you have a good fit and four Trumps, the triple raise should not be more than thirteen points. Remember you can force lightly, particularly so when the hands fit. If your point count is 13–16 and you do not wish to force you should employ the "delayed game raise". This is a temporizing bid say of two Clubs followed by a jump to four Spades. Further action is left to partner.

These two examples should teach you more than the principle that responses of two No Trumps and the double raise are non-forcing and, therefore, limit bids. They should teach you the cardinal rule of bidding. Make things easy for your partner. There is a corollary, "and difficult for your opponents", but that comes later. For the moment don't invite partner to take decisions you can take yourself. Don't assume he doesn't know what he is doing when he screams at you with three Spades over two No Trumps to shut up. Don't, in short, bid his cards for him.

Now let's go back to the beginning. Partner opens one of a suit and you look at your cards. His bid is limited only by the fact that he has not opened a two bid. It may still be of very great strength. For you to pass would be a wail of weakness. Worse still, it tells the opponents how bad you are. Still, it's cheaper to pass on nothing: for if you bid you will probably deceive your partner and not your opponents. How little should you have to respond? The answer normally is about five and a half points. Say, a King, a Queen and ten. Less if you have a good shape or support in his suit. More if you have not. The minimum response is called a courtesy bid. Probably if you have a weak hand, you have been in the habit of responding with one No Trump. It's an old-fashioned bad idea and you must drop it. No bid is so uninformative as the one No Trump response. Always, if you can, bid a suit—even a bad four card one at the level of one. If partner opens a Diamond, bid—

One Heart on: One Spade on:

(e) ♠ x.x.x.   (f) ♠ A.10.x.x.
    ♥ K.J.x.x.   ♥ x.x.x.
    ♦ x.x.x.   ♦ x.x.
    ♣ K.x.x   ♣ J.x.x.x.

One No Trump on:

(g) ♠ Q.x.x.
    ♥ Q.x.x.
    ♦ x.x.x.
    ♣ Q.x.x.x.

Remember then, that a response of one in a suit shows no more points than a bid of one No Trump. It may, of course, be more. It may be just fractionally under a forcing take out. But it may even be less than five and a half points. A response of one Spade is correct (if you decide to bid at all) on:

(h) ♠ K.x.x.x.x. or (i) ♠ A.x.x.x.x.x.
    ♥ Q.x.x.   ♥ x.x.
    ♦ x.x.x.   ♦ x.x.
    ♣ x.x.   ♣ x.x.x.

To bid at the two-level your normal minimum should be eight points. This is a common-sense precaution against the dangers of the higher level. If in hand (*h*) you reverse the Spades and Clubs, you should pass the opening one Diamond bid.

The opener in his turn must realise how weak you may be and tread delicately until you tell him more. There are hands with more than five and a half points on which it is sounder to pass. Usually, these hands either fit very badly with partner's suit, or involve bidding a ragged suit at the level of two. For example, if partner again opens one Spade, I would certainly pass on:

(*j*) ♠ x.
    ♥ x.x.x.x.
    ♦ K.x.x.x.x.
    ♣ K.x.x.

The no trump bid with a singleton of partner's suit is to be avoided if at all possible and I can't risk the weak Diamond suit at the two level. I may, of course, be wrong to pass. There may just be a game in Hearts if partners hand is ideal. But the pass is, on balance, a good deal safer. Naturally, if an opponent intervenes you need not scrape up a courtesy response, for your partner will have another chance. Consequently if you do bid it as a "free" bid and must be rather stronger. Say eight to nine and a half on balanced hands. For example, if your partner bids a Diamond and the next hand a Heart, bid one No Trump on:

(*k*) ♠ Q.x.x.
    ♥ Q.10.x.x.
    ♦ x.x.
    ♣ A.x.x.x.

With unbalanced hands, as far as possible ignore the intervention, although noting as a warning, particularly if they are vulnerable, that the opponents are strong enough to bid.

Although then you should prefer a suit, particularly a major suit response to a No Trump Response, and although the suit response may be no stronger than the No Trump bid yet it must be replied to where the No Trump bid can be passed. The reason, of course, is that the range is much greater. The one No Trump should have a ceiling of nine and a half points. The one-over-one or two-over-one suit response may be up to sixteen. It is then a one round force whether the level be one or two, irrespective of the opponent's bidding, unless you have passed. The opener cannot, then, pass any of these situations:

(*l*)	N	E	S	W	(*m*)	N	E	S	W
	1♣	—	1♥	—		1♥	—	2♦	—
	?					?			

(*n*)	N	E	S	W
	1♥	1♠	2♣	—
	?			

but he can pass:

(*o*)	N	E	S	W	or	(*p*)	N	E	S	W
	1♦	—	1NT	—			—	—	1♥	—
	?						1♠	—	?	

The last two bids are strictly limited. The first by the nature of the bid, the second by the fact that North has already passed. The opener can also pass a one-over-one response if an opponent's intervening bid ensures that partner will have another chance. Indeed, by doing so, he can usefully indicate a minimum hand.

Whether a bid of a third suit continues to hold this forcing situation is a matter of system opinion. Most systems say firmly, "Yes". Just as firmly Acol says, "No". Acol is a system that dislikes the straitjacket approach. We prefer to leave discretion to partner. Of course normally if we bid a third suit, partner will respond. But he may not want to. Let's leave it to him. He's not a robot. Or if he is, he shouldn't be playing Acol.

If you cannot bear the thought of partner passing your bid, you mustn't make it. You must force (i.e. bid one more than necessary in another suit). And this is the third leg of the Acol bidding tripod. Because Acol insists on opening lightly it must be able to pass easily. Because it can pass easily we must force lightly. None of those awful one-over-one responses on a huge hand because "partner can't pass". None of those cunning reverses to show strength. None of those terrible second or third or even fourth suits bid not because you want to show them but because "a change of suit is forcing". Just bid naturally. As soon as you know there is a game or a slam, and where it is, bid it. If you know there is a game or a slam, but don't know enough about the hand, force. It's pure illusion to think you save time by bidding only One Spade over One Heart, if you have a whale of a hand. Sooner or later, you will have to gamble or force and lose the bidding space. In fact, usually you lose more because the situation is not established until the second or third round. Crawl along in the bidding if you want to, be as subtle and delicate in your inferences as you like, but force first.

How good then to force? Easy. Good enough for a game even if partner has a weak opening. No particular point count, because shape enters into it too much. No rigid high card qualifications for the same reason. The better your hand fits the less you need. Normally a force should have at least one first round control and usually two or more. On balanced hands the minimum count should be around sixteen. But the force is usually on an unbalanced holding. Normally, but by no means invariably, it shows some sort of fit. These then are forces over a bid One Heart:

(q)	♠ A.K.J.x.	(r)	♠ none.
	♥ A.Q.x.x.x.		♥ K.Q.x.x.x.x.
	♦ K.x.x.		♦ A.J.x.x.x.
	♣ x.		♣ x.x.
	(2♠)		(3♦)

(s)	♠ A.Q.x.	(t)	♠ A.K.Q.10.x.
	♥ A.x.x.		♥ none.
	♦ Q.x.x.		♦ A.Q.J.x.x.
	♣ K.Q.10.x.		♣ K.x.x.
	(3♣)		(2♠)

but these, for the reasons shown, are not:

(u)	♠ K.Q.x.x.	(v)	♠ A.J.x.
	♥ K.J.x.x.x.		♥ A.x.x.
	♦ K.x.		♦ Q.x.x.
	♣ K.x.		♣ K.J.10.x.

(Too dangerous without an Ace)   (Too Weak)

63

(w) ♠ A.K.x.x.x.
♥ none.
♦ A.x.x.x.x.
♣ Q.J.x.

(not strong enough in view of the void)

Subsequent bidding over a force belongs to the chapter on Slam bidding.

PRE-EMPTIVE RESPONSES

Sometimes, particularly on weak hands, it is necessary to crowd the bidding. These bids should be perfectly natural. They say exactly what they mean and they promise no honour strength. Bid then Four Hearts over one Club on:

(x) ♠ x.
♥ A.J.10.x.x.x.x.x.
♦ Q.x.x.
♣ x.

Any other bid is fatuous, and in view of the probable enemy action in Spades, dangerous. The leap to three in a major or four in a minor in a suit other than the one opened is also pre-emptive, but obviously slightly weaker. Over a Club bid three Hearts on:

(y) ♠ x.x.
♥ A.J.10.x.x.x.x.
♦ Q.x.x.
♣ x.

or four Diamonds on:

(z) ♠ x.
♥ Q.x.x.
♦ A.J.10.x.x.x.x.x.
♣ x.

or, of course, on similar values. These bids are strictly limited and must not be made on hands with good defensive values. Subsequent action is left to partner.

NO TRUMP RESPONSES

When we were examining the theory of responses we gave $5\frac{1}{2}$ to $9\frac{1}{2}$ as the range for a one No Trump response. There is one exception. As we always bid a suit, even a weak one, if we can, it follows that over one Club the one No Trump response shows no biddable suit. This is an example of the logic that is Acol. For the four-card suit is now almost certain to be Clubs and yet we have not given a single raise. Obviously because the hand is quite reasonable, say a minimum of eight points. Maximum remains around 9½. And as a footnote, of course, if you only have about 6–7 points and a four-card Club suit, raise to two Clubs.

The two No Trump response is agreed as a limit bid. The range is 11–12½. The immediate three No Trump is also a limit bid. Range 13–15½. Don't bid it on more: you may miss a Slam. And be chary of bidding it on a blank thirteen points. Remember how bad the opening bid can be, and hunt for an alternative if possible. Examples over one Club bid:

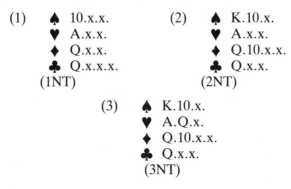

(1)	♠ 10.x.x.	(2)	♠ K.10.x.
	♥ A.x.x.		♥ A.x.x.
	♦ Q.x.x.		♦ Q.10.x.x.
	♣ Q.x.x.x.		♣ Q.x.x.
	(1NT)		(2NT)

(3)	♠ K.10.x.
	♥ A.Q.x.
	♦ Q.10.x.x.
	♣ Q.x.x.
	(3NT)

Partner is in no difficulty over these bids. With balanced hands he reverts to the 25/26 No Trump yardstick and raises one No Trump to two on seventeen and a half, and to three on a very good nineteen. If partner has opened one Club and you bid one No Trump he knows you have at least eight points and can bid two on sixteen and three on seventeen. Two No Trumps are raised to three on fourteen. If you have responded one No Trump and partner raises to two, rebid to three on eight points unless the opening bid was one Club when you need nine points.

With unbalanced hands, the action is up to him. You have announced your hand within fairly exact limits, and control goes to him. If he thinks there is a game he must bid it or force. If he thinks there isn't, he passes or signs off. In either case you accept his decision.

Sometimes he needs more information. Now he will consult with you. You have, of course, already limited your hand. But partner is now saying, "There may still be a game". Obviously, then, if your bid was minimum discourage him. If it wasn't, encourage him. After that, it's on his own head.

There remains the category of hands in which you have a choice of bids. Assuming the situation is uncomplicated, either by a part score or the necessity of stopping your partner playing the hand, always follow one rule. Make the cheapest bid. And don't go galloping into a game in No Trumps until you've had a sniff at a major suit game. Don't, for example, bid three No Trumps over one Club on:

> (4) ♠ K.10.x.
> ♥ Q.10.x.x.
> ♦ A.Q.x.
> ♣ Q.x.x.
> (see hand 3)

Four Hearts may easily be the only make, and three No Trumps go down on a Spade lead. Bid one Heart. Again holding:

> (5) ♠ A.x.x.x.
> ♥ K.J.x.x.
> ♦ A.x.x.
> ♣ Q.x.

bid one Heart—the cheapest of the alternatives—over one Club. Partner may respond one Spade which you raise to four. If he bids anything else you can always still bid three No Trumps. Be careful not to carry this principle of the cheapest bid too far. There is a school of experts who tell you holding:

> (6) ♠ A.J.x.x.
> ♥ x.x.x.
> ♦ x.x.x.x.
> ♣ x.x.

that the correct bid is one Diamond over one Club. And some of them even purport to be playing Acol when they do it. That way madness lies. Remember first that a far larger—and more successful—number of master players think that such super science is crazy. Secondly, that even if the scientific bug bites you, only an expert player with an expert partner dare bid like that. Don't muddle your thinking. Pass on the hand or, if you must, bid one Spade.

One final word of warning. Don't bid a suit for fun or to show your knowledge or because it's safe. If you are sure three No Trumps is right, bid it at once. By the time you've finished bidding your suits, you'll have told the opponents what to lead and you'll go down. Serves you right too. You should have made the natural bid.

CHAPTER X

TRIAL BIDS

I give a special chapter to Trial Bids. Partly because I have a paternal interest in them for I christened them and helped to develop them. Partly because they are an essential part of Acol. What is a Trial Bid? It is any bid in any other suit after a suit has been agreed. For expert players add the proviso that sometimes a suit can be agreed by inference. Why use Trial Bids? To answer the doubts about game or slam that the previous bidding has shown. Trial Bids are to Acol what Asking Bids are to Culbertson. Typically though, Trial Bids have requirements neither for the bidder nor for the responder. There are no rules. Each case is different. They will require then a little effort to master them for you cannot find the answer to the questions in any book. You must apply the principles I will give you to each situation. Soon though, you will find a new delight in Bridge for these are the most delicate and precise of all bidding aids.

GAME TRIAL BIDS

The standard Trial Bid situation is after the simple raise in a major, say one Heart–two Hearts. If you can bid game now of course you bid it. Suppose you can't. Suppose you want to be in game if partner's raise to two of a major is a maximum, not if it is a minimum. What now? Well you can, of course, bid three Hearts. Sometimes that might be the way out, but on most hands it's a clumsy uncouth method. For it tells partner very little. It doesn't tell him where you would like his strength to be. It answers for the hands where you hold a maximum, and where it is immaterial where your side strength lies. For Acol players, this isn't good enough. Suppose I have bid one Heart on:

(a) ♠ x.
     ♥ K.Q.10.x.x.x.
     ♦ K.x.x.
     ♣ A.10.x.

and partner bids two Hearts, a game is almost certain to succeed if he has:

(b) ♠ J.x.x.
     ♥ A.x.x.x.
     ♦ Q.J.x.x.
     ♣ x.x.

and almost certain to fail if he has:

(c) ♠ Q.J.x.x.
     ♥ A.x.x.x.
     ♦ J.x.x.
     ♣ x.x.

How can we distinguish between these two hands? They are identical except for the better fit in the first hand. The answer lies in the Trial Bid. This can be Two Spades or Three Diamonds or Three Clubs. Any of these bids must be unconditionally forcing for clearly on the information we have at present we are going to play the hand in Hearts. You select the one in which you would like some help. The help can be honour trick strength (Jacks and tens are rarely of value) or a singleton or even doubleton. In the case we've given then, you bid Three Diamonds. This says, "Partner, I know you've a weak hand on your bid of Two Hearts. If you're very weak sign off with Three Hearts, and I'll pass. If you've got a really good Two Heart bid give me game with Four Hearts. And if you're just between the two, then it looks as if Diamonds are the danger suit. If you can help a bit here, then have a go at Four Hearts. If you can't, we'll play in Three Hearts." That's a really remarkable amount of information for one bid to convey. And you can see at once how it solves all these very difficult bidding problems.

Look how easy it is for the responder. Hand (b) is a poor hand, but the Diamonds just tip the scale and the bid is Four Hearts. Hand (c) is a poor hand and the Diamonds are a liability. So Three Hearts only. The hand might have been:

(d) ♠ x.x.
♥ A.x.x.x.
♦ x.x.x.
♣ K.Q.x.x.

which is a maximum Two Heart bid and so an automatic Four
Heart bid in spite of the Diamonds. Again it might be:

(e) ♠ x.x.x.
♥ A.x.x.x.
♦ Q.x.
♣ x.x.x.x.

which is a bad Two Heart bid and so a sign off to Three Hearts
even with the Diamonds. Now look back to the original idea of
bidding Three Hearts instead of a Trial Bid. The various combinations partner's cards can take, pivoting on A.x.x.x. in trumps,
and the chances of game are:

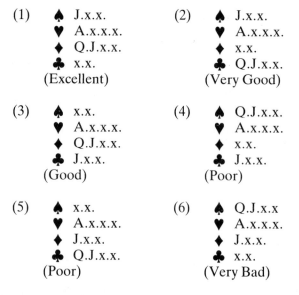

(1) ♠ J.x.x.
♥ A.x.x.x.
♦ Q.J.x.x.
♣ x.x.
(Excellent)

(2) ♠ J.x.x.
♥ A.x.x.x.
♦ x.x.
♣ Q.J.x.x.
(Very Good)

(3) ♠ x.x.
♥ A.x.x.x.
♦ Q.J.x.x.
♣ J.x.x.
(Good)

(4) ♠ Q.J.x.x.
♥ A.x.x.x.
♦ x.x.
♣ J.x.x.
(Poor)

(5) ♠ x.x.
♥ A.x.x.x.
♦ J.x.x.
♣ Q.J.x.x.
(Poor)

(6) ♠ Q.J.x.x
♥ A.x.x.x.
♦ J.x.x.
♣ x.x.
(Very Bad)

Let's assume the first three just make game and the second three
go one down. The Trial Bid player, after Three Diamonds, will
bid the first four and play the last two in Three Hearts. The
Punter over the uninformative Three Hearts from the opener will

bid all six. The Safe player will bid none. Non-vulnerable, giving 300 for game and 50 for a part score, this is our balance sheet:

	Acol	*Punter*	*Safe player*
1.	420	420	170
2.	420	420	170
3.	420	420	170
4.	−50	−50	140
5.	140	−50	140
6.	140	−50	140
	+ 1,490	+ 1,110	+ 930

Vulnerable the difference is more marked and the figures work out at plus 2,040, plus 1,560 and plus 930. Of course, if there is any doubling or redoubling of the game contracts, we will gain more because we are in five good contracts out of six. Note too, that the opening bidder gains nothing by himself gambling Four Hearts over Two. If the hands are as shown, he will score the Punter's points. If the responding hand is better, we will all reach every game whether we bid a direct Four Hearts or Three Hearts or Three Diamonds. But if they are worse than the hand shown—say without the Queen—he will go down on all six where we can stop in Three and make at least half the contracts. The figures show two things. First of all, it is better to go for a doubtful game, especially if vulnerable, than play safe. Secondly, that it is much better than either not to have to guess.

So the Game Trial Bid is, in essence, an invitation to partner to bid game in the agreed suit. The important thing for partner to consider is not that his hand is weak—he's said that already with Two Hearts—but whether it is rather better than it might be. If so, bid Four Hearts. If you bid only Three, partner having made a Game Trial Bid must pass. No "ifs" no "buts". Expert or dub, you must pass. For if you do not, then there is an end of Bridge logic and of partnership. If you say, "I can't bid a game—can you?" and partner says, "Sorry I can't" you daren't go on to say, "O.K. then I will". But thousands of players do.

Let's take it one stage farther. As soon as the level of Three Hearts is passed you are in game. Till then the field is yours. Suppose then, the bidding goes:

N	E	S	W
1♥	—	2♥	—
3♣	—	?	

and you just don't know whether to go Four Hearts or not. You have a little more than a minimum, but not much, Clubs you can help but not much. What now? Gamble or play safe? You needn't guess. Pass the buck back to partner. Bid Three Diamonds. And that says as clearly as if you spoke the words. "I'd like to go on, but I'm not sure. It's the toss of a coin for me. I'll do what you say." And then the opening bidder can decide to play for game or part score. Don't use this ultra subtle method as a coward's way out. If you possibly can, decide yourself. Only if you are in an agony of indecision, and if you can bid under the safety level, in this case Three Hearts, are you justified in putting the onus on partner.

There is one situation to watch carefully. Take the bidding:

N	E	S	W
1♥	—	2♥	—
2♠	—	?	

Now Two Spades is, of course, a Trial Bid. It may or may not also be a suit. It is also possible that Four Spades can be made and not Four Hearts as in the following hands:

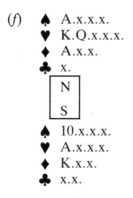

(f)   ♠ A.x.x.x.
     ♥ K.Q.x.x.x.
     ♦ A.x.x.
     ♣ x.

♠ 10.x.x.x.
♥ A.x.x.x.
♦ K.x.x.
♣ x.x.

Here the 3/2 break in Spades may enable South's losing Diamond to be thrown on the long Heart. In Hearts four tricks must be lost. But South must not assume that North has a Spade suit:

he may have only three or even two Spades. So the response of Four Spades is out. So is the bid of Four Hearts which would close the door on Spades. The answer, of course, is Three Spades. This says, "Partner, I'm interested. We'll have a try for game. But I have also four Spades. Does that interest you?" And North should now respond Four Spades on the hand given or Four Hearts if he has not a Spade suit. In either case, of course, he cannot pass for Three Spades (being over the safety level of Three Hearts) is inferentially a game force. South then must never bid Three Spades in this sequence without having four of them. With three—however good they are—he bids Three or Four Hearts, or perhaps buck passes with three of a minor.

Game Trial Bids in a minor suit are unlikely after the simple raise. Eleven tricks are a lot to contract for if partner can do more than raise the suit once. But they can be very useful. Holding say:

(g)   ♠   x.
     ♥   A.x.x.
     ♦   K.Q.10.x.x.x.
     ♣   A.10.x.

If partner bids Two Diamonds over your one bid there may be a game either in No Trumps or in Diamonds. Or there may only be a part score. Check up by Trial Bids. Bid first Three Clubs. If partner signs off to Three Diamonds, bid Three Hearts. Partner with:

(h)   ♠   J.10.x.x.
     ♥   Q.x.x.
     ♦   A.x.x.x.
     ♣   J.x.

or similar hands should try Three No Trumps. Obviously the opener hasn't a Spade guard. With:

(i)   ♠   x.x.x.x.
     ♥   x.x.
     ♦   A.x.x.x.x.
     ♣   K.x.

he should jump to five Diamonds. Slightly better—say K.Q. of Clubs—he should jump to four Diamonds over the first Trial bid of three Clubs. Notice by the way, that if you make the "cheaper" Trial Bid of two Hearts you cannot bid Clubs under the level of four, and so shut out the game in No Trumps.

The minor suit Game Trial Bid is, however, more usual after the double raise, say 1D-3D. Here a bid of three of a major or of four Clubs invites a five Diamond response. Work out the possibilities on exactly the same principle as the major suit Game Trial Bids. Remember always not to underestimate a weak hand. The fit is what counts.

SLAM TRIAL BIDS

We have poured scorn on the player who barges on to game over our sign off. But suppose it happens. And suppose the player who after:

N	E	S	W
1♥	—	2♥	—
2♠	—	3♥	—
?			

still bids Four Hearts is Harrison Gray or Jack Marx. Have they gone crazy? No. Then am I wrong to say an expert or a dub who has made a Game Trial Bid must pass this sequence? No. How come then? You've seen the catch by this time: The Two Spade bid wasn't a Game Trial Bid at all: it was a slam try. At the two level! Obviously he was going to game anyway, minimum or no minimum from you, but he decided to have a sniff at a slam on the way. He has something like:

(j) ♠ A.Q.10.x.x.
　　　 ♥ K.Q.x.x.x.x.
　　　 ♦ A.
　　　 ♣ x.

This hand may well be a certain slam if partner lifts Two Spades to Four Hearts say on:

(k) ♠ K.x.x.
　　　 ♥ A.x.x.x.
　　　 ♦ J.x.x.
　　　 ♣ x.x.x.

There are three key cards missing. The two Aces and the King of Spades. If partner can find a Four Heart bid, you can bid six confidently. At the very worst it will be an even money Spade finesse. But if he only bids Three Hearts he cannot have two out of the three cards. At the best there will be a Spade finesse for the contract: at the worst, two Aces are missing. The odds aren't good enough, and you bid Four Hearts quietly.

The classic Slam trial bidding in this field is a hand held by S. J. Simon. He had:

(*l*) ♠ A.K.x.x.
       ♥ x.x.x.
       ♦ x.x.x.
       ♣ x.x.x.

and raised his partner's one Spade to two. Partner bid three Hearts and Simon three Spades. Partner now bid four Hearts. What on earth can this second trial bid mean? Clearly both the trial bids were slam tries for the bidding is already at the level of game. The opener still hasn't given up even though you have twice said your hand is shapeless and weak. He is making a second slam try without the A.K. of trumps. Now obviously you can have nothing more than the A.K. of trumps or you would not have signed off in three Spades. So it follows that your hand is now the strongest it can possibly be. So—Six Spades. And partner held.

(*m*) ♠ Q.J.10.x.x.
       ♥ A.K.Q.10.x.
       ♦ A.x.
       ♣ x.

This is a perfect illustration of how good a bad hand can become.

The responding hand, of course, never assumes, at least until the second trial bid, that the opener is slamming. He takes it as a game try and replies accordingly. When in the slam zone, cue-bidding and trial bidding merge into each other. Usually a cue-bid shows a particular feature, Ace or void, or sometimes a King. Trial bids may or may not show particular features. Cue-bids in fact, are always trial bids except when they are used defensively to signal a lead. Trial bids on the other hand are not always cue-bids.

Look at this hand, bid in a match, to Three No Trumps:

(n) ♠ A.Q.10.x.   ♠ K.x.
     ♥ J.10.x.   ♥ A.x.x.
     ♦ K.   [W E]   ♦ A.Q.x.x.
     ♣ K.Q.8.x.x.   ♣ A.9.x.x.

with E–W vulnerable and East dealing. The bidding in the match was:

E	S	W	N
1♦	—	2♣	—
2NT	—	3NT	—
—	—		

This, of course, is bad bidding, and a bad result. But if the bidding starts with a one Diamond bid—and many players, perhaps most, would open one Diamond—the Three No Trump contract is difficult to avoid. Guy Ramsey noted the hands down, gave one to Jack Marx and one to me, and invited us to try. This was our sequence:

E (Macleod)	W (Marx)
1NT	3♣
4♣	4♠
5NT	6♦
7♣	No.

Acol bidding and the opening No Trump which limits my hand, makes it easier to show strength later, knowing that my hand cannot be overestimated. The really interesting bids are the two by Jack Marx after the suit was agreed. Let's read the bids:
1. 1NT (16–18 points).
2. 3♣ (Game force. The alternative is 2♣ calling for a four-card major. Perhaps it's best to get the force over in view of the strength of the hand, but the decision is close.)
3. 4♣ (Agreeing the suit. Three No Trumps in view of the fit and the three Aces would be very bad.)

76

4. 4♠ (A cue-bid because it shows an Ace. A trial bid because it asks for a slam in Clubs. Almost certainly it denies the red suit Aces: in cue-bidding one normally bids the lowest control to economize in bidding time.)
5. 5NT (The ideal hand for this bid. It pin-points my three Aces and my Spade King. It, of course, accepts a small slam and invites the Grand Slam.
6. 6♦ (The perfect Grand Slam try bid. It is higher than 6♣, but, as bids aren't made for fun, it denies the ability to bid 7♣. This is what it says, "I can't myself go seven even though I know about the four cards you hold. Have you something goodish in Diamonds? If so, bid 7♣. If not Six No Trumps looks safe and I'll pass that.)
7. 7♣ (Obviously).

I bid the Grand Slam because I had the Queen of Diamonds. Not just because I had a Queen. With the Queen of Hearts, for example, I bid Six No Trumps. Again, if Jack's Hearts and Diamonds were reversed, he would bid six Hearts and not six Diamonds. The point is that the Grand Slam is on because we have the precise cards, and because we use a system flexible enough to show them.

I'm afraid then that this chapter must be left a little in the air. No tidy little table of holdings on which you should make a Trial Bid or Cue Bid. And no commands from one partner to another which call for blind obedience. Something much better. Judgement in difficult situations. Partnership instead of dictatorship. And, above all, logic. First, last and all the time, logic.

Finally, here are half a dozen illustrations. I add no comment. Read them several times until you're sure that you have mastered the logic of Trial Bids:

(1)
♠ J.x.x.x.
♥ A.x.x.x.
♦ K.x.
♣ x.x.x.

W E

♠ A.10.x.
♥ K.10.x.x.x.x.
♦ A.x.x.
♣ x.

Bidding:

	W	N	E	S
	—	—	1♥	—
	2♥	—	2♠	—
	3♠	—	4♥	

(2)
- ♠ J.x.x.x.
- ♥ K.x.x.
- ♦ Q.x.x.x.
- ♣ Q.x.

W   E

- ♠ A.Q.x.x.x.
- ♥ A.x.x.
- ♦ x.
- ♣ K.J.x.x.

Bidding:

	W	N	E	S
	—	—	1♠	—
	2♠	—	3♣	—
	3♥	—	4♠	—
	—	—		

(3)
- ♠ A.x.x.
- ♥ K.J.x.x.
- ♦ A.J.x.x.x.x.
- ♣ none.

W   E

- ♠ J.x.x.
- ♥ A.x.
- ♦ K.x.x.x.
- ♣ Q.x.x.x.

Bidding:

	W	N	E	S
	1♦	—	2♦	—
	2♥	—	2NT	—
	4♦	—	5♦	—
	—	—		

(4)
- ♠ A.K.x.x.x.
- ♥ A.J.x.x.
- ♦ none.
- ♣ A.J.x.x.

W   E

- ♠ Q.J.x.x.
- ♥ x.x.
- ♦ A.J.x.x.x.
- ♣ Q.x.

Bidding:

	W	N	E	S
	1♠	—	3♠	—
	4♣	—	4♦	—
	4♠	—	—	

(5)
- ♠ K.x.
- ♥ A.Q.x.x.x.x.
- ♦ x.
- ♣ A.K.x.x.

W   E

- ♠ A.x.x.
- ♥ K.x.x.x.x.
- ♦ J.x.x.
- ♣ Q.x.

Bidding:

	W	N	E	S
	1♥	—	3♥	—
	4♣	—	4♠	—
	5♣	—	6♥	—
	—	—		

78

(6)

	West		East
♠	A.x.	♠	x.
♥	A.x.x.x.x.x.	♥	K.Q.10.x.
♦	K.J.x.x.	♦	A.x.x.
♣	K.x.	♣	A.Q.x.x.x.

W E

Bidding:

W	N	E	S
1 ♥	—	3 ♣	—
3 ♦	—	3 ♥	—
3 ♠	—	4 ♦	—
4NT	—	5NT	—
6 ♣	—	7 ♥	—
—	—		

CHAPTER XI

COMPETITIVE BIDDING

USUALLY in Bridge books pre-emptive bidding, overcalls and doubles are each given a separate niche. They are, of course, all part of the same problem, the problem of competitive bidding. The first point to learn is so obvious that most players never bother with it: there can be no competitive bidding unless you bid. So get into the bidding. Get in as quickly as you can and as safely as you can, but get in. Nearly always it's poor play to "trap" by passing on a big hand. Nearly always it's silly play to hold back from the bidding until the opponents' bidding peters out. It may or may not do so, and even if it does the level is sure to be higher. Suppose your right hand opponent bids a Heart and you have a fair hand, but you belong to the school of the strong overbid and pass. Your other opponent bids three Hearts and it's passed round to you. What now? Probably three Hearts is a make, and possibly you can do better—you may even have game. But if you interfere now you can equally well go down three doubled, or play it in the wrong suit. And so usually you just pass. That's why Acol bidders over and over again, even against the strongest international competition, get away with a partscore bid and made in both rooms. So you should intervene readily, and, if the balance of cards is against you, push the bidding as high as you dare as quickly as you can; you must steal bidding space from your opponents. It follows then, and this is essential to your partner's peace of mind, that an Acol player doesn't have to torture himself with doubt about re-opening on a poor hand when the opponents' bidding falters and stops. He knows perfectly well that partner hasn't got a big hand: if he had he'd bid. We must then be adventurous in our defence. We must—it's a favourite saying of Harrison Gray's—"contest those partscores". We must worry our opponents and give them neither space nor peace.

There must, of course, be some sort of safety level always in mind and Culbertson's "Rule of Two and Three", as he calls it, is the surest guide. A player should expect then for a defensive bid to get within three tricks of his contract non-vulnerable and two tricks vulnerable. He should assume reasonable breaks, but also that his partner's hand will be near worthless to him. And now if you're all set to be truculent to the opposition, let's start.

PRE-EMPTIVE BIDS OF THREE

Don't play these as a timid invitation to Three No Trumps. Play them, major and minor, as a shut-out bid on weakness. Usually they show a seven-card suit. I like playing them very weak indeed and would open Three Diamonds, non-vulnerable on:

(a) ♠ x.x.
     ♥ x.
     ♦ A.x.x.x.x.x.x.
     ♣ J.x.x.

but most people play them a shade stronger: say the Diamonds headed by A.Q.10. Within limits, the more you lose, even doubled, the more you save. Certainly it's much harder for the opponents to find their correct contract if they have to start at the level of three. Two words of warning. don't open with a three bid if you have a four-card major suit as well, unless partner has passed: there's a big danger of missing a game if his hand fits, and you'll probably shut him out. And don't bid them with too much high-card strength. An Ace and a King is about the maximum.

Responding to a three bid is easy enough, provided you remember always how weak the bid is. You should always invent a hand for partner, and then look at yours again. Suppose you have:

(b) ♠ A.K.x.x.
     ♥ A.J.x.
     ♦ x.
     ♣ K.x.x.x.x.

and partner opens Three Diamonds. Give him hand (a) even with the Diamonds strengthened and where do you go for honey?

81

Nowhere. So pass. Maybe the other opponent will protect and then you have a sound double. With J.x. of Diamonds you might try three No Trumps.

The second rule in responding is that if you want to be in a game in another suit you should bid it direct. Otherwise any suit bid is a mild slam try and partner can respond either with a minimum rebid or, if he has a maximum three bid with a jump. For example:

(c)	♦ K.J.x.		♠ x.
	♥ A.K.Q.x.x.	W E	♥ x.x.
	♦ A.x.x.		♦ Q.x.
	♣ K.x.		♣ A.Q.J.x.x.x.x.x.

Sensible bidding with East dealing would be:

E	S	W	N
3♣	—	3♥	—
5♣	—	6NT	—
—	—		

West's final bid is to guard against a doubleton Spade with East.

DEFENCE TO THREE BIDS

All that really matters here is to be quite sure that you and your partner are using the same defence. I am not at all dogmatic about it, but this is the way I like it:

1. The double is optional, but will normally be left in for penalties. Partner can always remove if his hand is unbalanced.
2. The overbid of Three No Trumps shows a desire to play in that contract. Partner should rarely disturb. This is the only way to cope with a holding like:

(d)	♠ A.J.x.
	♥ Q.x.
	♦ K.Q.J.10.x.x.
	♣ A.Q.

over an opening three bid either in Clubs or Spades.

3.   With a huge hand a direct overbid in the same suit, e.g.
     Four Diamonds over Three Diamonds on:

$$(e) \quad \spadesuit \quad \text{A.K.J.10.x.x.}$$
$$\heartsuit \quad \text{A.Q.J.x.x.x.}$$
$$\diamondsuit \quad \text{none.}$$
$$\clubsuit \quad \text{Q.}$$

If partner replies, as he probably will, with Five Clubs you
now bid Five Diamonds for him to choose between the
major suits. You should play one variation. Over an opening of Three Spades a bid of Four Spades shuts out the
most likely game bid Four Hearts. Accordingly Four
Clubs should be the conventional game force over Three
Spades, and should not guarantee a Club suit.

OTHER OPENING PRE-EMPTIVE BIDS

These are purely common-sense bids and need little comment. An opening bid of four shows one probable trick better
than a reasonably good bid of three. For example open Four
Spades on:

$$(f) \quad \spadesuit \quad \text{A.J.10.x.x.x.x.}$$
$$\heartsuit \quad \text{none.}$$
$$\diamondsuit \quad \text{A.x.x.x.}$$
$$\clubsuit \quad \text{Q.x.}$$

Without the Ace of Diamonds this would still be a sound bid of
Three.

OVERCALLS

I suppose "it was only an overcall partner", is the most fre-
quent excuse for disaster at the Bridge table. A moment's
thought, of course, kills the plea. For if the hand is not worth an
opening bid when the opponent's strength is unknown, it can
hardly be worth a bid (often at a higher level) when you know
one of the opponents has sufficient strength to bid and, by the
same token, there is less for your partner to share. No exact
rules can guide you as you try to steer between the rocks of cow-
ardice and foolhardiness. As a general guide though, an overcall
at the one level should be roughly a normal opening bid with a
point count around thirteen and most important, a fairly

compact suit. Say, as a minimum, non-vulnerable, Heart bid over one Diamond:

(g) ♠ Q.x.
♥ A.Q.10.8.x.
♦ x.x.
♣ A.x.x.x.

If you have to bid at the two level add one or two points and be a little more fussy about the small cards in your suit. Of course there are dozens of occasions when these "rules" are too severe and should be ignored. For example, over any suit bid a bid of One Spade, non-vulnerable, is perfectly sound on:

(h) ♠ A.Q.J.9.x.
♥ x.x.x.
♦ x.x.
♣ x.x.x.

This is partly to get a lead if your left-hand opponent plays in No Trumps, partly because of the pre-emptive value of Spades, and partly because (as with the three bids) if you are doubled and defeated you will surely show a profit against the enemy game or slam. Only experience will tell you when it is tactically sound to shade the requirements I have given, and you will find it pays to err on the side of caution till you're sure of yourself.

An overcall nearly always means a five-card suit. If you have to do it on four then K.Q.9.x. would be a normal minimum, but more often a double can be found. The simple overcall has fairly clear limits of strength. It cannot be as weak as an opening bid (except when used tactically), but on the other hand it cannot be as strong as a maximum one bid, for then a double or a jump overcall should be used. Be chary of over-calling a suit bid with one No Trump. In No Trumps the normal added protective values of your fourth and fifth trump do not exist, and you need a better point count to compensate. You should have sixteen points non-vulnerable and eighteen vulnerable. If your count is sixteen to eighteen and you are vulnerable, you should usually double or bid a suit.

The jump overcall 1H–2S or 1H–3D is, of course, a strong

bid, but it is not forcing, even for one round. Typical hands with the above sequences would be:

(i)   ♠   A.Q.J.10.x.x.   (j)   ♠   K.x.
        ♥   A.x.   ♥   x.
        ♦   K.J.x.   ♦   K.Q.J.10.x.x.
        ♣   x.x.   ♣   A.Q.x.x.

The pre-emptive overall 1H–3S on the other hand is a weak bid rather similar to a goodish opening bid of three.

The only way in which you can force to game after the opponents open is by overbidding their suit 1S–2S, or 1D–2D. This often, but not invariably, shows also the Ace or a void in the opponent's suit. Partner should not, however, rely on this unless a subsequent bid confirms it. When such an enormous hand is held the opening bid can often be a help in placing outstanding cards. For example:

(k)   ♠   K.x.   ♠   x.x.x.
      ♥   A.K.x.x.x.   ♥   Q.x.x.x.x.
      ♦   A.K.Q.x.x.x.   ♦   x.x.
      ♣   none.   ♣   J.x.x.

W   E

Bidding:

S	W	N	E
1♣	2♣	3♣	3♥
4♣	4NT	—	5♥
—	6♥	—	—

East should not be deterred from showing his five-card major suit on the first round. It's as much as he can expect to hold on the bidding. West knows the Ace of Spades is missing, but Spades may not be led in which case East's will be thrown on the Diamonds or, if they are, South is almost sure to have the Ace.

Partner's responses to the various overcalls cannot be tabulated. If he proceeds on the assumption that the simple overcall shows a reasonable opening bid with a fair five-card suit, he will have no difficulty, and he may, if necessary, shade his trump support in raising. If the overall was one No Trump a simple calculation will show him that non-vulnerable he can raise to three on about nine and vulnerable on seven to eight. The jump overcall should be kept open with equivalent values to a simple raise of one or two: again, of course, trump support can be shaded. For example, an overcall of Two Spades over One Heart should be raised to Three on:

(*l*)   ♠   x.x.x.
        ♥   J.x.x.
        ♦   Q.x.x.
        ♣   K.Q.x.x.(compare hand (*i*))

DOUBLES

More ink has been spilled on the question of "when is a double not a double" than any other Bridge topic. I'll add very little to it. There must always be a measure of discretion with partner, but these rules cover about 95 per cent. of all cases. A double is for penalties unless:

(1)   The partner of the doubler has not bid, and:
(2)   The double is made at the first opportunity, and:
(3)   The double is of a suit not above the level of three (and not at the three level bid pre-emptively).

If all these three conditions apply the double is for a take-out.

PENALTY DOUBLES

Doubles of No Trump contracts are always for penalties. Partner can remove the double if his hand is weak and unbalanced or if, for example, at a partscore, he sees a more likely profit in bidding game. A typical immediate double of a one No Trump bid would be:

(*m*)   ♠   K.J.x.
        ♥   A.Q.x.
        ♦   K.Q.J.x.x.
        ♣   Q.x.

The most fruitful doubles are usually the immediate doubles of an opponent's intervening bid. These doubles must, however, be regarded as tentative and the opener, particularly if his opening bid is a light Acol one, will frequently decline the offer. For example, if the bidding goes 1H–2C the next hand should surely double on:

(n) ♠ A.J.x.
         ♥ x.
         ♦ A.x.x.x.x.
         ♣ Q.9.x.x.

The point count is there for two No Trumps, but this is a stupid bid with the singleton Heart. On the other hand a singleton in partner's suit is a great asset in defence and indeed a double should rarely include more than a doubleton. For good players, especially vulnerable against non-vulnerable opponents, the double and the evident willingness to give up a chance of a rubber is prima facie evidence of a misfit. With a balanced hand, particularly if he has two or three small trumps, the opener should pass. He should be most suspicious of a singleton trump and should always remove the double with a void. A void does not mean that partner will have great length in trumps: much more often it means that dummy will turn up with three or even four unpleasant ones. Moreover, the disadvantage of not being able to lead at least one round of trumps through declarer is often fatal to the defence. In Auction Bridge days it used to be a maxim "never double anything unless you can double everything". It goes, of course, much too far, but there is a grain of truth in it. It is suicidal on the bidding 1D–1H to double on:

(o) ♠ x.
         ♥ K.Q.10.x.x.x.
         ♦ J.x.x.
         ♣ x.x.x.

Pass and hope that partner can double (for a take-out although, of course, you'd pass) or that opponents, if your partner rebids, can be lulled into a bid of two Hearts.

Don't distinguish too carefully between "free" and other doubles. A redouble and an overtrick or two can make any double expensive. Most Bridge writers say you should accept from time to time the doubling of opponents into game as part of the price you have to pay for speculative doubles, which on balance show a considerable profit. I'm a bit chary about it. First of all, a double more often than not gives information worth a trick to the declarer. Secondly nothing is so destructive of partnership confidence as to present the opponents with a game they could neither reach nor make, probably as well as losing a partscore of your own. I tend to be tight in my penalty doubles when a lost game is the price of failure, but if a freer game suits you here, play your own way.

Mr. Punch's advice to those about to marry applies to those thinking of doubling a slam—don't. The mathematical odds are hopelessly against you and by the time the slam zone is reached, the margin for error should be small. There are only three occasions when you should double a slam:

(1) When the bid is a sacrifice.
(2) When you are quite certain you can defeat it and any other contract the opponents can switch to.
(3) When your double is a call for a lead—the Lightner Double.

Lightner's Double is an admirable convention. It calls for an unusual lead against a slam. Just that. Partner's holding will almost always make it clear to him what lead you require. It may be you want to ruff or that you want a lead through a suit bid by dummy and not supported by declarer in which you hold a tenace, or that you are exposing a phoney bid. Suppose you are West with this holding:

(*p*) ♠ Q.x.x.
    ♥ x.x.x.
    ♦ x.x.
    ♣ Q.x.x.x.x.

and the bidding goes:

W	N	E	S
—	1♠	—	3♦
—	4♦	—	4♥
—	5♦	—	6♦
—	—	Dble	—
—	—		

The Club would be a normal lead, but the double rules that out. Your Spade Queen makes it most improbable that East has any tenace in the suit. The lead is surely the Heart. East will have either K.Q. of Hearts and the Ace of Diamonds, or he may even

have A.K. of Hearts and South's Heart bid have been to inhibit
a lead. Actually (this is a hand from play) the second possibility
was correct and South held:

$$(q) \quad \spadesuit \quad \text{K.x.}$$
$$\heartsuit \quad \text{Q.x.}$$
$$\diamondsuit \quad \text{A.K.J.10.x.x.}$$
$$\clubsuit \quad \text{A.x.x.}$$

without the Heart lead North's Spades are set up and the Grand
Slam made.

TAKE-OUT DOUBLES

The following are the most common situations in which the
double is for a take-out. In no case, however, does partner for-
feit his discretion to pass:

	S	W	N	E
(1)	1♠	Dble		
(2)	1♠	—	—	Dble
(3)	1♠	—	2♠	Dble
(4)	1♠	2♣	—	—
	Dble			

A take-out double, if at all possible, should be preferred to a
suit overcall. Obviously the safety margin is greatly increased if
you can offer partner the choice of three suits. Ideally, therefore, the doubler should have either a 5–4–4–0 or a 4–4–4–1
shape. You mustn't, however, wait for that to happen. Nor
should you worry too much about your point count. Long ago
Richard Lederer decided correctly that:

$$(r) \quad \spadesuit \quad \text{A.x.x.x.}$$
$$\heartsuit \quad \text{x.}$$
$$\diamondsuit \quad \text{K.x.x.x.x.}$$
$$\clubsuit \quad \text{K.10.x.}$$

was a good double of one Heart. So it is. Indeed, sometimes

89

tactically, particularly when partscores are about, you can shade the point count down to:

$$(s) \quad \spadesuit \quad \text{A.x.x.x.}$$
$$\heartsuit \quad \text{none.}$$
$$\diamondsuit \quad \text{A.x.x.x.}$$
$$\clubsuit \quad \text{J.x.x.x.x.}$$

over a bid of one Heart. Only experience (and a knowledge of your partner) can tell you how far you can safely go. Normally your minimum count should be eleven and your maximum about twenty. That is an enormous margin and partner must step warily with his first response. It isn't as dangerous as it sounds to double lightly, because of course as your point count drops so you must have better distribution to compensate. Partner should base his first response on the assumption that you have about fourteen points. Naturally, if there is an element of protection about your bid, as in example (2) of the situations given, partner will realise that you may be quite a bit weaker. It's difficult at love all if you are East to know what to do if the bidding goes:

S	W	N	E
1NT	—	—	?

and you hold about ten points. You may well be able to beat the contract a couple of tricks doubled: equally, if North has a maximum pass you may get into trouble. On the whole it is best to pass. If your opponents are strong players they will be quick to double you, and if they are not, it often happens that South's No Trump opener was far stronger than it should have been. You also know that partner—who would bid if he possibly could—has passed. At match point duplicate you usually have to chance your arm: otherwise you'll show a profit passing. With twelve points or more, however, you should always re-open.

RESPONDING TO TAKE-OUT DOUBLE

Assuming first of all that the intervening opponent passes, let's look at the correct action on different hands. First of all if you're very weak. Acol used to play a Two Club bid as a "bust" response: correctly, for it's a pity to advertise weakness and invite a double, this has been dropped. On a hopeless hand make the best of it. Over a double of One Spade followed by a pass bid:

    (*t*) 2♣ on: ♠ x.x.x.
                                  ♥ x.x.x.
                                  ♦ x.x.x.
                                  ♣ x.x.x.x.

         2♦ on: ♠ x.x.x.x.
                                  ♥ x.x.
                                  ♦ J.x.x.x.x.
                                  ♣ x.x.

         2♣ on: ♠ Q.x.x.x.
        (not 1NT)   ♥ x.x.x.
                                    ♦ x.x.x.
                                  ♣ x.x.x.

The one No Trump response should show a hand like:

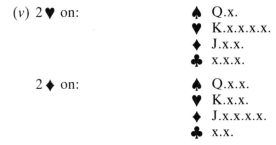

           (*u*) ♠ K.10.x.
                 ♥ x.x.x.
                 ♦ Q.x.x.
                 ♣ Q.x.x.x.

Ordinary hands present no problem and you bid:

        (*v*) 2♥ on: ♠ Q.x.
                                ♥ K.x.x.x.x.
                                ♦ J.x.x.
                                ♣ x.x.x.

              2♦ on: ♠ Q.x.x.
                                  ♥ K.x.x.
                                ♦ J.x.x.x.x.
                                ♣ x.x.

A little stronger than this you should jump the bidding. You can feel quite safe doing this, as your jump bid is not forcing even for one round, although of course the doubler will be strongly encouraged to go on unless his hand is minimum. Here (and everywhere else) if you can make a game, bid it yourself. A double nearly always shows major suit strength, and when a major suit is doubled guarantees strength in the other major suit. Accordingly on the same sequence 1S-double–No Bid, you should bid:

3♥ on:	♠ Q.x.
	♥ A.J.x.x.x.
	♦ Q.x.x.
	♣ x.x.x.
3♦ on:	♠ x.x.x.
	♥ K.x.
	♦ K.Q.x.x.x.x.
	♣ x.x.
4♥ on:	♠ Q.x.
	♥ A.J.x.x.x.x.
	♦ Q.x.x.
	♣ x.x.
2NT on:	♠ A.J.x.
	♥ x.x.
	♦ K.Q.x.x.
	♣ J.x.x.x.

Very rarely should you make a penalty pass, particularly if the suit is ragged. With the same sequence you should bid One No Trump on:

(x) ♠ K.J.x.x.x.
     ♥ x.x.x.
     ♦ Q.x.x.
     ♣ x.x.

but pass on:

(y) ♠ Q.J.10.8.x.x.
     ♥ x.x.x.
     ♦ Q.x.
     ♣ x.x.

A penalty pass, if undisturbed, calls normally for a trump lead.

The only response you can make (anyway in Acol) that is forcing to game is the overbid of the opponent's suit as in the sequence 1H-Dble-2H. Typical hands are:

(z)	♠ A.Q.x.x.	♠ x.	♠ A.J.x.x.
	♥ x.x.	♥ x.	♥ A.
	♦ K.Q.x.x.x.	♦ A.J.x.x.x.	♦ x.x.x.x.
	♣ Q.x.	♣ K.Q.x.x.x.x.	♣ K.x.x.x.

The subsequent bidding does not differ from any ordinary sequence where a forcing situation has been established. The important thing is to agree your suit as quickly as you can. Three No Trumps, although of course, sometimes the only hope of game, should very rarely be attempted without a minimum of two stoppers. The opponents have got their bid in and the attack is apt to be a tempo ahead—with the lead—in clearing their suit. If the intervening player redoubles you should ignore the bid. Proceed then exactly as if he has passed. It follows that a pass from you in such a situation remains a business pass perhaps on:

$(a2)$ ♠ K.J.10.9.8.x.
♥ Q.x.
♦ J.x.
♣ J.x.x.

if one Spade is doubled and redoubled. This is the original Acol theory and I see no good reason to change it, although a number of Acol players now believe that a pass should show a worthless hand. Actually this last method creates more problems than it solves and, if only for simplicity, I prefer our first thought.

DEFENCE TO THE DOUBLE

Systems again vary greatly here although it is now common to almost all systems that the redouble is a "leave the next round to me, partner" bid. It does not guarantee a fit in the opening suit and indeed more often than not is based on high card, strength in the other three suits. An ideal redouble of One Spade would be:

$(b2)$ ♠ x.x.
♥ A.J.x.
♦ K.Q.10.x.
♣ K.10.x.x.

especially if opponents are vulnerable. The opener need not, and will not if his bid was based a single suit, pass a suit bid by the fourth player. Minimum count for an Acol redouble should be ten points.

93

If the third hand cannot redouble his alternatives are:

Pass—This is usually weak, but on rare occasions may be a trap.

Simple Take-Out—This is a normal bid ignoring the double. As a redouble has not been made its count has a normal maximum of ten.

Simple Raise—Almost certainly very weak and purely defensive.

Jump Raises—e.g. 1S–3S. These may be slightly under strength with the usual object of cramping the opposition's bidding.

Jump bid in a New Suit—Again ignoring the double, and nearly always game forcing. The double here may be semi-psychic and it is more economical to carry on with normal bidding rather than waste time exposing it. On the next round a rebid of the same suit, e.g.:

S	W	N	E
1♥	Dble	3♦	—
3♥	—	4♦	—

can be passed—just.

PSYCHIC BIDDING

In a book about systematic bidding there is not much to be written about psychics. They are unregimented and there is no formula for success. It is easier to say what you should not do. If for example, you pick up:

(*c2*) ♠ x.x.x.
        ♥ x.x.x.
        ♦ x.x.x.
        ♣ x.x.x.x.

and in a moment of irritation open the bidding with One No Trump or any other fantasy, you are sure, sometimes, to bring off a coup and muddle the opponents. For every coup you will crash at least ten times and your loss will be very heavy. And this points the only real lesson in psychic bidding—don't attempt too much. Look at it in terms of war. If you are hopelessly outgunned and outnumbered and if, even more important, your opponents know it, an attack all along the front is aimless. You may, though, persuade your enemy that one particular feature is held in greater strength than is the case, or even capture a minor post by concentrating your forces. One Bridge writer described a psychic bid as "an attempt to persuade the opponents that they do not hold the cards they can see in their hands". But these are the stupid psychics and we will waste no more time on them. Your psychic should then not only have a definite but a limited objective. And finally, if possible, it should have all the appearance of a genuine bid. The best psychic I remember in match play was one made by Jack Marx playing with me in the team of four match a year or two before the war. He dealt as South. E–W were vulnerable, and these were the hands:

(d2)

		♠ K.J.10.x.x.x.		
		♥ x.x.		
		♦ J.10		
		♣ J.10.x.		

♠ A.	N	♠ none.
♥ A.Q.10.9.x.x.	W E	♥ K.J.x.x.x.
♦ Q.x.	S	♦ A.K.x.x.x.x.
♣ K.x.x.x.		♣ A.x.

		♠ Q.9.x.x.x.x.		
		♥ none.		
		♦ 9.x.x.		
		♣ Q.9.x.x.		

The bidding started:

S	W	N	E
–	1♥	1♠	3♦
4♦	4♠	6♠	?

Before we look at East's problem it is worth looking at the effect of the defensive barrage we managed to put up. Many of the lessons of this chapter are illustrated here:

(1) The importance of intervening at the earliest moment.

If North·does not bid One Spade it is certain his side can never bid and E—W select their Grand Slam at their leisure. This indeed is what happened in the other room. When South passed and I had such a useless hand it was clear, if any spoke was to be put into the bidding, there would be only one chance.

(2) The hand illustrates the pre-emptive value of the Spade suit.

(3) The defensive bidding obeys the chief rule in Competitive bidding—"if you are weak deny bidding space to your opponents and make them guess". Notice that we have allowed them only three bids and they are already up to the Grand Slam level. In this particular case we reap no profit from this because East—West can in fact make three Grand Slams (No Trumps, Hearts or Diamonds), but if only one of these contracts could be made, then East—West would have an unhappy guess. South's bid—on the face of it an announcement of a Diamond void—is, of course, clearly based on a fit in Spades.

Now take East's cards remembering you cannot see the other three hands. He reasons something like this. "My partner's strong overbid of the opponent's suit shows almost surely both a good Heart suit and a fit in Diamonds. It's a nuisance of the opponents to crowd the bidding, but obviously we have everything. Seven Hearts is certain, seven Diamonds very likely and seven No Trumps (unless West's cue-bid is a void which is just possible) also a good chance—except for that four Diamond bid. For if South is void of Diamonds (and with my six-card suit he may well be) then Seven Hearts is defeated on the Diamond lead and the other two contracts probably fail if North has all the Diamonds. So if South's bid is genuine—and there is no evidence that it is not—we can only double and take a penalty. I don't think I should pass and let West take this decision for, apart from the doubt about his Spade holding, he can hardly think my hand as strong as it is. So it's a guess. I'd rather take a penalty than bid Seven Hearts and go one down, and hear partner's caustic comment, "Didn't you hear the bidding?" So—I double.

The result of four down 700 points was a clear profit to us of 1,510 for, of course, Gray and Simon in the other room bid Seven Hearts.

The particular merit of Jack Marx's bid was that he would have made exactly the same bid if he had in fact a Diamond void. The stupid psychist—obviously South's position, when I have shown Spades and East—West are vulnerable and bidding strongly, is ideal—would perhaps bid Three No Trumps. Far better to plant a reasonable doubt in the opponent's mind. Let them guess.

The other main rule for intelligent psyching is to read your partner's bid as phoney before the opponents find out, and to thicken the smoke screen. One of my happiest Bridge memories comes from a pre-war rubber. I was South and I had cut Eric Leigh-Howard, a good player who likes a gamble. West was a very sound player and East a "Mrs. Guggenheim". East—West had game and thirty when the bidding opened:

W	N	E	S
1NT	Dble	2NT	?

My hand was:

(e2)   ♠ K.10.x.x.
         ♥ K.x.x.
         ♦ Q.10.x.x.x.
         ♣ x.

There is something very odd about this. I have eight points and two tens. The other players' bids add up to about 43. It's impossible. Check back. I know I've got my points—I can see them! The sound player sitting West wouldn't shade his bid by a Knave playing with his partner. The glorious fatuity of the Two No Trumps bid itself guarantees a firm point count. So my partner is trying something. Obviously again, it's in Clubs. So I bid Three Clubs on my singleton. West doubled and I stood it. One may comment in passing that it must be rare to bid a suit for the first time at the three level on a singleton and—unsupported—stand the double. North had seven Clubs to the A.Q. and six small cards. The cards, except for West's K.J.x. of Clubs lay badly for us and if North had played the hand he would surely have gone two down. Or East—West would have taken an easy rubber in No Trumps or Hearts. By concealing my pieces I achieved two successes. First of all West faced with a blind lead chose the Ace of Hearts. Secondly, East was so unnerved by the stream of trumps in dummy ("What are trumps, partner?"—"Oh, but I thought Mr. Macleod bid those—. . .—well I don't understand it") that I was in due course presented with a Diamond for my ninth trick. Again the point of the story is that the bidding is made to sound natural—a weakish double by North, and a save on, say, Six Clubs to the Queen.

The situation in which it is almost standard bidding to be psychic starts 1D–Dble–?, when partner has a very weak hand and Diamond support. Two hints here. First a barrage bid is more effective than a psychic if you can go high enough. On:

$(f2)$ ♠ x.
        ♥ x.
        ♦ Q.10.x.x.x.x.
        ♣ J.x.x.x.x.

Five Diamonds is best. At least the opponents have little chance of probing for their best contract; they must plunge. Secondly, if your hand is not so freakish, by all means make a psychic bid. No matter that it will probably be shown up; that can even be an advantage. Make your bid then as a rule in a suit where you have some little strength—later the opponents will assume your partner holds the honours. On the sequence given then bid Two Spades not Two Hearts on:

(g) ♠ K.10.x.
       ♥ x.x.
       ♦ J.x.x.x.x.x.
       ♣ x.x.

THREE-CARD SUIT BIDS

These are more strategic than psychic. S.J. Simon before he died and since then Terence Reese and Adam Meredith have been perfecting the theory. They are dangerous tools except in expert hands, but you may care to experiment with them. From time to time then try bidding One Heart third in hand on:

(h) ♠ K.10.x.
       ♥ Q.10.x.
       ♦ A.J.x.x.x.
       ♣ x.x.

98

and try overbidding with One Spade on:

(i2)   ♠ J.x.x.
        ♥ x.
        ♦ A.Q.10.x.x.x.
        ♣ K.x.x.

The opening strategic bid is most valuable when you have a part-score. If, of course, you are raised by your partner you don't attempt to rescue. Indeed, you'll probably make your contract, especially as opponents are bound to miscount the hand. You ought to be able to make a profit in ordinary rubber Bridge with an occasional flight of this nature.

Finally on psychic bidding remember this. It is too easy a judgment to say that the only measure for a psychic bid is its success or failure. Even if you succeed there is a price to pay that doesn't appear on the score sheet. If you make psychic bids frequently your partner is almost sure to lose something of the confidence he has in your bids. No temporary triumph is worth that.

A FAIRY STORY

This has been a long chapter and I dare say hard work too. Let's end it with a fairy story which, like all fairy stories, is perfectly true.

Once upon a time before the war there was a Lithuanian timber merchant who was a very nice fellow but a very bad Bridge player and liked playing for very high stakes. He sat playing East with a partner who knew him not. I was South and, more fortunate, had Edward Mayer as my partner who knew the L.T.M. well. The L.T.M. dealt and opened One Spade and I, after a brief glance at my hand which contained eight small cards and the A.K.Q.J.10. of Spades, passed. By the time bidding came round to me again it had gone:

E	S	W	N
1 ♠	—	4 ♠	Dble
Re-dble			

Still there seemed nothing I could do about it. "My lead?" I asked carefully before opening the King of Trumps. The full hands were:

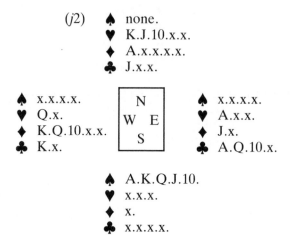

(j2)
♠ none.
♥ K.J.10.x.x.
♦ A.x.x.x.x.
♣ J.x.x.

♠ x.x.x.x.
♥ Q.x.
♦ K.Q.10.x.x.
♣ K.x.

N
W   E
S

♠ x.x.x.x.
♥ A.x.x.
♦ J.x.
♣ A.Q.10.x.

♠ A.K.Q.J.10.
♥ x.x.x.
♦ x.
♣ x.x.x.x.

Perhaps you think Edward's double a little shaded? You don't know the L.T.M. Edward knew:

(1) That his hand should take two tricks.

(2) That the L.T.M. always lost two tricks in the play.

(3) That trumps were badly placed for the declarer.

Just how badly placed he couldn't very well guess, but I've seen worse doubles. The redouble surprised no one: as long as the timber lasted the L.T.M. always redoubled. I played four rounds of trumps, Edward throwing three Diamonds and a small Club. Then I led a Heart and the Ace was forced out. You might think now that declarer would at least take his Club tricks and hold the defeat to five tricks. Not a bit of it. I told you the L.T.M. always lost two tricks in the play. He led a Diamond. Seven down, redoubled, vulnerable.

"I make that exactly four thousand," said Edward, after a short pause, "Plus a hundred and fifty honours," I murmured.

CHAPTER XII

TECHNIQUE IN RUBBER AND DUPLICATE BRIDGE

Most books on Bridge seem to assume that four talented players called North, South, East and West are engaged in an endless pair competition. As if Howard Schenken and George Rapee were for ever opposed to Terence Reese and Boris Schapiro. Bridge, especially rubber bridge, happily isn't like that. You have a partner. It is because you have to have a partner at Bridge that Poker is such a popular game. If you cut an expert or a sound player you can go your way rejoicing, but with one warning. The skill percentage is anyway on your side. Don't try barrages or psychic bids, or spectacular sacrifices. You will win anyway. It's when you cut a weak partner not a strong one that you should play an abnormal game.

MATHEMATICS OF RUBBER BRIDGE

Counting the points you score for your bid, the game values in rubber Bridge are roughly:

First Game	410
Second Straight Game	510
Rubber Game	610

These then are the measures for your doubles and your sacrifices. These—and the ability of your partners. Culbertson tells you that all rubber Bridge is really played for game points and that the rubber is an "artificial abstraction". So it is if the four players are anywhere near equal in calibre. But if your partner is the "dud" of the four all calculations go overboard, and the rubber should be grabbed however tempting the penalty. Equally if you and your partner have a clear lead in skill it does no harm to prolong the rubber and take a small penalty even if, mathematically, it looks a poor investment. Other things being equal though you should as a rule prefer a penalty, say one which looks like being five hundred points to a fairly sure rubber game. There are two reasons for this:

(1) Your win on the game bid is known to within a very few points; your win on the penalty may be much greater. Your safety margin too on the double is wider.

(2) If you take the penalty, at least you will have a plus score. The game may fail on bad breaks or duplication. There is great psychological value in a few hundreds entered above the line, and partner will take no comfort from the theoretical correctness of your bid if he has to chalk up a minus score.

Not enough attention is paid by rubber Bridge players to this point of scoring something on the hand. Indeed, this is one of the main reasons why some of our expert duplicate players are poor money players. George Morris, certainly the most effective and successful money player in this country since Contract started, always used to say in his thin, high voice in the face of some long explanation from his partner, "I like to score on the hand".

Don't be upset if now and then—I know it's infuriating—the opponents go down a few hundred to save the rubber, and win it next hand with a cold slam. No subsequent result condones or justifies a bad sacrifice. Next time they'll lose both the sacrifice and the slam. In an even rubber play each hand and each game as it comes; if your decision to take a penalty is sound, it's still sound whatever happens on the next hand. Remember too, that a penalty doesn't wipe out the success below the line. If you win the first game the odds are 3–1 on you winning the rubber. On the next hand the opponents may save the rubber fairly cheaply; you are still 3–1 on to win it, and you have a penalty as well. Much the same sort of thing happens when you have a partscore. The partscore—apart from its scoring value—can only be roughly assessed but it is worth around 100 points. Again, when you have taken your penalty, the partscore with its double value (shown and hidden) remains.

This is a field in which you have to play your players; a field in which the really expert players glean a fine harvest. Don't bother to defend a rubber bid of say, Two Spades, unless you can defeat them at Three or at least at Four Spades, otherwise you merely offer your opponents a free second string to their bow, the choice of the double. Personally, I don't sacrifice a great deal to save the first game or, if I've lost the first, the second straight game. Partly because of the mathematics of the situations, partly because my opponents are usually ready to snap a penalty. It's in the rubber game you have most chance. Carefully calculated overbidding here will make the rubbers you win very large, and those you lose tiny. Over and over again until they get into a rhythm of overbidding, can you push even good players just one too high when the rubber points are dangled before them. Indeed, I believe if you broke down an expert's winnings over the year into all the different phases of the game, you'd find that this is where he gains most.

RUBBER BRIDGE CONSULTANT

If something goes wrong with your inside, you can see your doctor. If you start slicing or socketing, your golf pro may put it right. I've never heard of a Bridge consultant. If you play the game intelligently you can, I believe, be your own. For the disease of playing Bridge badly, diagnosis is almost the same as cure. Once recognize your faults and it's easy to remove or at least minimise them. It is an immense source of strength to a Bridge player to know what his own weaknesses are. I don't know yours, and however long I played with you I probably wouldn't pin-point them all. But I know mine. The main ones are:

(1) A tendency to leap into Two No Trump and Three No Trump contracts without exploring other possibilities—especially if I'm going to play the hand.
(2) A habit of thoughtless and pointless falsecarding that often fools my partner.
(3) An expensive habit of placing exact cards in my partner's hand during competitive bidding, and bidding further on the strength of them. It's expensive if they aren't there.
(4) A tendency, when I'm tired or thinking of something else, not to bother to think out defensive plays.

Now what about yours? Next time you feel you lost more than you should have done on your cards in a session, jot down what went wrong. Do it a dozen times and you'll find two or three threads running through the notes you have made. Fasten on to these and study them. I don't pretend to have cured myself of the four faults I've listed, but—just knowing them—I've reduced enormously my loss on them. When such situations crop up at the table, memory nudges me—and I bid or play as I should. When I was a very small boy (around five) I remember perfectly well a nurse telling someone a story of how a small boy in her charge had choked to death because a bit of toast got into his windpipe as he ate it lying down in bed. From that day to this if and when I have breakfast in bed, whatever position I consume the rest in, I'm bolt upright for the toast. Memory nudges me. Or think of the story of Archie Jackson, one of the most brilliant young Australians ever to play Test cricket. He had a risky habit of flicking at balls on the off before he was well set. Every time the bowler bowled at him in the early overs, Jackson would mutter to himself. "Don't cut it, Archie. Careful, Archie, don't cut." However brilliant you are, there are flaws in your play. Try, then, a close analysis of your game, sift and list your faults and when the time comes, you will find at least that you stop and think. And you will find something else too. You will find that you save a great deal of money.

PARTSCORE BIDDING

The partscore, if you have a good hand, can be a darned nuisance. Yet the rules are simple enough and can be tabulated:

(1) An opening force (say Two Clubs) is always a force, whatever the score, at least for one round. It should not be shaded in strength. An ordinary force (1H-3D) is unconditionally forcing for at least one round whatever the score.

(2) Two of another suit may be slightly shaded (in total playing tricks but NOT in the quality of the suit), and if it is a game bid, can be passed on a very weak hand. A courtesy raise or Two No Trump response should, however, be scraped up even on a fairly weak hand if there is some slight hope of a slam.

(3) Slam Tries should be made by taking the bidding one trick (for a mild slam try) or two (for a strong try) over the score needed for game. At a partscore of sixty you, at South, should take the following action on the hands given:

104

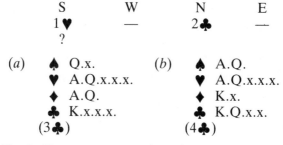

S	W	N	E
1♥	—	2♣	—
?			

(a)   ♠ Q.x.   (b)   ♠ A.Q.
        ♥ A.Q.x.x.x.   ♥ A.Q.x.x.x.
        ♦ A.Q.   ♦ K.x.
        ♣ K.x.x.x.   ♣ K.Q.x.x.
       (3♣)   (4♣)

(4) Tactically you may sometimes have to raise out of weakness. In particular (say at partscore seventy) the opener, pending confirmation, should not assume that a raise of One Heart to Two or Three shows a strong hand.

Apart from these situations the usual rules of competitive bidding apply. In particular—get in quick.

TYPES

Every card-room suffers from them. Every club shelters them. Bad Bridge players are not really difficult to cope with provided you know what form their madness or badness takes.

(1) George, for example, is a hog. He loves playing the hands. Usually he's a hog for No Trumps (yes, I remember the first weakness of mine listed!) but if you've bid No Trumps then he'll try a suit contract. Don't fight George. First because you won't win, and secondly because he plays the cards rather well. I expect it's because he gets so much practice.

(2) Bill and Clarence we'll take together. Bill overbids and Clarence underbids. Ely Culbertson has some baffling theory which I've never been able to understand, that you should overbid with Bill and underbid with Clarence. It's too complicated for me, though I dare say it's got some sound psychological basis. I'm quite sure it's too deep for Bill and/or Clarence. I'm a simple soul. If my partner overbids I underbid, and vice versa—but I don't tell them I'm going to.

(3) Charlie is much more difficult. You never know whether he's going to overbid or underbid or bid normally. If he is a hopelessly bad player you just apply all treatment

105

recommended later for the "Mrs. Guggenheims" of Bridge. Sometimes though, he's a fairly intelligent player who lacks consistent judgement. I tend to underbid a shade with such a partner. The tragedies of Bridge come from overcalling not from undercalling. If he is, in fact, bidding too strongly, your moderation will correct it. And if he is not, no great harm is done. Underbidding usually produces no worse result than a partscore for a game, or a game for a cold slam. So at least you score on the hand and that's money in your purse. If your cards are a shade over average, you'll take the rubber. Not such a quick nor such a large rubber as it should be, but you'll take it. With Charlie I'm satisfied. In defence—unless he's made an overbid in which case you must be wary, you can usually loosen up a little. Not too much though; you don't really want to prolong the rubber with Charlie sitting opposite you.

(4) Nigel is the real horror. Nigel has read a book on Bridge. Probably more than one. His mind is a bird's-nest of half truths, useless scraps of knowledge, and ill-digested Bridge tips. He will suggest that you play "Acol with the strong No Trump and Blackwood"—as if such a combination were possible. He bids prepared clubs, he reverses and he makes inferential cue-bids before you've any idea which suit to play in. He can play a double squeeze to land a bid of One Club, and he can't draw trumps to land Six Hearts. One particular "Nigel" has or had a remarkable method. Over and over again normal bidding would go perhaps One Spade—Three Spades—Four Spades, and after deep thought and with infinite meaning, this Nigel would double. All the species, by the way, cheat by vocal inflexion. Redouble and an overtrick was more or less routine. Purely by accident I discovered the reason. "You know," said our hero after one disaster, "I don't think Simon's theory of doubling is sound," "Which theory?" "Well, he wrote that the biggest doubles were when the defending strength wasn't concentrated, and you could double on strength in your partner's hand. But it doesn't seem to work." Bridge writers have much to answer for! Nigel, of course, had grasped 10 per cent. of a very complicated argument. That's his normal form.

What then to do with him as your partner? First of all agree to play whatever fantasy he suggests—and don't use it. Secondly, simplify your bidding and defensive play to the point of inanity. Thirdly—and this is the only exception to an otherwise universal rule of praising your partners—never under any circumstances congratulate him on anything. If you do the very next hand he'll surely show what he really can do if he tries.

(5) Finally there's a menace. Pinned like a butterfly in S.J. Simon's books the immortal Mrs. Guggenheim (absurd to invent another name) delights everyone except her partners. Yet your technique playing with her, or him, is an essential part of winning rubber Bridge. And it's an easy one to learn. Mostly, of course, it consists of dont's:

(i) Don't bother her or lecture her or hector her or reproach her. Above all, never be sarcastic. Whenever you can praise her. It pays enormous dividends.

(ii) Never issue an invitation to game or slam. Never bid Three Spades over her One Spade or Two No Trumps over her opening bid. She'll always go on to game—partly because she's never quite sure if your bid is forcing or not—and she'll often be doubled. If you think a game or a slam can be made, bid it yourself—and on the first round. Don't worry that she'll go any further:she'll think your bid is a stop signal. As long as she can, till game is reached, she'll keep the bidding pottering along because she has a vague idea that as you are a good player your bids must have a little more strength than the next fellow's. Heaven knows why, but she does. Bid No Trumps, of course, much more freely, and if a slam is inevitable use direct bidding without slam conventions. And however glittering the penalty take a sure rubber and be thankful.

(iii) Because you can't sign off with Mrs. Guggenheim you can't afford light opening bids. Bid solidly, and always play the strong No Trumps. Even with "Acol".

(iv) Naturally you want to play as many hands as possible. Be careful which you choose. Never try and take a slam hand from her. She can take a finesse as well as you can, and your superior end-play knowledge is not enough compensation for an inferior contract. Grab the low contracts. This is the golden rule though most players do exactly the reverse. Re-bid that weak five-card major, rather than let her play the hand in One No Trump. Don't give preference if you can find an excuse for taking the bid yourself. Pass as quickly as you can, unless you are certain a game can be made, if the pass leaves you declarer. The reason is simply that no bad player can cope with weak hands. They are far too impatient. They bustle around playing suits with Q.x.x.x. in one hand and J.x.x. in the other, when they ought to be sitting back and letting the opponent's work. They snatch all the early ruffs they can see, and run short of trumps before they can draw them or establish a side suit. They have no conception of the countless end-plays that land the small contracts. There is a whole pile of points here for you if you can arrange to be declarer in the part-score hands.

Two other matters to finish. First, neither moan, nor grumble, no one cares, and suits don't always break for them. Secondly; playing with Mrs Guggenheim, or Nigel, or Charlie, or any of the others, always remember (and in moments of stress you can intone it to yourself) that "for every time they cut with me they'll cut against me twice".

DUPLICATE BRIDGE

There are two main varieties of duplicate Bridge, team matches and pairs tournaments. The first is usually played on aggregate and the second on match points. The difference is rather like the difference between a knock-out tournament of golf and card-and-pencil play against bogey or par. I greatly prefer the first variation, partly because I enjoy the sense of personal combat it brings, but partly also because in match points one often has to play deliberately unsound Bridge in order to get a good score; to reject the safe suit contract for a speculative No Trump bid all because of the extra ten points, or to take absurd risks to garner an overtrick. In theory luck is eliminated in duplicate because each team (or pair) can score just as high points however the cards are dealt. In practice, of course, luck remains; a bad lead can still defeat a perfectly sound contract, a bad duplication can wreck a well-judged bid. There is little to be said about team of four matches. Presumably you are playing with a partner you know well and no special technique is called for. But the vagaries of match point play do need study.

The bonuses given for each hand are:

Partscore	50
Non-Vulnerable game	300
Vulnerable game	500
Non-Vulnerable Small and Grand Slam	500 and 1,000
Vulnerable Small and Grand Slam	750 and 1,500

As nothing is carried forward to the next hand so sacrifices become an exact science. If the opponents have a certain non-vulnerable game, say in Spades, it is worth 400 to save it, but not 500. The odds you need for a slam bid are mathematically evens for a small slam, and 2–1 on for a grand slam. There is an important point to watch here, and because of it the Acol team used to make a habit of NOT bidding a small slam that appears an even chance, say a simple finesse. The snag is that usually something else is needed as well; perhaps a normal break in trumps or the avoidance of a ruff. Superficial analysis would describe this hand as an even chance—on the Spade finesse:

♠ x.x.x.		♠ A.Q.J.
♥ J.x.x.x.	W E	♥ K.Q.x.x.x.
♦ A.K.x.		♦ x.x.
♣ A.x.x.		♣ K.Q.x.

Actually it's a thoroughly bad bet. A 4–0 trump break which occurs 10 per cent. of the time will beat you, and a singleton Club lead will also probably defeat you when the opponents get in with the Ace of trumps. Nor does it help if South opens a Spade from the King; he will still take his winner. So make your odds at least 5–4 on as near as you can judge and perhaps 3–1 on for a Grand Slam.

Match point scoring, when you are perhaps playing against a dozen or more pairs, is difficult at first to grasp. I think the easiest way to look at it is to consider a number of objectives—peaks I call them—which you must try to surmount.

1. When the cards run fairly evenly and your side (N–S or E–W, whichever it may be) have a shade the better of them your attacking peak is 110 *points*. You must aim to score no less than this and if possible rather more. The peak here represents the ordinary partscore contract (Two Spades or Three Diamonds made 60 plus 50). For this reason if you can make Two No Trumps (120) it is nearly always an excellent score. Better still, of course, is to squeeze an overtrick in the suit contract (130 or 140). It follows naturally that opponents must not be allowed to get away with partscores where undoubled they would lose 50 or 100. The safety factor in doubling must here be relaxed. These relative chances must be carefully weighed. A policy of gambling always for a top score will win very few tournaments in good class Bridge, and the steady score of a shade over 60 per cent. is the perfect target. You will, of course, note the great advantage of the majors over the minors (Two Spades equals Three Diamonds and Three Spades beats Four Diamonds) and steer your course accordingly. Again here two of our earlier hints on competitive bidding crop up; remember to contest the partscore hands, and remember the pre-emptive value of Spades.

2. If a game (or slam) is on for your side your attacking peak is the full score and bonus say 620 *points*. Only a 700-point sacrifice will satisfy you in exchange. Here again you must weigh the possibilities of making Four No Trumps (630) as against an overtrick in Spades (650). Here, in particular, a minor suit game can rarely be a good score. Never though, let the glitter of match points lead you into bidding that you know is bad: on balance you'll lose. Witness this hand from a match point pairs bid by only one pair, playing

Acol, into the good and—on this occasion justice was done—the only makeable contract:

♠ x.x.		♠ A.x.x.
♥ A.Q.x.	W E	♥ K.x.x.x.
♦ A.x.x.x.		♦ K.
♣ J.x.x.x.		♣ K.Q.10.x.x.

Their bidding was:

E	S	W	N
1♣	—	3♣	—
3♥	—	5♣	—
—	—	—	

The lure of No Trumps and Hearts proved too much for all the other pairs.

DEFENSIVE PEAKS

1. When you have rather the worst of the cards you should get a good result by losing 100 *points,* a bad one by losing 150; in the latter case you have lost to all the normal part-score results. The moral is that you must take risks when playing the hand, ignore safety plays, try bluffs, anything to secure the magic 100 *points* result.
2. Your second defensive peak is, of course, the game score against you. This is a mathematical decision, but I find it pays to be a little bold. Not always just because you hope to lose less than the game points, but because most opponents will bid one more and you may be able to win a top score defeating them. Here as in rubber Bridge you must play your opponents, and offer the greedy ones a chance to try too much.

The point that you must keep constantly in mind is that you must avoid a worse score than the normal result at the other tables. Whether your score is worse by 10 points or 2,000 points is a secondary consideration.

Here is a good illustration of match point technique which illustrates the struggle for the "peak". Incidentally, it also illustrates the unsound bidding and play you may have to indulge in. Taken from the November, 1950, Pairs Championship following the Bermuda World Championship event. John Crawford and George Rapee won the event by half a match point and Crawford sat South:

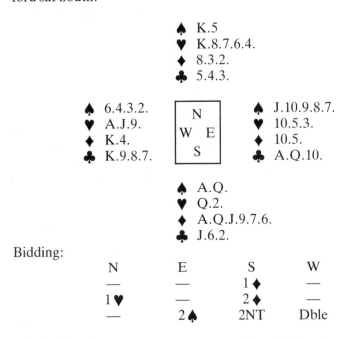

```
                    ♠ K.5
                    ♥ K.8.7.6.4.
                    ♦ 8.3.2.
                    ♣ 5.4.3.

    ♠ 6.4.3.2.          N          ♠ J.10.9.8.7.
    ♥ A.J.9.                       ♥ 10.5.3.
    ♦ K.4.          W     E        ♦ 10.5.
    ♣ K.9.8.7.          S          ♣ A.Q.10.

                    ♠ A.Q.
                    ♥ Q.2.
                    ♦ A.Q.J.9.7.6.
                    ♣ J.6.2.
```

Bidding:

N	E	S	W
—	—	1♦	—
1♥	—	2♦	—
—	2♠	2NT	Dble

You see clearly here the lure of the 110 and 120 point scores. The Two of Spades was opened and Crawford could see seven tricks only; the Diamond finesse was surely wrong. So he won in his own hand and calmly led a small Heart. West played low and Crawford grabbed the King and switched to Diamonds. West played another Spade for a game to North–South. West's play, of course, is sheer lunacy. If he takes the first Heart as he should the contract goes four down. If—in with the Diamond King—he plays Clubs which is equally obvious, it goes two down. Now do you see why I think match point pairs a bad imitation of real Bridge? It's an utterly different game. Give Crawford all the credit you like. Call his play brilliant if you will. But no one, and least of all Johnny Crawford, could call it Bridge.

CHAPTER XIII

LUCK AND ODDS

THERE is really only one rule to learn about odds: however long a series has run one way or the other, an even chance remains an even chance. Flip a coin in the air and suppose it comes down heads forty-nine times running. On the fiftieth throw the bet is still even money. Don't tell me this is a childish point. From people's ignorance of odds many others have made fortunes. Long ago someone discovered that all you had to do was to pay out 35–1 at roulette on what is in fact a 36–1 chance. The percentage is not noticeable on a single coup. A state's prosperity has been built on its effect over a period. Just that. And every system ever invented breaks down on one simple fact—a roulette wheel or a penny or a pack of cards can't remember. But you can. Let's start with that.

The exploitation of odds has a place in Bridge. But odds are only to be used when the inferences and deductions available to you at the card-table fail. I've put some tables of odds at Appendix "B". They are there to settle arguments, to be studied if the theory of odds attracts you, but rarely for practical use. If we can, let's keep the odds working for us. Lord Yarborough knew what he was doing when he used to bet £1,000–£1 against a player holding the worthless hand, containing no honour in any suit, which now bears his name. The real odds are over 1,800–1.

The expert players don't really bother consciously with odds at all. They play a hand a certain way because they have played thousands like it before, and because they know which line of play yields the best results. Here and there a knowledge of odds may find the best play. Take this hand for example;

♠ A.Q.x.		♠ K.J.x.x.
♥ x.x.x.	W E	♥ A.x.
♦ A.x.x.x.		♦ K.x.x.x.
♣ A.J.10.		♣ x.x.x.

Suppose you play in Three No Trumps. The Two of Hearts is opened. Hearts, you must hope, are divided 4–4. You have eight tricks on top and must play to develop one more either in Diamonds or Clubs. You have no time to try both. Which is the better chance—that Diamonds are 3–2 or that South has one Club honour in which case two finesses in Clubs make the contract. The percentage advantage is, in fact, very slight. Diamonds will be 3–2 68 per cent. of the time and South will have at least one Club honour 75 per cent. of the time. Actually the difference is closer still: for the 5–0 Diamond break occurs in 4 per cent. of hands and you would still have time to switch to the Club play if either hand shows out on the first round. And so the percentage in favour of the Club play is very small. Negligible? Yes and no. It is true that these sort of situations are very rare. It is also true that your Club play gives you more than the advantage the bank has at roulette and it is more than enough to make them—over anything but a very short time—certain winners.

Where the odds are of real value is in helping you to determine whether to finesse or play for a drop. First of all the general theory of distribution is of importance. About 65 per cent. of all hands contain neither a singleton nor a void. Most players believe that where one hand is a freak, the others will tend to be freakish: that where one hand has one or more singletons so will the others. As a result they tend to finesse, against the odds, in a freakish hand instead of playing for the more normal drop. How much importance you attach to this theory of symmetry must vary according to your inclinations. There can be no certainty about it. Ely Culbertson elaborates what is at best a theory into a pompous Law of Symmetry. Terence Reese, on the other hand, is much more tepid and goes no farther than "The opinion of most expert players is that unbalanced patterns do tend to co-exist in one deal". If this is true, rank me with the minority. Firstly because there is no mathematical basis whatever for the theory. There is no reason why the distribution of cards in your opponents' hands should vary from the normal percentages because your hand is, or is not, a freak. It is, of course, obvious that if your hand consists of very long and very short suits the other hands have to restore the balance, but there is nothing freakish in this. Secondly, there is an inevitable tendency to remember the unusual which gives a pseudo support to the theory. We remember almost as a manifestation of the supernatural the odd occasions when we have been thinking of someone—and on the instant they have telephoned. We forget the tens of thousands of times that there was no such dramatic denouement. Suppose you have a six-card suit. The odds say that the other seven cards will be held 6–1–0– on about 1 per cent. of hands, 5–2–0– in 4 per cent. and 5–1–1– in 4 per cent. Tragedy may result from any of these divisions and you remember them. But after all they make up, according to the odds, nearly 9 per cent. of all hands and that is a large percentage. You forget the 34 per cent. of hands that break 3–2–2, and the others stick in your mind. So I ignore altogether the theory or law symmetry. True I often reject the odds and make an unusual play, but I do this on an inference or a hunch and not in deference to any theory or distribution. The argument is not of any great importance and if you want to become a symmetrician, then by all means do.

There are many pitfalls in the use of odds and a little learning here is a most dangerous thing. For example, when you and your partner have nine cards, say:

A.K.J.x.x.x. | W   E | x.x.x.

the odds are that the other four will be divided:

4–0	10 per cent.
2–2	40 per cent.
3–1	50 per cent.

Dozens of Bridge articles on the strength of these figures have said that with this holding you should finesse for the Queen because the 3–1 division is the most likely. There is an important fallacy here. First of all the 3–1 break will only occur with the three cards in the South hand on half the occasions. Secondly, the odds vary as the cards are played. Suppose you play the King and both opponents follow. The 4–0 divisions are now eliminated. You then lead a small card from East and South follows with a small one—if he doesn't there is, of course, no problem. Now you know North did not start with three and the odds favour the play for the drop. Always provided that is, that

115

there are no contrary inferences to be drawn from the bidding or play of the hand so far.

LUCK

Do you sit on your handkerchief? Or always take the blue cards? Or move your seat because, "the others have won the last four rubbers?" You do, I expect. Nearly all card players do. Nearly all card players have a pathetic belief in their powers to command success. "Tis not in mortals . . . ". The best you can do is to deserve success. Personally, since I first started playing cards I have never, for myself, changed my seat unless I have to, and I always deal with the first pack ready. I might, of course, change my seat because it is too hot or too cold, or because the light isn't good—never for reasons of luck. And again, I am always willing to move if my partner wants me to, not because it will do any good, but because it keeps him happy. Besides it saves me from his plaintive, "I told you so" if things go wrong. So I agree cheerfully that in part I do not court my Lady Luck because I am idle. Much more important, I don't court her because (in the sense in which the word is usually used) I don't believe she exists. Do you remember what we agreed at the start of this chapter? A pack of cards has no memory. It doesn't know you have had a dozen bad hands running, nor does it care. And you, when you trip round the table to the lucky seats, are making exactly the same error as the small system players in the Casino. You are going to sit not where luck is, but where luck was. And the chances of good cards are even wherever you go, just as the chances of heads or tails remain constant however long the series. One more reflection. The cards you are going to get on the next deal depend on only one thing. Where the player who cuts the pack puts his finger and thumb. and if you think, sitting on your handkerchief is going to move his thumb up a bit or down a bit, then go on sitting on it. I've done my best.

There is a real Bridge lesson behind this diatribe against superstition. The best rubber Bridge players I know, Kenneth Konstam, Terence Reese, Colin Harding, never bother about seats or cards because they have achieved the essential equable indifference to good or bad fortune. Their finesses come off or fail, suits break kindly or devilishly. Neither triumph nor disaster excites or depresses them unduly, because they know the luck will even out. They know too that skill won't. And so

116

month in month out, year in year out, they are big winners. Not because they are luckier, but because they are better players than their opponents. When you hear someone called a lucky player, it nearly always means he's a good one. A contract perhaps to an average player, depends on a finesse. It is an even money chance. But the expert may be able to try two or three different ways for his last trick before he is driven to the finesse. It isn't luck that lands those contracts.

TO STOP OR TO PLAY

Most Bridge books—and S. J. Simon's in particular—advise you to play as long as you can when you are in luck and stop playing when you are not. Here the assumption is that when you are winning you play better and vice versa. Personally I don't. I play my best Bridge, duplicate or rubber Bridge, when things are running against me. If you can be blandly indifferent to bad luck you will not go to pieces when the cards are heavily against you. You will just sit tight and wait for the storm to blow over. This, of course, is a counsel of perfection, but if you can bring yourself to give up your cherished Bridge superstitions you have at least taken a long step forward. For if you know that your chance of being dealt the best hand at the table is exactly the same as anyone else's, whatever the state of that rubber may be, then you need not fear that your judgment will deteriorate in a bad run. It should get keener.

Very few players are either good enough analysts or equable enough in temperament to try and puzzle out why they have had a series of misfortunes. They blame their partner and distrust themselves. Then they start playing badly. If they reach this point Simon is probably right—they should go home. But if they clear their mind they will often see that their play is perfectly reasonable, that their partner is quite sound. All that has happened is that a series of odds against chances have turned up. Once recognise this and the sense of panic goes.

In any case the advice to play less or more according to your luck is irrelevant to the overwhelming majority of Bridge players in this country. They play Bridge because they always do on Tuesdays, or because it's a wet afternoon, or because they've finished early at the office. Of course, they like to win and they

117

would like to play better and win more, but the stakes are rarely a first consideration. So they will play anyway. Quite right too.

The advice isn't even sound for what is called the professional. He is a professional because he is a winner, and he is a winner because his bidding and play give him a percentage advantage over the average player. Say his advantage is about 7 per cent.—that's twice as much as a roulette wheel has. His advantage is there whether he is winning or losing. He will be winning more and losing less than the average player. And so he ought to play just as much as he can for his percentage works every hand he plays. You cannot sit out your bad luck. The pack of cards not only hasn't a memory: it hasn't got eyes.

This is not to argue that you should not adjust your play to all the numerous situations at the card-table. Of course you should. That is part of rubber Bridge technique and was discussed in the last chapter. You must make concessions to the other players, to the score, even to your mood. But no concessions, please, to luck. There ain't no such animal.

CHAPTER XIV

ON BECOMING AN EXPERT

THIS is a short chapter but, for a few of you, the most important. Let's assume you have studied and mastered the use of the bidding weapons in this book. It doesn't follow that you understand bidding, any more than it follows that a deep knowledge of the mechanics of cricket makes you a batsman. Out of the competent run-of-the-mill Bridge players—and it's very easy to become that—perhaps one in fifty goes on to become a really good player. Out of the really good players perhaps, again, 2 per cent. become Master Players. There aren't more than twenty or so in the British Isles. So the odds against you are heavy. Still, if you want to climb from the ruck of goodish players this chapter is for you.

THREE PRINCIPLES

As I understand bidding and Acol bidding in particular, three principals are essential to success:

> The Principle of the Limit Bid.
> The Principle of the Lesser Risk.
> The Principle of Consultation

The Principle of the Limit Bid

Acol theory holds—it is its first commandment—that whenever a limit bid accurately reflects your hand you should make that bid. A limit bid is of course one that shows your general strength, and sometimes your point count, within narrow limits. If then you have a choice between two equally "sound" bids or responses, select the one which defines your hand most closely. Life then is much easier for your partner. For example, if you hold:

(*a*)   ♠   A.J.10.
      ♥   K.J.x.
      ♦   A.K.x.
      ♣   A.J.x.x.

either one Club or Two No Trumps is perfectly correct. Always you should bid Two No Trumps and tell partner at once, not only the truth but the whole truth. Again, if partner bids one Club and you hold:

(b) ♠ A.x.x.
     ♥ K.10.x.
     ♦ A.Q.x.x.
     ♣ J.x.x.

all cunning players bid one Diamond: Bridge players bid three No Trumps. Apart from the fact that there is no need to tell the opponents not to lead a Diamond, all sorts of unpleasant things can happen if you keep the bidding low. Opponents may be able to indicate cheaply a lead in a major suit. They may even, if partner has something like:

(c) ♠ x.x.
     ♥ x.x.
     ♦ K.x.x.
     ♣ A.K.Q.x.x.x.

have a cheap save against you. You may go down outbidding them in Five Clubs even though four No Trumps are on. Far more important though than all these considerations is the partnership understanding and absence of strain that easy natural bidding produces. Don't carry the principle too far though. Shuffle the suits a little to:

(d) ♠ A.Q.x.x.
     ♥ A.x.x.
     ♦ K.10.x.
     ♣ J.x.x.

and one Spade is correct, both because partner may well have four Spades, and because the pre-emptive value of the Spade suit makes an overbid at the two level improbable.

These then are the principal limit bids:

(1) All No Trump bids unless used conventionally.
(2) Any direct raise to any level of partner's opening suit bid.
(3) Any bid which, after the first round of bidding, explicitly denies ability to contract for game or slam, e.g.:

1 ♥   —   1 ♠   —
3 ♥

120

(4) Any direct game bid in any contract where a forcing bid situation does not exist, e.g.:

$$1\ \heartsuit \quad\quad\quad - \quad\quad\quad 4\ \spadesuit \quad\quad\quad -$$

(5) Any pre-emptive opening bid or response.
(6) Any sign off.

Note that except for the last category a limit bid need not be a sign off as well.

The limit bid has two great advantages. First it pin-points the strength of the hand. Secondly, it enables the player in later rounds to bid as freely as he likes, and his strength remains limited by his earlier bid.

Essentially the principle of the limit bid is the principle of simplicity. Don't footle about with clever bids if the final goal is clear. Don't show features in your hand only because you have them, or you want to display your knowledge of technique. I remember a classic example in rubber Bridge at the old Lederer's Club when Kosky was partnering one of the cunning species. The bidding had got up to Four Spades with Kosky to play the hand when suddenly his partner produced a Four No Trump bid. Kosky managed to head him off the slam, and the bidding stopped in Five Spades. One down. "I had to show you my three Aces," pleaded the guilty one. "Couldn't you wait," said Kosky wearily, "till you put your hand down?"

The Principle of the Lesser Risk

S. J. Simon analysed this principle carefully in his *Design for Bidding*. His argument was that bidding is not an exact science, but an assessment of probabilities. There are not enough bids, and there is not enough bidding space, to exhaust the alternatives. All bidding is, therefore, a calculation of risks. To add that one should take the lesser risk is at first sight platitudinous: actually it is the key to a philosophy of Bridge.

This theory will help you to understand bidding in general and Acol in particular. It is a lesser risk to open the bidding on the first round than overbid on the second. It is also the lesser risk—spreading the risk—to make a weak informatory double if at all possible rather than nail your fortunes to one shaky suit. You must then have a system which can open easily and stop quickly. The theory will lead you to pre-emptive bids and to early direct raises, both to simplify the issue for your partner and to embarrass your opponents by denying them both information and bidding space. A definite part of your bidding equipment should be devoted to making life difficult for your opponents. Hustle them, cramp them, make them guess. Sometimes they must guess wrong. The theory will lead you to force early and to force lightly; to crawl along with your inferential and approach bids after and not before the suit is agreed, and you know the opponents cannot harrass you. The more natural your bidding, the more difficult it is for your opponents to upset you.

Three examples should make the principle clear to you.

(1) If you hold:

(e) ♠ K.x.
    ♥ A.J.x.x.x.x.
    ♦ A.Q.x.x.x.
    ♣ none.

and your bid of One Heart is raised to Three you should bid Six Hearts. You might not make it I agree, but it's much better than an even money chance. Again, you might, if partner has the ideal cards, make seven and the way to find out is by bidding Four Diamonds. If you do, you will surely stop a Diamond lead, and you may lose the small slam. Tell your opponents nothing at all. Bid six and let them find a lead.

(2) You hold, as South:

(f) ♠ A.Q.10.x.x.x.
    ♥ x.
    ♦ A.J.10.x.x.
    ♣ x.

Vulnerable against non-vulnerable opponents you open One Spade:

S	W	N	E
1♠	2♥	2♠	3♥
?			

What now? Four Spades is very probable, but the sacrifice of Five Hearts may be on and must be cheap. On no account make the fatuous and revealing bid of Four Diamonds. Bid Three Spades only, and if it's passed out take you partscore. It's the lesser risk.

(3)   (g)   ♠ A.x.x.
                        ♥ x.x.x.x.
                        ♦ none.
                        ♣ x.x.x.x.x.x.

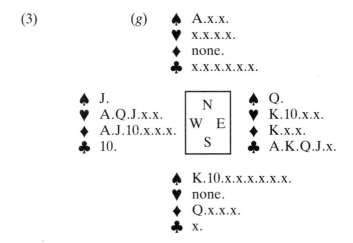

West		East
♠ J.		♠ Q.
♥ A.Q.J.x.x.		♥ K.10.x.x.
♦ A.J.10.x.x.x.		♦ K.x.x.
♣ 10.		♣ A.K.Q.J.x.

                 ♠ K.10.x.x.x.x.x.x.
                 ♥ none.
                 ♦ Q.x.x.x.
                 ♣ x.

I was North when West dealt this hand at love all.

W	N	E	S
1♦	—	3♣	3♥
Dble	—	—	4♠
5♥	—	6♥	—
—	6♠	Dble	—
—	—		

My partner's Three-Heart bid stakes a claim for a Heart lead against a slam in Diamonds. Six Hearts can, in fact, be defeated by the underlead of the Spade Ace and the Diamond return, but Six Spades is the obvious insurance. In fact we made our sacrifice bid, for West made the (stupid) lead of the Ace of Diamonds.

The Principle of Consultation

There are two sorts of system, those which dictate and those which consult. And there are two sorts of Bridge player—those who irritate and those who soothe their partner. It is the third essential principle of good bidding that the strong hand should not lay down the law to the weak. In every bidding sequence there comes a time for decision: it is the mark of a fine partnership that, as often as not, the weaker hand produces the key bid. There's a very sound reason for this and the reason again is the shortage of bidding space. Suppose I have a King and a Queen and nothing much else. You sit opposite me with a rockcrusher. It doesn't help in the least for you to announce your hand with a forcing bid, and then crash on to ask me how many Kings and Queens I have. Principally because you won't know which they are; it was a similar objection we raised to the Blackwood convention. Even if by Asking Bids you do discover exactly what my little treasures are, you still won't let me tell you about a void or a singleton or even a doubleton which may be much more important. Now, of course, I can't paint a picture for you of my weakness—the bids available aren't descriptive enough. What *you* can do, however, is not waste time asking me questions, but tell me exactly what you have and exactly where you would like support. And when you've done that, trust me. That method is not only much better for partnership confidence, it's much more efficient as well. This book and the collection of hands, "Acol in Action" at the end are studded with examples. One more here will do. Love all, East deals:

(h)
♠	x.x.x.x.
♥	Q.10.x.x.
♦	x.x.
♣	K.x.x.

W E

♠	A.
♥	A.K.J.x.x.
♦	A.K.J.x.
♣	A.Q.x.

	ROOM 1					ROOM 2		
E	S	W	N		E	S	W	N
2♣	—	2♦	—		2♣	—	2♦	—
2♥	—	3♥	—		2♥	—	3♥	—
4NT	—	5♦	—		4♦	—	4♥	—
6♥	—	—	—		5♣	—	6♥	—
					7♥	—	—	—

A perfect illustration from a 1950 match of the two approaches. In Room 1 E–W played Two Clubs with an Ace response and Blackwood. In Room 2 Acol. The Blackwood bid in Room 1 is for Kings (Two Diamonds denied an Ace) and one King is located. Spades or Clubs? East doesn't know nor does he know about the vital doubleton in Diamonds. He's too high to explore and he gambles Six. If West had:

(i)   ♠   K.x.x.
         ♥   10.x.x.x.
         ♦   x.x.x.
         ♣   x.x.x.

the small slam even may not be there.

Then look at Room 2. Study how East says, "I know you're weak. Don't bother about Aces, but can you help a bit in Diamonds and Clubs?" The first time West says, "No": the second trial bid of Five Clubs shows him that weak as he is, everything he has is in the right place, and he takes the decisive step of bidding the small slam. Note that he would not bid six if he had, for example, his Spades and Diamonds reversed, but I think he might (in view of his Club fit) temporise with Five Diamonds under the safety level of Five Hearts. The Grand Slam from East on the original bidding is automatic.

The last rung

The three principles I have given you add up to a plea for simple logical bidding. No bidding that is illogical or inconsistent with the earlier rounds can be good bidding. If you bid with these principles always in your mind, you just must bid well.

Suppose then you are one of the really good players who have climbed above the normal standards. How do you climb the last rung? How do you become a Master? The answer is almost certainly that you don't. Not, that is, unless you're prepared to let a game eat all your leisure and much of your sleep. Unless you're prepared to seek out better players than yourself and play always with them, or if you cannot play with them, watch them. Unless you're prepared to play in every tournament you can find, and argue Bridge hands endlessly with three other maniacs who form your team. I don't suppose you are prepared to do this, and I don't blame you. But there's no other way. Helen Sobel, the best woman player in the States, in her excellent book, *Winning Bridge* says this:

"Don't scoff at talking Bridge hands. The all-night 'bull' sessions after the first contract tournaments some twenty years ago proved to be, if not the birthplace, the proving ground for almost all of the well-known players in the two decades since. And the winning bidding methods they were developing by replaying the evening's hands with the aid of pencil and table-cloth (and maybe a few highballs) are the methods used all over to-day."

Except that usually we couldn't afford the highballs, that is exactly what happened in this country as well.

CHAPTER XV

THE UPDATE

YOU can happily play the Acol system today exactly as it was set out by Macleod thirty years ago, and you'll be well-equipped with the near perfect system.

In his inimitable style, Iain has emphasised the personal attributes you need to play Bridge well. Without beating about the bush, he's stressed that Acol is NOT a system with a series of bids which you learn parrot-fashion; it's a set of logical principles and rules which you use in conjunction with your own common-sense and judgment. When, and only when, you've become competent and experienced in playing the system, you're allowed to break the rules—but you must never try to change the principles.

Macleod was no great lover of master point pairs Bridge, and he showed this at the end of his chapter on duplicate technique (Chapter XII). So it's just as well that he didn't devote too much space to the subject, as we'd have almost certainly been in disagreement. I love pairs competition, certainly as much as rubber, and probably more than teams Bridge. It's very much a part of real Bridge, but it has an artform of its own, which isn't generally understood.

In Pairs play, you have two sets of opponents to think about—the pairs against whom you actually play, and those who are sitting the same way as you and playing the same cards. In total, they all represent "the field", and where you finish in the field is determined by the comparison of your results with theirs. People think, and even say, that you need luck to win a pairs event; that's partially true, but there's a smaller element of luck in doing well at pairs than at teams or rubber. You can always guarantee to finish in the top half of the field simply by playing steadily and unimaginatively, following the basic Acol principles, and not making the wrong bids and plays. Often you'll find yourself winning using this formula, for your opponents will continue to make mistakes, and throw good results at you. So you've won without really trying it seems, and it's irritating when this is called *luck*. What you've actually done is given your opponents the opportunity to make mistakes—and they've taken it!

Trying to win is always disastrous, for it first and foremost means you overbid and usually get doubled, then you unsettle your partner and he starts making mistakes, and finally you end up near the bottom. So, until you have become quite proficient at playing the cards and feel an all-round grasp of the game, play "passive" and watch the good results keep rolling in.

There is an "active" technique for pairs play, but there are very few players in the world who can use it successfully and consistently. In addition to very sound judgment and a lot of experience, you need to have flair. Flair comes with the ability to recognise special situations quickly where you can make an unusual, even unorthodox bid or play, which gains you a cheap sacrifice or extra tricks. Flair is not random "psyching", nor is it anything which disrupts or confuses your partner.

Let's take Macleod's example on page 112 to illustrate our differing viewpoints on the pairs game:

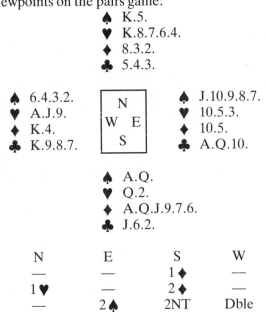

Bidding:

N	E	S	W
—	—	1♦	——
1♥	—	2♦	—
—	2♠	2NT	Dble

Iain suggests that the North–South bidding is unsound and that the opponents' defence is lunatic; but surely, it's East who hazarded a very questionable intervention after an innocuous auction had finished. South clearly is good enough to bid again, and Two No Trumps seems to me to be a more descriptive bid than Three Diamonds at any form of Bridge. Apart from the obvious ten-point bonus for playing in No Trumps, there's nothing to suggest that an extra trick can be made in Diamonds. From the bidding, South might expect partner to have the King of Clubs rather than the King of Spades, in which case Two No Trumps makes and Three Diamonds fails. As the cards lie, E–W can make Three Spades, so the most unsound bid must be West's penalty double, especially when he doesn't plan to beat the contract! Total credit goes to South's flair in making the only play to give himself a chance from the inferences of West's Double. West should have risen immediately with his Ace and switched to Clubs, but even good players get it wrong when they are put under pressure, before they have a count of partner's hand.

Purists of Bridge have the same attitudes to master point pairs as do the connoisseurs and technocrats of Cricket towards the "limited over" game. They don't like the improvisation and calculated risks which have become necessary to gain a good score. Just as batsmen have introduced a new range of strokes to penetrate defensive field settings and take "suicide" runs which they would never dream of doing in a Test Match, so declarers will favour a dodgy game in No Trumps to a sounder one in a minor suit, or forgo a safety play for the tempting prospects of making overtricks. Both games have tremendous appeal, and each has contributed a great deal to the development of skills among its players.

More significantly, there are thousands of social players who take Bridge holidays each year. Whether it is a fortnight in Torremolinos, a cruise to the Caribbean, or a weekend at a local hotel, the Bridge will generally be in the form of pairs competitions. The leisure industry has woken up to the potential of the Bridge market, and big names in special interest holidays such as Ladbrokes and P&O have for some time been running an extensive programme of weekends and cruises.

There is no escape from the fact that the style of Bridge generally has been influenced by the duplicate game. Most of the professional Bridge teachers are competition players and some have never even played rubber Bridge; so it follows that their students start to play rubber Bridge with a duplicate Bridge attitude—and using duplicate Bridge style. Duplicate style will cost you money if you try to use it in clubs at cut-in rubber Bridge but, apart from that, there are two standard features of the modern pairs game—Weak Twos and Transfer Bids—which clearly have merit for any form of Bridge. You may well find that their use won't be permissible in rubber Bridge clubs, but there is no harm in their adoption for your regular "school".

This leads me to perhaps the most important, and certainly the most controversial part of the book—my philosophy of bidding. Important, because you won't find it ever appearing in my column, and controversial, because many bidding theorists disagree with me. It is based fundamentally on recognition of the risk factor. Risk is an integral part of Bridge; it is probably the ingredient which adds more excitement to the game than any other—so why not include it as one of the skills in your armoury? Taking a calculated risk is not the same as gambling; you have to know what you're doing, so I'm not recommending it for the inexperienced or faint-hearted. Experts often take calculated risks and, when they come off, it's called skill; when a "rabbit" does the same thing, it's called luck—so there's no justice! The main purpose of taking a risk at master point pairs is to get a good or better result, and, ironically another purpose generally is to reduce risk. Take the following example to illustrate what I mean:

(a) ♠ Q.J.4.3.
     ♥ Q.J.8.4.
     ♦ A.6.
     ♣ K.10.5.

After West opens One No Trump (12–14), East's textbook response with the above hand is a Stayman Two Clubs enquiry for majors, and when West bids Two Spades you raise to Four Spades, for it's considered technically more sound to play in a 4–4 suit fit. The "risk" bid, (which I'd make) is a direct raise to Three No Trumps—and we'll say West holds:

(b) ♠ 10.8.5.2.
     ♥ K.9.
     ♦ Q.J.4.
     ♣ A.Q.J.2.

130

Now let's calculate the risk factor:

(1) If Stayman is used, there is no escape from playing in Four Spades.
(2) If Trumps break 4–1 (and although that's only a 28 per cent chance, they always do when I play in Four Spades), the contract will almost certainly fail, but Three No Trumps has various chances of making.
(3) If Four Spades makes, so might Four No Trumps—for a better score at master point pairs.
(4) By bidding direct to Three No Trumps, the opponents have no inferences to help them in defence, and a Spade might even be led.

It is well known that authors construct model hands to illustrate their points, and there will be many occasions when Four Spades would play better. However, the two factors which I believe tip the balance in favour of my theory are:

(a) Giving no information to the opponents,
(b) The potentially random nature of No Trump openings.

My approach to bidding is practical, rather than scientific. It should be simple, direct and, above all, effective. I love opponents who go through pedantic sequences to reach their contract, at the end of which I have been given so much information about their hands that defeating the contract becomes a mere formality. Keep "scientific" sequences for your big hands, where you think there might be slam prospects, and you have lots of constructive information to exchange with partner. Recognising hands with slam potential is quite another topic, but you get relatively few of them to deal with. So we can move on to my favourite topic of No Trumps.

NO TRUMP BIDDING

First of all, you should re-read Macleod's Chapter VII, for this is the only one we need to update. Just as he relaxed the rigidity of No Trump requirements which were fashionable in the Culbertson era, I advocate an even greater relaxation on his style. Like him, I want to open a No Trump as often as possible, because this is the most versatile and effective bid in Bridge, especially if you happen to take up pairs play seriously. So, for starters, I would use a *weak* No Trump in virtually all situations, as you are three times more likely to have 12–14 points than 16–18 points. The two occasions when it might be wise to use the stronger version are:

(a)   At very high stake rubber Bridge,

(b)   When vulnerable in a teams match and your counterparts are playing strong No Trumps.

Occasionally, you can get caught badly, and a 1,400 penalty would be very hurtful. At master point pairs, the risk isn't so critical, for a bottom score gets you a "zero" whether you lose 1,400 or just 50.

The popular and standard range of the weak No Trump is now 12–14 points with tens counting as half a point. However, there is a lot of merit in the old range of 13–15 points for beginners, who need that little bit of extra strength behind them until they have practised declarer play. The No Trump range must not be more than three points, so you agree with partner which is going to suit you best.

A myth exists about the difficulty of playing in No Trumps. Whether it is the fear of the opponents running a long suit against you as declarer without the protection of trumps, or whether it is the fact that the experienced player in a partnership will tend to hog the bidding in No Trumps first so that he can be declarer—and the beginner rarely gets a chance to practise. I don't know why this myth exists, for playing in suit contracts is in principle far more difficult and intricate, due to the introduction of the ruffing element and trump management (see Chapter XVII on Planning the Play).

So Beginners—cast away your fears, and start opening One No Trump as often as possible—not only to get the practice, but also because it will greatly simplify your bidding problems at a time when you ought to be concentrating on counting and playing the cards.

Statistically—if you believe in statistics—most of the opening hands which you hold will fall in the 12–14 honour point range, and, of these, over half will be distributionally eligible for a No Trump opening. I'm not a statistician, and I only fall back on statistical probability as a last resort, but I open One No Trump on about 60 per cent of my 12–14 point hands (revealing the secret of a lifetime).

Hand patterns are shown in Table II of Appendix B and, of these, 1,2,3,4 and 6 are eligible for No Trump openings—

though not all hands within these patterns are necessarily suitable, and some judgment is required.

I would bid One No Trump on the following:

(c) ♠ K.x.　　　♠ K.x.　　　♠ K.x.　　　♠ K.Q.x.x.
　　♥ K.x.　　　♥ K.Q.J.x.x.♥ K.x.　　　♥ x.x.
　　♦ J.x.x.　　♦ Q.x.x.　　♦ Q.x.x.x.　♦ K.Q.x.x.
　　♣ K.Q.J.x.x.x. ♣ Q.x.x.　　♣ K.Q.x.x.x. ♣ Q.J.x.

but:

(d)　　　　　　(e)　　　　　　(f)　　　　　　(g)
　♠ A.K.x.x.　　♠ Q.x.x.x.　　♠ Q.x.　　　♠ A.K.x.x.
　♥ x.x.x.　　　♥ K.Q.J.x.x.　♥ x.x.　　　♥ K.Q.J.x.
　♦ x.x.　　　　♦ K.x.　　　　♦ A.K.x.x.x.　♦ x.x.
　♣ A.K.x.x.　　♣ Q.x.　　　　♣ K.Q.x.x.　♣ x.x.x.
　(Bid 1♣)　　(Bid 1♥)　　(Bid 1♦)　　(Bid 1♠)

I dare not be more controversial with hand types, because I do not want to encourage beginners to bite off more than they can chew to start with. But you can use your imagination to work out the permutations, which are available, once you have got the hang of No Trump play. When your 12–14 point hand has no sensible re-bid other than re-bidding your suit, bid One No Trump. And remember that you don't need a stopper in each suit, but you have got to hope that partner's hand is going to fill the gap of your weakness. Recognise that you might occasionally find yourself playing in No Trumps with a small doubleton in the same suit in both hands. That's the risk factor—but the opponents still might not lead that suit!

Here is a re-cap of the merits of the weak No Trump.
(a) It is a limit bid so you won't have to bid again unless partner forces you to.
(b) It is a bid which will describe a large proportion of your opening hands.
(c) It is higher ranking than the other suits and, apart from scoring more, it forces the opponents to overcall at the two-level.
(d) It is the most difficult contract against which to defend.

One No Trump doubled is my favourite contract in bridge. Except when the player on lead reels off a seven-card suit, there is always the prospect of a really exciting challenge, which

I'll hope to win more often than not. This deal came at a critical point in a teams final. South dealt and both were vulnerable:

```
                    ♠ Q.J.2.
                    ♥ 5.2.
                    ♦ J.10.4.
                    ♣ 9.7.5.4.3.

  ♠ A.K.8.6.3.    ┌─────────┐    ♠ 10.9.7.
  ♥ A.Q.8         │   N     │    ♥ K.J.9.7.4.
  ♦ 8.5.          │ W   E   │    ♦ Q.9.2.
  ♣ K.10.8.       │   S     │    ♣ Q.6.
                  └─────────┘
                    ♠ 5.4.
                    ♥ 10.6.3.
                    ♦ A.K.7.6.3.
                    ♣ A.J.2.
```

West doubled my hazardous No Trump opening and led a low Spade. After I had run the Diamond suit successfully, West got his discards wrong and let me make an overtrick for +380. Our partners sitting E–W reached Four Hearts after South opened One Diamond, and East made +620. Looking at all the hands, you can see that I should not have made more than four tricks, but that would have meant West making the improbable lead of a Heart or Club. Most doubled No Trump contracts can be beaten at double dummy, and in this case I could have afforded to go two down and still gain on the hand.

I don't think the statisticians have yet worked out the odds in favour of the defence, when it has a clear balance of points and the initiative of the lead. Declarer certainly starts with an enormous psychological advantage, first with a chance of making, and then with the insurance buffer of sacrificing against the opponents' contract. This example will be controversial because, apart from the very dodgy No Trump opener, many will say that either North or South ought to have tried to rescue into a minor. Not so, for once you've made your bed, you must learn to lie in it. There is nothing to suggest that Two Clubs or Two Diamonds will not be equally disastrous for you — at a level higher, and you will have lost part of your psychological advantage.

Clearly the "risk factor" is at its highest level in this situation, because I have taken an extreme example. There will be many others where the odds are less heavily stacked against you, and you have quite a comfortable and enjoyable ride to an overtrick or two. The point to be made is that this isn't "bad Bridge" — it's using the risk factor as a skill. Quite a lot of experts use this style, especially against less experienced opponents, so it's important that it should be "made public".

THE ONE NO TRUMP RESPONSE TO PARTNER'S BID OF A SUIT

Refer back to Chaper IX which covers this generally. There are two important further points to be borne in mind, especially by those who start to play in competitions, where the need for bidding accuracy is greater, and each trick is valuable:

(1) If the contract is to be played in No Trumps, it's generally better to try to have the stronger hand as declarer; first, to keep the greater strength concealed from the opponents, and secondly, to have the initial lead coming up to strength, instead of through it—thus being more likely to gain a tempo for declarer.

(2) Limit bids should logically be confined to the narrrowest practical range, and certainly not exceed three points. The possible No Trump range of 5-10 points in response to a suit opening is unwieldy, and so I would recommend the following:

(i) Over a minor suit opening, 7½–9½ with no four-card major.

(ii) Over a major suit opening, 5½–7½ preferably with a half stop in the other major.

With less than 7½ points in (i), you must decide whether to pass, or raise the minor suit. With more than 7½ points in (ii), you can make a bid at the two-level.

Remember that these are only guidelines for your consideration and, if you're happy with your present style, stick with it. As always, in Acol, your judgment determines what you should bid, and you must never become a slave to points.

In response to a One Heart opening, bid:

(h)	(i)	(j)	(k)
♠ Q.10.x.	♠ x.x.	♠ 9.x.x.x.	♠ Q.x.x.
♥ x.x.	♥ x.x.x.	♥ J.x.	♥ x.x.x.
♦ Q.x.x.x.	♦ K.x.x.x.	♦ Q.J.x.	♦ J.x.x.
♣ Q.x.x.x.	♣ K.x.x.x.	♣ Q.x.x.x.	♣ K.Q.J.x.
(Bid 1NT)	(Bid 2 ♥)	(Bid 1 ♠)	(Bid 2 ♣)

In response to a One Diamond opening, bid:

(l)	(m)	(n)	(o)
♠ Q.x.x.	♠ J.x.	♠ Q.J.x.	♠ Q.x.x.
♥ Q.10.x.	♥ 10.x.x.	♥ 10.x.x.x.x.	♥ Q.x.x
♦ J.x.	♦ Q.x.x.	♦ J.x.	♦ x.x
♣ Q.10.x.x.x.	♣ K.x.x.x.x.	♣ K.J.x.x.	♣ K.Q.J.x.x.
(Bid 1NT)	(Pass or bid 2 ♦)	(Bid 1 ♥)	(Bid 2 ♣)

Note that, at rubber Bridge, a No Trump response would also be feasible on all these hands except (i).

THE ONE NO TRUMP OVERCALL

This is only touched on briefly in Chapter XI (page 84) and there's a fair bit more to say on this aspect, especially for those playing in competitions. Like all No Trump bids, this is a limit bid with a three-point range. In the immediate overcall position, it is a strong bid showing 15–17 or 16–18 points, according to taste. More importantly, it guarantees at least one, and preferably two controls in the opponents' bid suit (A–Q or K.Q.x., etc). Apart from these mandatory requirements, it will fall among the hand patterns used for No Trump openings.

Bid One No Trump over One Heart on:

(p)			
♠ Q.x.x.	♠ Q.x.	♠ A.x.x.	♠ K.x.x.
♥ A.Q.	♥ K.Q.x.	♥ Q.J.x.x.	♥ A.K.x.
♦ Q.10.x.x.	♦ A.Q.x.x.x.	♦ K.x.x.	♦ Q.x.
♣ A.Q.x.x.	♣ Q.J.x.	♣ K.Q.x.	♣ K.Q.x.x.x.

In the fourth (or "protective") position, however, the One No Trump overcall is *weak*, showing 10–12, 11–13 or 12–14 points, according to preference, but you must have an agreement to use

136

one of them. The bid does not guarantee a stop in the suit opened, though it's preferable to have at least half a stop. The reason for this difference in strength is logical; your left-hand opponent has opened only at the one-level and his partner is too weak to respond. So the chances are that your partner has some values but has no suitable overcall. Of course, the opener might have as many as 19 or 20 points for his one-bid with his partner holding 4 or 5; that's the small risk factor you have to take, against the more probable chance that your side holds the balance of strength and ought to be playing the contract. If you hold more than your agreed point range for a No Trump in the "protective" position, you'll normally be expected to make a "take out" double and partner, who sits over the opening bidder, will decide on the best course of action. The opener's suit might also be your partner's suit, in which case he can pass the double for penalties.

Opener bids One Heart, and the next players pass; you hold:

(q)	(r)	(s)	(t)
♠ Q.J.x.	♠ Q.x.	♠ K.Q.x.x.x.	♠ A.x.x.
♥ K.x.x.	♥ Q.J.x.	♥ Q.x.x.	♥ Q.x.
♦ J.x.x.x.	♦ Q.x.x	♦ Q.x.	♦ K.J.x.x.
♣ K.J.x.	♣ K.Q.x.x.x.	♣ J.x.x	♣ K.Q.x.x.
(Bid 1NT)	(Bid 1NT)	(Bid 1♠)	(Double)

THE TWO NO TRUMP RESPONSE TO AN OPENING BID

This is the hand which Macleod uses to illustrate a Two No Trump response to a One Club opening bid (page 65), and it's still a good Acol response, which I would use in many situations—for the reasons which were explained:

(u) ♠ K.10.x.
     ♥ A.x.x.
     ♦ Q.10.x.x.
     ♣ Q.x.x.

Yet most teachers will tell you that the standard Acol response is One Diamond, which is also correct, if you are playing master point pairs. This is the best possible example I could find to highlight the influence which competition-style bidding is having on Bridge, and perhaps that's why Iain didn't like master

137

point pairs. I tend to sympathise, for Two No Trumps conforms to my philosophy of being "simple, direct, and effective". On the other hand, One Diamond is also simple, direct, and, for purposes of the accuracy needed in Pairs bidding, more constructive. So you pays your money and takes your choice!

Styles do change; take, for example, the following hand on which Terence Reese advocated a Two No Trump response to One Heart:

(v) ♠ K.J.7.3.
♥ Q.10.8.
♦ Q.5.
♣ A.9.8.4.

This was over 25 years ago. Terence, who was another of the original pioneers of Acol, and who is still one of the world's leading bidding theorists, wouldn't advocate the same bid today any more than he would fly to the moon.

Personally, this Two No Trumps bid is the only one in the game about which I have mixed feelings, and I still use both versions according to the circumstances. However, I don't agree with the "scientists" who want to integrate what is known as the Baron Two No Trumps into the Acol system; Baron uses Two No Trumps response to show a balanced hand with 16–18 points, preferably also agreeing the suit opened. Of course, this has Bridge merit, but for inexperienced players I believe it offers them a minefield in which they will often blow themselves to a level beyond their playing competence. "Scientists" are now all competition players, and they play an important role in the development of bidding theory generally—even if it isn't always practical. It does seem a bit daft that one should have two alternative bids to describe the same hand accurately—unless we assign one to rubber and one to master point pairs. I designed my own format for the use of Two No Trumps in tournaments some years ago, but it hasn't yet crept into the hit parade. This would be my typical Two No Trumps response over One Heart:

(w) ♠ K.Q.x.
♥ x.x.
♦ Q.J.x.x.
♣ Q.J.x.x.

Whilst being a limit bid and quite obstructive, it gives a lot of constructive information to partner; it shows:

(i)   Balanced hand with 10½-12½ points, without more than two controls.

(ii)   A doubleton in partner's bid suit (possibly three-card suit).

(iii) A stopper in each of the other suits.

What alternative sequence do you have for this type of hand— Two Clubs and then Two No Trumps after partner rebids his Hearts? That would offer an almost irresistible temptation for your opponent to intervene with Two Spades!

OPENING BID OF THREE NO TRUMPS

At last, here's an Acol bid which the influence of pairs play has improved (see Chapter VII). Taking Macleod's logic a step further, it is wasteful (of bidding space) to make pre-emptive bids on strong hands. The example (x) and (y) on page 39 could be opened with Two Diamonds and One Club respectively, and they are both much too strong for the modern style Three No Trumps, which shows a solid seven-card minor suit and not more than one defensive trick outside. Take the Ace of Clubs from hand (x) and the King of Diamonds from hand (y) and you have got a Three No Trumps opener. You are always living dangerously with this bid, but think of the pressure you put on your opponents. If you get doubled, partner is in a good position to judge whether to take out into your suit (which ought to be marked), or, with some sort of stop in the other suits, he will "risk" that you're going to make nine tricks. He will know that you're going to make eight if you get the lead quickly.

TRANSFER BIDS

There's nothing new about the concept of transfer bidding. It's been an integral part of tournament systems for well over thirty years, but its use isn't normally permitted in rubber Bridge clubs. I can well understand Iain not making any mention of this subject, because the book is about simple, natural Bridge, without frills. Transfers are not natural bids, but they are simple, harmless, not really artificial, and have great Bridge merit; so they must be explained. They have also become an integral part of the Acol system and most duplicate players now use them. Transfers are only used in response to No Trump bids and their purpose is to ensure that the stronger opening hand is still going to be declarer and remains concealed, when the contract is to be played in a suit. Take this example:

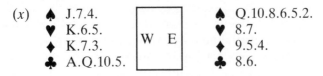

(x) ♠ J.7.4.   ♠ Q.10.8.6.5.2.
     ♥ K.6.5.   ♥ 8.7.
     ♦ K.7.3.   W E   ♦ 9.5.4.
     ♣ A.Q.10.5.   ♣ 8.6.

(See hand (n) on page 36). Over West's opening of One No Trump, East would naturally bid Two Spades, which isn't likely to make, unless South holds both red aces and The King of Clubs. The contract might go three down, if North has these cards, but, whatever the distribution, the chances are bound to be better if the lead comes up to West's unsupported Kings or into his nice Club holding. So East makes a transfer bid of Two Hearts which tells partner to bid Two Spades, thus invariably ensuring that declarer will make at least one trick more than if an attacking lead is made initially through the vulnerable red suits. If the One No Trump was doubled by either North or South, it's even more important to have the trump suit in dummy, and so the transfer bid would still apply. A 300 or even 500 penalty would not be serious in this situation as the opponents would themselves be able to make a certain game and probable slam.

You transfer by bidding the suit below the one in which you want partner to play. I recommend at this stage that you only consider using transfers for the major suits, as transferring to the minors will mean playing at the three-level; and, in addition, there are alternative versions of the transfer mechanism, which can give rise to partnership misunderstanding, or forgetfulness. If the No Trump gets doubled, you can now make a two-level transfer to the minors, by using a "re-double" for Two Clubs, and Two Clubs (which isn't Stayman in this position) for Two Diamonds. Note, however, that if you use "re-double" as a transfer bid, you've changed its natural meaning, which shows 9+ points.

The transfer bid can be used in exactly the same way over a Two No Trump opening bid. It improves on the well-known

Flint convention, for it uses Three Hearts as well as Three Diamonds as transfer bids.

Any mechanism which improves the performance of a bidding system consistently and unambiguously should be generally acceptable for use, unless its use causes offence or confusion to opponents. In the case of rubber Bridge clubs for example, the use of transfers would normally be undesirable, for there will always be members who will not or do not play them, and any suggestion that they should would be a cause of friction.

Once people start playing transfers, it is extremely difficult for them to confine the use simply to the weakness take-out situation we've discussed. For the bids can also be used constructively to show hand-types, which cannot easily be described with "straight" Acol. Beginners must read this section for interest and future reference only. However appealing and simple the ideas might sound, it is NOT a good idea to try to use them until the *natural* basics of the system have been learnt and fully understood. The further use of transfers correctly is not automatic; it requires a fair bit of experience and the usual sound judgment—but it's worth knowing about.

Look again at the East hand of our example on page 36, and add a few more points to it, say the King of Spades and Ace of Hearts. After One No Trump, with 9 points and a good six-card suit, it is too strong for a mere weakness take-out, yet not strong enough to make an immediate jump bid. Bidding naturally you would have to use your non-forcing sequence via Two Clubs (Stayman) followed by a jump to Three Spades, which partner is likely to assume shows a five-card suit and 11–12 points. A transfer sequence enables you to fill this gap neatly and effectively; after Two Hearts and partner's Two Spades response, you raise to Three Spades, which shows 9–10 points plus a six-card suit, and you have the stronger hand as declarer; this is invitational to Four Spades only.

Next, let us take the situation where you have 11–12 points and a five-card suit opposite the One No Trump opening—something like:

(y) ♠   A.K.8.6.5
        ♥   Q.8
        ♦   Q.10.4
        ♣   8.6.4

Using transfers, you show your five-card suit by bidding Two Hearts, and over the forced Two Spades response, you show your 11–12 points by rebidding Two No Trumps. Partner now has a precise picture of your hand, and the added advantage, which this sequence offers over the natural one, is that he can pass at the two-level, where eight tricks may be the limit of the hands, and Three Spades will go down. Put this hand opposite West's in our example, and West, holding three Spades, would have a borderline decision whether to bid Three or Four Spades. Add the King of Clubs to the above hand and you are not going to stop short of game, so you rebid Three No Trumps over Two Spades.

Finally, a third situation for the constructive use of transfers is to show two suits on hands unsuitable for play in No Trumps. What do you bid on this hand after partner has opened One No Trump?

(z) ♠   A.K.4.3.
       ♥   K.Q.8.7.6.
       ♦   6.
       ♣   K.7.6.

Presumably a Stayman Two Club enquiry for majors—and when partner responds negatively with Two Diamonds?— Three Hearts would normally be invitational so, as you can not afford to miss game, you have an awkward decision between bidding Four Hearts or Three No Trumps. Using the transfer bid sequence you can *show* your shape, instead of *asking* about partner's; you bid Two Diamonds (showing five Hearts) and over the Two Hearts response, you re-bid Two Spades, which is forcing.

Try this one:

$(a2)$ ♠   A.K.8.4.3.
       ♥   6.
       ♦   K.Q.10.4.
       ♣   K.7.6.

The natural Acol response to One No Trump would be Three Spades and, if partner has three-card support he will bid Four Spades, otherwise Three No Trumps. In either case, would you consider showing your Diamond suit beyond game level? Possibly Four Diamonds over Three No Trumps, but certainly not Five Diamonds over Four Spades. The transfer bid sequence solves the problem—Two Hearts over One No Trump, followed by Three Diamonds after the Two Spades response, again forcing, but note that the second suit is shown naturally. The important caveat with these last two examples is that your hand should be at least strong enough for game, and, when the second suit is a minor, have a possible slam interest. If the No Trump hand is good—something like:

$$(b2) \quad \spadesuit \quad Q.7.$$
$$\heartsuit \quad A.9.2.$$
$$\diamondsuit \quad A.J.8.6.$$
$$\clubsuit \quad Q.J.8.4.$$

You have got good play for Six Hearts in the first case and even better play for Six Diamonds in the second. As already mentioned, I am not a great one for scientific bidding theory, but this system of simple transfers is too useful to be ignored, especially by duplicate players; if you work it out, there is a whole extra stratum of bidding available to show hand-types over the No Trump opening. And since I have advocated the more liberal and versatile use of weak No Trump openings, the transfer bid becomes an even more valuable additive!

WEAK TWOS

First of all, re-read Macleod's splendid reference to this subject (Chapter VIII, page 50), especially his explanation as to why Weak Twos were, and still are, banned from use in most rubber Bridge clubs. I have never quite understood the logic of this ban, when Weak Threes have always been universally acceptable as part of "natural bidding", yet the three-level preemptive bid is far more difficult to cope with than the two-level pre-empt. It has always been my opinion that all natural bidding, which has Bridge merit should be, in principle, permissible everywhere in Bridge circles. Where there is an imbalance of playing standards, or an invividual reluctance to have change, these can be treated as exceptions in accordance with the normal courtesies and protocol, which are associated with a healthy club environment. However, it is an archaic principle which allows amnesia and ignorance to restrict use of the natural features of the game. (Note that this differs from my view on the restricted use of transfer bids, which are not truly natural bids, and require further explanation).

The broad logic of Two Bids being played as Weak and preemptive is that they are used for the same purpose as Weak Threes, i.e. to obstruct the opponents, but show a different hand-type. Weak Threes show a seven-card suit with very few points (not more than an Ace and a King, and maybe only a Queen and a Jack) (see Chapter XI, page 81); Weak Twos show a six-card suit with an agreed point range, which is normally 6–10, but may be 5–9.

Although the use of Weak Twos had been popular in America from the early days of contract Bridge, it wasn't until 1962 that a Scot, Albert Benjamin, designed a modified version of the American Weak Twos, and, all of a sudden, Acol became "Benjaminised"! That's the way to become immortalised in Bridge! Benjaminised Acol, or "Benjy" as it's affectionately called, is now a standard form of Acol, used predominantly in master point pairs. When I asked Albert recently about the original version of his system, he couldn't remember, as it was so long ago since he had played the system himself, and it was only on the insistence of an Englishman that he had bothered to license it!

"Benjy" Weak Twos only apply to the major suits; Two Clubs and Two Diamonds are used to show strong hands. A Two Spades or Two Hearts opening would promise the following:

(a) Six-card suit with one of the top three honours.

(b) 6–10 (or 5–9) points.

(c) No other four-card suit; if partner hasn't already passed.

A response of Two No Trumps by partner is forcing, and asks opener to describe the strength of his hand on the following scale:

Three Clubs—Minimum points (6–8 or 5–7) and one honour in his suit.

Three Diamonds—Minimum points with two honours in the suit.

Three Hearts—Maximum points (9–10 or 8–9) with one honour in the suit.

Three Spades—Maximum points with two honours in the suit.
Three No Trumps—Suit headed by the three top honours.

Responder's raise of the opener's suit is pre-emptive and non-forcing. You have an option as to how you use a response in another suit; Macleod advocates it as forcing for one round; I prefer to treat it as non-forcing, but showing a suit, which should be at least as good as the suit opened, and not more than a singleton in the other suit. The following hands qualify for Weak Two openings with appropriate rebids after Two No Trumps response:

Two Hearts and rebid Three Clubs on:

(c2)   ♠   x.
        ♥   K.x.x.x.x.x.
        ♦   Q.J.x.
        ♣   J.x.x.

Two Hearts and rebid Three Diamonds on:

(d2)   ♠   J.x.
        ♥   A.Q.x.x.x.x.
        ♦   x.x.
        ♣   x.x.x.

Two Hearts and rebid Three Spades on:

(e2)   ♠   x.
        ♥   K.Q.10.x.x.x.
        ♦   K.x.x.
        ♣   Q.x.x.

Two Hearts and rebid Three No Trumps on:

(f2)   ♠   x.x.
        ♥   A.K.Q.x.x.x.
        ♦   x.x.
        ♣   x.x.x.

As with all Acol bidding, you must use your judgment and not automatically make a bid just because you have the technical requirements. For example, it would be folly to open Two Hearts on hand (c2) if you were vulnerable and the opponents were not. But hand (f2) would be a sound opening in any position, and the valuable information about your solid suit, which you show with Three No Trumps, might enable your side to make game on very slender values.

Now we come to the strong hands, which are covered by bids of Two Clubs and Two Diamonds. Since Two Diamonds does not have much merit as a weak pre-emptive bid, we assign it to the big game forcing hands on which you would normally open Two Clubs in basic Acol (see Chapter VIII, page 43). The negative response to Two Diamonds is Two Hearts, and the requirements for a positive are exactly as have been laid down for the normal Acol Two Clubs. The "Benjy" Acol Two Clubs shows either an eight playing-trick hand, or a No Trump hand with 21+ points. The negative response is Two Diamonds, and the requirements for a positive response are similar to those of the normal Acol Two Clubs (see page 43). Note that, even though the Two Clubs opener is likely to have the eight playing-trick hand, I recommend that you should have stronger values to show a positive, than you might have for a positive over an Acol Strong Two Bid. The reason is that bidding space is extremely valuable when you need to investigate slam possibilities, and it is always a good idea, if you are to force opener to show his suit at a level higher, that you promise one of the following holdings:

(1) An Ace and a King.
(2) Two K.Q.s.
(3) K.Q. and two Kings.
(4) Four Kings.

Without one of these requirements but with 8–10 points, you can respond Two No Trumps, or Three No Trumps with 11–12 points.

Study this example;

(g2)   West
  ♠ J.4.
  ♥ A.K.Q.10.7.4.
  ♦ A.K.10.4.
  ♣ 4.

which is just worth a "Benjy" Two Club opener.
  Now look at two possible responding hands;

(h2)	East	(i2)	East
♠	K.Q.10.6.5.3.	♠	A.K.10.6.5.3.
♥	J.6.5.	♥	J.6.5.
♦	8.7.	♦	8.7.
♣	8.6.	♣	8.6.

On hand (*h2*) you bid a negative Two Diamonds and over West's Two Hearts, you raise to Three Hearts. On hand (*i2*) you bid a positive Two Spades and, over West's Three Hearts, you raise to Four Hearts. Note that in both cases you must show support for partner's suit immediately on a three-card suit, rather than rebidding your Spades. If you make the mistake of bidding Two Spades on (*h2*) instead of Two Diamonds, partner will think you have a "positive", and will make a slam try, after you raise his Three Hearts to game, and the contract will be too high. Hand (*i2*) has got that vital extra control, which makes the slam a very good prospect. If we take the Five of Hearts away from the above hands and make it the Five of Clubs, the bidding sequences would alter appropriately:

W	N	E	S
2♣	—	2♦	—
2♥	—	2♠	—
3♦	—	3♥	—
4♥	—	—	—

W	N	E	S
2♣	—	2♠	—
3♥	—	3♠	—
4♦	—	4♥	—
4♠	—	—	—

Here are a few examples of Benjaminised Acol Strong bids:

Two Clubs then Two Spades on:
(*j2*) ♠ A.K.x.x.x.
        ♥ A.K.x.x.x.
        ♦ A.x.
        ♣ x.

Two Diamonds then Two Spades on:
(*k2*) ♠ A.K.Q.x.x.x.
        ♥ A.K.Q.x.x.x.
        ♦ none.
        ♣ x.

Two Clubs then Three Hearts on:

(l2)   ♠ x.
       ♥ A.K.Q.J.10.x.x.
       ♦ x.x.
       ♣ A.K.x.

Two Clubs then Two No Trumps on:

(m2)   ♠ A.Q.x.
       ♥ A.K.x.
       ♦ Q.10.x.x.
       ♣ A.Q.x.

Two Diamonds then Two No Trumps on:

(n2)   ♠ A.Q.x.
       ♥ A.K.x.
       ♦ K.Q.10.x.
       ♣ A.Q.x

The two-tier means of showing No Trump ranges provides a useful bonus for the three or four times in your Bridge life when you hold most of the points in the pack (I recall holding 35 once—and went down in the inevitable slam!). With the extra levels of bidding available on the following scale, you might still have time to find a suit fit!

21–22	2♣—2♦—2NT
23–24	2♦—2♥—2NT
25–26	2♣—2♦—3NT
27–28	2♦—2♥—3NT
29–30	2♣—2♦—4NT
31–32	2♦—2♥—4NT
33–34	2♣—2♦—5NT
35–36	2♦—2♥—5NT

With this valuable information, the responder can more easily reach a slam holding a Yarborough.

The Weak "Benjy" Two bids are very simple to use provided you obey the rules for their limits. Although their purpose is mainly obstructive, they are also useful to take care of some hands where you would otherwise open at the one-level and rebid the suit. If you find yourself defending against Weak

Twos, you do not have the same difficulties as you do against the higher three-level pre-empts. Your best method of defence is to treat them as if they were one-bids. But remember that, when you make a take-out double, partner will expect you to have a good holding in the other major suit.

THE MULTI-COLOURED TWO DIAMONDS

Reference to this terrible "gadget" is by way of obituary notice and health warning, rather than an accolade for Bridge merit. There's nothing new about the artificial bid of Two Diamonds, for it has always been an integral part of the artificial Club systems (Blue and Precision). The bid is "at home" within the framework of these systems, but its transplant into the body of a natural system such as Acol is a threat to the basic infrastructure of that system.

The Multi Two Diamonds as it's commonly known, was licensed as a convention several years ago by the Laws and Ethics Committee of the English Bridge Union, and since then it has grown in popularity among tournament players at all levels. Fortunately, it's never likely to appear at the rubber Bridge table. So this synopsis is for the benefit of tournament newcomers who suddenly find themselves confronted by opponents who are playing it.

Very basically, the Multi Two Diamonds can show any of the following hand types:

(1) A Weak Two in a major suit.
(2) A Strong Two in a minor suit.
(3) A 4–4–4–1 or 5–4–4–0 distribution with 17+ points.
(4) A strong balanced hand with 22+ points.

The convention combines the use of any three of these options, and the choice of the one to be left out is a matter for partnership agreement. Within these options there are about a dozen variations in the responses so the chances of two random partners playing the same style are fairly remote. But that does not concern the average user for whom the main appeal of Multi seems to be the element of confusion which it causes the opponents.

The legendary Rixi Markus, who is never short of a positive opinion on Bridge matters, once said to me "This Multi is almost cheating", and I know what she means. Any convention, which has little Bridge merit, other than to gain an advantage over less

149

experienced opponents, can hardly be called Bridge—and certainly not Acol. The Multi Two Diamonds replaces natural Acol bids and sequences, which are basically more efficient. Notably, its use as a Weak Two doesn't give the same pre-emptive value as "Benjy"; and bidding on the strong 4–4–4–1 type of hand can not stop below the three-level; there are other flaws, but these are the main ones.

Many former converts to Multi have reverted to normal methods, once the novelty of this colourful gadget has worn off, but there are still plenty of devotees, so I had better recommend a defence for those who meet it on the first occasion. The best defence is to Pass if you possibly can, for the opponents will usually "hang" themselves through mis-use of the convention. If you are too good to Pass, bid simply to show one of the three main hand-types, as follows:

(1) Good single-suited hand—bid the suit naturally.
(2) Two- or three-suited hand—bid the unusual Two No Trumps, for partner to show his lowest biddable suit.
(3) Strong balanced hand with 16+ points—Double for take-out, but partner can Pass it for penalties.

HYBRID ACOL

There is a trend among the "scientists" of Bridge to impregnate Acol with features from the artificial Club systems, and notably the Precision Club.

I call this modern version of Acol theory "hybrid Acol", because some distinction must be made between the system explained in the previous chapters and that which Eric Crowhurst, one of Bridge's most respected and brilliant analysts, calls "Acol in the 'eighties" or "precision bidding in Acol". Hybrid Acol is totally unacceptable to rubber Bridge, and it should also be avoided like the plague by social duplicate players. For the remainder—scientifically and statistically minded competitors —there will always be an irresistible fascination for "precision bidding", and the Crowhurst theories are unbeatable in this context.

If your inclination is to become a "scientist" always remember that the formulae look great on paper, but, when put to the test, they are highly vulnerable to attack and sabotage by competent opponents using natural methods.

One of the great appeals of Bridge is the freedom of choice which you have in selecting your style of play. It is a game where you actually can mix chalk with cheese and still get successful results. No two players could have more diametrically opposed views on bidding theory and practice than Eric and me, yet, many years ago now, I recall that we convincingly won the County Pairs for at least three consecutive years together—and I've learnt a lot from him about the other side of the coin!

CHAPTER XVI

THE THEORY AND PRACTICE OF OPENING LEADS

IN play the declarer, who can see all the twenty-six cards in his own and his partner's hand, has the advantage. But he has not the initiative: by virtue of the opening lead that lies with the defence. It is small enough compensation and it must never be wasted. Start then always with a plan. You have the information of the opposition bidding, and perhaps of your partner's. Even your partner's silence can be of importance. You know the score, and probably the ability of the declarer. Very often the opening lead will appear to be automatic. Even then you should pause for a moment and glance at the other possibilities. The decision you have to make is in three parts. If you are a beginner, or if the hand is particularly difficult, you will find it best to take each decision in turn.

Is my lead to be busy or passive?
From which suit?
Which card?

BUSY OR PASSIVE DEFENCE

These terms are the ones employed by S.J. Simon. Ely Culbertson calls them "attacking" or "protecting" but I find Simon's terms more descriptive. When you reach a good standard of play your cards and the opposition bidding will be a sure guide. Usually you will be right to get busy and the passive game though common enough should be the exception.

THE LEAD AGAINST NO TRUMPS

If your partner has bid you should normally lead his suit. It is true that the opponents have announced that they hold the suit at least once, but the opening lead gives you the advantage in knocking out a stopper, and this "tempo" (or advantage in time) as it is called, may be decisive. Remember too, that partner may have taken a risk in bidding at all, so that he can indicate a lead. These considerations are nothing, of course, if you have an established or near-established suit of your own, but in any close decision you should allow them to settle the point. At the worst it makes for partnership harmony to lead his suit, rather than gamble on your own. If you decide to lead his suit you should lead your highest unless you have three or more to a honour (Q.10.*x*., J.x.*x*., A.x.*x*.), in which case the lowest is led. There is a simple reason for this. The stoppers in the suit are presumed to be on your right. Study how in each of these examples the lead of your lowest card gains a trick:

(*a*)   x.x.
    Q.10.*x*.   A.x.x.x.x.
            K.J.x.
(*b*)   x
    J.x.*x*.   A.Q.9.8.x.
            K.10.x.x.
(*c*)   x.x.
    A.x.*x*.   J.10.9.8.x.
            K.Q.x.

If you have four or more cards you should lead the fourth best unless you have an obvious sequence lead, e.g. K.x.x.*x*. but *Q*.J.9.x.

More often the opponents' bidding will have been undisturbed. Decide first if the bidding is confident or not. 1NT-3NT obviously is: just as obviously.

1♥	—	1NT	—
2♦	—	2♥	—
3♥	—	3NT	—

is not. Clearly if in the second sequence given you have only three or four points your partner must be pretty good. It may—probably will—pay you to play to his hand. Suppose you have:

    ♠ J.x.
    ♥ Q.x.x.
    ♦ x.x.x.
    ♣ J.x.x.x.x.

153

and the second sequence given above has been bid against you. Obviously partner is good. Look closely at the bidding. It shouts aloud that neither of them has a four-card Spade suit—so your partner has five, perhaps six. The Jack of Spades is your lead. There is an important secondary lesson to be learned here. If you have a choice between the lead of a major and a minor suit, other things being equal, pick the major suit. The reason is that a four-card minor suit is often suppressed in the bidding, a four-card major very rarely.

There are two occasions when a passive lead and a negative defence are best. The first when you—as leader—hold such a good hand that your partner can have very little, and when you have no particular suit of your own, e.g. against the bidding 1NT–3NT from:

♠ 9.8.x.
♥ A.Q.x.
♦ K.J.x.x.
♣ K.10.x.

the nine of Spades is best, not because (as in the last example) you hope to hit your partner's suit, but because it is your best chance of giving nothing away. The second range of hands is when you hold a moderate point count (about 7-8 points) when it is clear your partner has about the same, and your opponents will be struggling for tricks. In this case the ideal safe lead is something like *J*.10.9.

FOURTH BEST

The standard lead from a long suit against No Trumps is the fourth best. By the application of the Rule of Eleven partner can calculate how many higher cards than the one led are held by the declarer. For example:

K.J.x.

West leads 7.   A.10.x.x.

East can see in his own hand and in Dummy's four cards higher than the lead, and so South cannot beat the seven. Accordingly if declarer plays low from North, East also ducks and the seven holds the trick. The only trouble with the Rule of Eleven—discovered in 1889 and so far older than Contract or Auction

154

Bridge—is that declarer also can use it. On the whole this is of less importance than giving accurate information to your partner. You should, however, sometimes vary your game (particularly when your partner is weak and unlikely to be deceived) by leading fifth best instead of fourth best or—with a four-card suit—the third best. For example, Q.9.x.x._x._ or A.x._x._x. The deuce as a fourth best lead is rarely a happy selection: it gives too much away, and opens a wide choice of safe throw-in plays to an expert declarer. Still, on balance, there is far more to be said for the fourth best lead than against it, and it should be your standard play. The combinations to avoid opening are four to an unsupported honour, especially a Jack, and four-card suits headed by broken honours, e.g. A.J.x.x.

THE CHOICE OF CARD

Leads are fairly standardised once the suit is selected, and few cases offer any difficulty.

(a) The normal lead from an inner sequence is the middle card: Q._10_.9., A._J_.10., K._J_.10., A._Q_.J., A._10_.9.

(b) The normal lead from outer touching honours, if supported is the top card, e.g. _K_.Q.10., _Q_.J.10., _Q_.J.9., but you should lead fourth best from K.Q.x._x_., Q.J.8._x_., etc. From A.K. combinations, however, the King is the usual lead unless consideration of entries make a fourth best lead desirable, e.g. from A.K.x._x_.x. Lead the King from A._K_.x.x.

(c) If you decide to lead a short unbid suit, you should lead the highest card from a worthless doubleton or trebleton, but the lowest card from three to an honour, K.x.x. or 10.x.x. If more than one honour is held rules (a) or (b) apply. Be sure, however, that your trebleton really is worthless before you lead the top card: for example, with 9.4.2. the nine may well be an important card in the end game, especially in a suit contract, and the four is probably a better lead.

(d) The lead of the Ace against a No Trump contract is a conventional request to partner to throw his *highest* card on it to unblock the suit, e.g. _A_.K.Q.10.x.x. or _A_.K.J.x.x.x.x.

155

1.   The bidding goes:

N	E	S	W
1NT	—	3NT	—
—	—	—	

and you have to lead from:

♠ A.x.
♥ J.x.x.x.
♦ x.x.
♣ 10.8.x.x.x.

Prospects, of course, are not rosy, but equally they are not hopeless. Let's try the three steps:

(a) Busy or Passive? Busy, of course: we'll never get five tricks here by waiting.

(b) Which suit? Spades are out. The Heart combination is one we are firmly prejudiced against. The fourth best Club looks attractive but, even if partner can help, your entry will probably have been forced out before the suit can be established. So that leaves us Diamonds, and the gamble on a fit in partner's hand.

(c) Which card? Top of a worthless doubleton.

2.   The bidding goes:

N	E	S	W
1♠	—	2♠	—
2NT	—	3NT	—
—	—	—	

East has:

♠ 10.x.x.
♥ J.x.
♦ K.Q.x.x.
♣ A.J.x.x.

(a) Busy or Passive? I have a good hand which looks well placed. The opponents can't have much to spare. I plump for a quiet lead.

(b) Which suit? We want to pick the one that risks least and clearly that must be Spades.

156

(*c*) Which card? The small one: it's just possible that to play the ten may ruin a combined guard in the two hands.

3.   The bidding goes:

N	E	S	W
1 ♦	—	1 ♥	1 ♠
1NT	—	2NT	—
3NT	—	—	—

East holds:

♠ J.x.
♥ 10.9.8.x.
♦ Q.x.
♣ Q.10.9.x.x.

(*a*) Busy or Passive? The opponents have just been able to scrape up a game bid, and you have a safe passive lead of the ten of Hearts. This is a superficial view. Left to himself, the declarer will probably come to nine tricks. You must attack.

(*b*) Which Suit? Clubs or Spades? It's very close. Partner must have risked a penalty to tell you about his Spades, and you have possible tricks in all the other suits. Take his word for it: lead a Spade.

(*c*) Which card? The Jack.

LEADING AGAINST A SUIT CONTRACT

It is more difficult to find the best lead against a suit contract, although the same approach is best.

WHEN TO OPEN TRUMPS

With a little study you can easily recognise the occasions when a trump lead is called for,. These are the main occasions:

(*a*)   When the bidding indicates a cross ruff. The ideal lead is something like A.x.x. which may enable you to draw three rounds of trumps, but K.x.x. is often effective and in these circumstances even Q.x.x. or J.x.x. will probably not lose in the end.

157

(*b*) When your partner has opened with One No Trump and you have a balanced hand. Here the object is to force the opponents as soon as possible into a No Trump game.

(*c*) When you have an abnormal number of trumps, say five against declarer's 4–4 holding.

(*d*) When your partner passes your take out double for penalties, e.g. you hold:

♠ A.Q.10.x.
♥ x.
♦ A.10.x.x.
♣ K.x.x.x.

If you double an opening Heart bid on your right and everyone passes you should start with your trump. This is a busy, not a passive, lead with the same object as in (*b*) of forcing a No Trump game.

There is also a residue of hands covered by the old rule, "when in doubt, lead trumps". It's a sound enough adage if you take it not as an excuse for sloth, but a final refuge when anything else looks unattractive.

SIDE SUITS LEADS

When partner has bid and you decide to lead his suit, the only difference at trump contracts as against No Trumps in the card you would lead, is when you have three to an honour. Here you normally lead the highest, e.g. *A*.x.x., *Q*.10.x., *K*.x.x., etc.

We have now given all the situations which can be classified and for which "rules" (however incomplete) can be given. The first test of a real Bridge player in defence comes when defending a suit contract he has neither a bid from partner to guide him nor an obvious combination of his own to lead.

Usually the leader has to select one of these three plans:

The Ruffing Game.
The Forcing Game.
The Waiting Game.

RUFFING GAME

This is the easiest to recognise, and also the one most likely to upset a "certain" contract. A perfect illustration will be found in

158

Hand No. 19 in Acol in Action. When you hold A.x. or K.x. in your partner's suit, your prospects are excellent. If you are going to open such a holding in an unbid suit you should only do it as a desperation lead, or when you have an early trump trick such as A.x. or K.x.x.

FORCING GAME

This is the strongest defence of all. It is the defence which is most likely to secure a very large penalty. The essence of the forcing game consists in a battle for tempos. Either you or your partner should have four trumps and a long strong side suit which is led at every opportunity. Typical forcing leads against a Four-Heart contract are:

(1)	♠	x.x.	(2)	♠	none.
	♥	K.10.x.x.		♥	A.J.x.x.
	♦	x.x.		♦	_K_.Q.10.x.x.x.
	♣	_A_.Q.J.x.x.		♣	x.x.x.

(3)	♠	A.K.
	♥	J.10.x.x.
	♦	_Q_.J.10.x.x.
	♣	x.x.

WAITING GAME

Try and find a waiting lead if your hand is studded with tenaces. Lead the doubleton Spade against Four Hearts from:

♠ _x_.x.
♥ Q.10.x.
♦ A.Q.x.x.
♣ K.10.x.x.

A waiting lead is often a trump lead, but avoid a singleton or such combinations as Q.x. and J.x.x.x. which may make partner's honour into a stopper.

LEADING AGAINST A SLAM

Against small contracts you may be able to correct an opening blunder. Against a slam you are unlikely to be reprieved. Many difficult problems will be solved for you if you play the Lightner Slam Double (see hand *p* in Chapter XI). Probably the opponents' bidding will indicate their weakness particularly if they are using slam conventions. Against a Grand Slam and with no obvious lead, play passive and safe. As a rule attack against a small slam. The best leads here are the ones that are so poor against No Trump game contracts K.x.x.*x*. or Q.x.x.*x*. The lead from the King is better than from the Queen, because of course partner needs less to build up a trick. If you can tell that the opponents are missing an Ace a singleton is an excellent lead, and you are likely to defeat the slam if partner has either the Ace of the suit led or the Ace of trumps.

EXAMPLES OF LEADS AGAINST TRUMP CONTRACTS

1. As East you hold:

♠ x.x.x.
♥ A.J.x.
♦ K.x.x.x.
♣ K.Q.10.

and have to lead against the bidding:

N	E	S	W
1♠	—	3♠	—
4♠	—	—	—

(*a*) Busy or passive? If partner can provide one trick or even good plus values you should beat this contract. Your aim, therefore, should be to give nothing away. Find a passive lead.

(*b*) Which Suit? Having made your first decision the choice is Spades or Clubs. The Club lead looks safe, but if Dummy turns up with J.x.x. you have almost certainly lost the vital trick. The Spade is safe.

(*c*) Which card? Top of a worthless trebleton.

2. As East you hold:

♠ x.
♥ J.x.
♦ K.Q.x.x.x.x.
♣ K.Q.J.x.

160

and have to lead against the bidding:

N	E	S	W
1♠	2♦	—	3♦
3♥	—	4♠	Dble
—	—		

(a) Busy or passive? Must be busy—and quickly. There may be a big penalty here for the forcing game: partner is likely to have four trumps.

(b) Which Suit? Diamonds not Clubs, for it is the early force (especially against the long trump hand) which wins, and partner is more likely to have the Diamond than the Club Ace.

(c) Which card? King.

3. As East you hold:

♠ x.x.
♥ J.x.x.
♦ K.x.x.x.
♣ Q.x.x.x.

and the opponents have bid:

N	S	W	E
1♥	2♠	—	—
3♠	4♥	—	—
4NT	5NT	—	—
6♥	—		

(a) Busy or passive? The slam is confidently bid and they seem to have all the controls. You have a possible trick in trumps (if partner has, say, Q.x.) and your partner may have a trick in Spades to win on a finesse. But the chances of both these coming off is not very good, and you must seek to build up a trick in a minor suit. Therefore a busy defence.

(b) Which Suit? Diamonds are better than Clubs.

(c) Which card? A small one. Probably the third best is correct especially if you have the deuce.

I don't suggest you should always go through these steps. Often you will take all the steps in one jump, and arrive at the right lead. But when the bidding has been confused or intricate, when you have no obvious lead then try thinking systematically. Set yourself deliberately to answer the three questions. Having done so at least you will not make an aimless lead, and very rarely will you make a bad one. And that will save you a vast number of points every year.

WHEN PARTNER DOUBLES

Many tragedies result from the selection of the wrong lead when partner doubles the final No Trump contract. No rules can cover every situation, but these will serve for at least 95 per cent. of hands.

1. If partner has bid a suit lead his suit.
2. If you have bid a suit lead your suit.
3. If neither of you have bid you should usually lead the first suit bid by the hand that is to be dummy.

For the other occasions there is probably no lead-directing significance in the double: partner just thinks you can beat the contract.

CHAPTER XVII

PLANNING THE PLAY

UNLESS a contract is laid down there is usually an appreciable pause after dummy has exposed his cards. The declarer plans the play of the hand, and the defenders calculate cheerfully or gloomily their prospects. Don't be in a hurry to play to the first trick. I'm no advocate of slow play and I believe that excessive analysis at Bridge usually muddles the analyst. There is a great advantage in the smooth speed of such players as Kenneth Konstam and Leslie Dodds. But that is after the plan is made. For the moment we are studying dummy and making an appreciation of the relative values of the different lines of approach to a doubtful contract. You should do as much of your thinking as possible at this stage so that later you can play as confidently and easily and naturally as possible. Unexpected distributions or an unorthodox defence may, of course, make you switch your plans later. At least you should have a plan to switch. There is no surer mark of the bad—of the losing—player, than a hasty play from Dummy at the first trick. Chew for a few moments over the oponent's bidding remembering, of course, that there is often as much to be learnt from a pass as from a bid, study the inferences you can draw from the opening lead, and then sum up your chances. Bridge hands defy exact classification if only because the combinations are too numerous. Experts play a hand as declarer more by drawing on the well of their experiences, than by book lore. Yet there is much about the approach to play that can be taught. In particular, there are two principles that should always guide you as declarer:
1. Play always so that any decision you have to take is taken as late as possible in the hand, and any decision the defenders have to take is presented to them at the earliest moment.
2. Always scheme and play to give the defenders as many chances of guessing wrong as you can contrive.

The essence of a No Trump contract is the battle for entries and for tempos. The first weapon at the disposal of the declarer is the hold up designed either to leave the lead in a safe hand or exhaust one opponent of the suit. In its first and simplest form the play is called the Bath Coup.

x.x.

<u>K</u>.Q.10.x.x.   x.x.x.

A.J.x.

By refusing to win the opening lead of the King with the Ace, South forces West either to switch to another suit or concede a second trick to the Knave. The second example is less obvious:

x.x.x.

Q.J.10.x.x.   x.x.

A.K.x.

If South refuses to win the first trick he can be forced to take the second, but East cannot continue the suit if he is thrown into the lead. A typical situation would be:

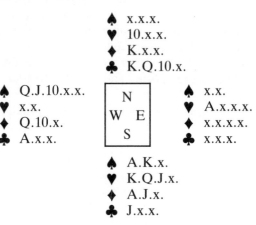

In Three No Trumps, South—if he wins the opening Spade— can only make nine tricks if he guesses that West's Ace is Clubs and attacks that suit. On the other hand, if he refuses the first trick it is immaterial which suit he selects for East will be unable to put West in. If East has a third Spade there is equally no

164

danger for the suit has now broken 4–3 and the contract is still safe.

A much more advanced example of a hold up is to keep the lead in a safe hand, even at the cost of a trick, is shown:

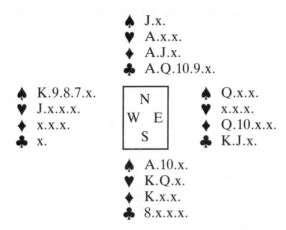

♠ J.x.
♥ A.x.x.
♦ A.J.x.
♣ A.Q.10.9.x.

♠ K.9.8.7.x.
♥ J.x.x.x.
♦ x.x.x.
♣ x.

♠ Q.x.x.
♥ x.x.x.
♦ Q.10.x.x.
♣ K.J.x.

♠ A.10.x.
♥ K.Q.x.
♦ K.x.x.
♣ 8.x.x.x.

Against Three No Trumps East puts the Queen of Spades on West's opening lead of the Seven. This gives South two tricks in Spades if he plays the Ace. But if he does he will loose the contract For East in with the Jack of Clubs will play a second Spade and West will duck. South must now loose three Spades and two Clubs. Declarer then must duck the first trick and when they are continued, duck again. The contract now is safe, for the Club finesses are taken into East's hand and the Spades cannot be continued.

There may, of course, be occasions when although the correct play in isolation may be to duck, yet the menace of another suit makes the play dangerous. For example:

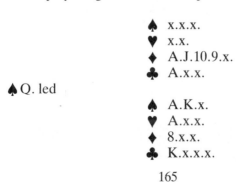

♠ x.x.x.
♥ x.x.
♦ A.J.10.9.x.
♣ A.x.x.

♠ Q. led

♠ A.K.x.
♥ A.x.x.
♦ 8.x.x.
♣ K.x.x.x.

Here you dare not concede the opening trick for a Heart switch will surely defeat you. You must win at once and rely on divided honours in Diamonds or on West having both the King and Queen.

Sometimes, again in No Trump contracts, consideration of time must lead you to abandon an attractive play or finesse. South played Three No Trumps against the lead of the nine of Hearts:

♠ A.9.x.x.
♥ x.x.x.
♦ A.x.x.
♣ 10.8.x.

♠ J.10
♥ A.K.Q.
♦ K.x.x.
♣ K.J.9.x.x.

Declarer carelessly crossed to dummy with a Diamond to finesse the Clubs. But West won with the Queen and a Diamond continuation beat the contract. South should, of course, play Clubs at once from his own hand (the King is correct in case either defender has a lone Queen) and the contract is then safe.

Declarer in No Trump contracts can often block the defender's long suit: For example in this situation:

A.6.

5. led

10.9.7.3.

South should play the Ace from dummy. The lead cannot be from K.Q.J. and therefore East has at least one honour. If the honour is a doubleton which is probable the suit is now blocked. A very common example–often missed in play–is the following hand. The contract is Two No Trumps after East has opened with one Heart. West leads the two of Hearts:

166

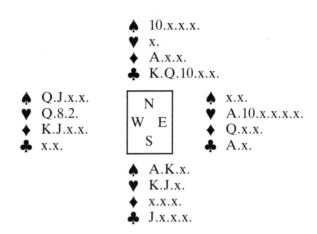

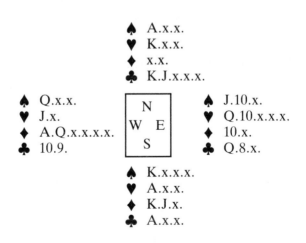

East plays the Ace and returns his fourth best. If now South plays the Jack the suit is cleared and he must be defeated. The situation should be clear to him and the play of the King at the second trick blocks the suit and ensures the contract.

The last group of special plays in No Trump contracts are those designed to avoid a lead through a known weakness. When West opened the eight of Diamonds and East played the ten, South (in a contract of Three No Trumps) knew he was lost if East obtained the lead. And yet the natural play in Clubs was into the danger hand:

There is no escape from trying the Club suit, and the ordinary good player would remember to play off the Ace and King in case East has Q.x. South was an expert player and went one better. He crossed to dummy and played the Jack of Clubs. East covered and South won and allowed West to win the next trick with the ten. South's play succeeds if West has two or three Clubs to the Queen, and can only lose against four which in view of the Diamond length, is most improbable. If East has Q.10.x. or even Q.9.x. (and West throws his 10) nothing can be done. The hand is a perfect illustration of a master's determination to have the odds in his favour.

PLANNING A SUIT CONTRACT

The introduction of the ruffing element, and the problems of trump management make the play in a suit contract far more difficult and intricate. The range of choice is wider, the margin for error usually smaller. We are mainly concerned here with the normal, with hands that can be made on reasonable distribution. Sometimes you will be in a "hopeless" contract. If you can afford to do so (that is assuming the penalties for failure are not too severe), you should see if such a contract can be made with any given distribution and division of high cards in the opponent's hand, and then you should assume such a distribution or division, and play accordingly. Take a simple example. If you cannot afford to lose a trick in trumps which are divided:

A.x.x.

Q.10.9.8.x.

you must assume that West has the singleton King. No other distribution provides five tricks for you. Again—a more common situation—if a suit is divided:

J.x.x.

A.Q.x.x.x.

168

only K.x. with East saves you losing one or more tricks. The point here is not that these distributions are probable—they are not—but simply that they provide your only chance of success. Once the assumption is made you build your plan round it, but it is not necessary to test it at once. If you are wrong you fail anyway. An example of three such assumptions being made in one hand is the following:

♠ none.
♥ 10.x.x.x.
♦ 10.x.x.x.
♣ A.Q.J.8.x.

```
┌───┐
│ N │
│   │
│ S │
└───┘
```

♠ A.Q.
♥ A.x.x.
♦ K.Q.J.9.x.
♣ 10.9.x.

South reached Six Diamonds and West led the King of Hearts. East followed, and South announced, "I shall make my contract if East has a singleton Heart and the Ace of Trumps, and if West has the King of Clubs". And they had.

COUNTING THE HAND

An expert Bridge player, it is said, is anyone who can count up to thirteen. There is a large grain of truth in the saying. Most of the plays that to the average player look like wizardry are essentially simple. Most of them come from a simple process of addition and subtraction. I hope you won't set out to count every hand you play. It is a frightful waste of time and the quickest route to unpopularity. I doubt if you should make a conscious effort to count more than one hand in thirty. I assume, of course, that you register trumps as they are played more or less automatically. Actually, in counting a hand, the negative inferences are usually far more important. Suppose, for example, West leads a Spade, you and dummy have six between you, and East trumps the first round. The bad player just says, "Damn!"

and leaves it at that. The ordinary player says, "West has seven Spades" and again goes no farther. The expert has much more to think about. That West has seven Spades is not particularly interesting because you're not playing in Spades. That he has only six cards in the other three suits is very important. Again you know that East has thirteen cards in three suits and that if any suit is to break badly—and one at least will—the length will almost surely be with East. So each card played tells you a little more. If West follows to three rounds of trumps (say Clubs) he has only three cards in Hearts and Diamonds. Now you can narrow the hunt still further and you may be able at the end to tell with absolute certainty whether you should or should not finesse, and if so, against which hand you should take the finesse. For example:

♠ J.10.x.x.x.
♥ x.x.x.x.
♦ x.
♣ A.10.x.

```
┌───┐
│ N │
│ S │
└───┘
```

♠ A.K.Q.x.x.x.
♥ x.
♦ A.x.x.
♣ K.J.x.

West opens with a pre-emptive Four Hearts, but you find your slam in Spades. West leads the King of Hearts. The contract depends on the Queen of Clubs. Remember the rule to postpone a finesse as long as possible. Suppose on the second Heart East discards a Diamond. You know seven of West's cards. If you lead a trump and East again discards you know nine of West's cards. If then you ruff out Diamonds and West follows each time, you know twelve of his cards and he is void in Clubs or has a Singleton. Accordingly you play the Ace and (if the Singleton Queen does not drop) announce the finesse through East. West, of course, will rarely be so obligingly informative with his discards. Nevertheless, you can usually be sure that at the moment of decision the odds are on your side. For instance, if in the last hand West had only followed to two Diamonds, you are now not sure where the Queen of Clubs is. But you are sure that East started with five and West with two, and that the finesse through East is 5–2 on. Never then be satisfied with the discovery that an opponent has five or six or seven in a suit. Take away the number from thirteen and see what you can deduce about his other suits. That's much more valuable.

THE SUIT TO CLEAR

It may well have been true in the days of Whist that hundreds of players were walking the Embankment, because they never drew trumps. It may even be true to-day. Certainly in normal hands it should be the first line to examine. Sometimes it must be rejected. Perhaps the surest sign that a player is beginning to climb above the average in card play is when he begins to understand when he should and when he should not draw trumps. Experience is the only real guide, but there are certain principles that can be laid down.

First of all when playing a two-suited hand, it is usually correct to establish—or at least explore—the side suit before drawing trumps. Probably you cannot cope with a bad division (say 5–2 or 4–1) in both your suits, but you should try and cover it in at least one and if possible in either. Take first the simplest case. You play, for example, in Four Spades;

♠ 10.x.x.
♥ x.x.x.
♦ K.J.10.x.x.x.
♣ x.

```
+---+
| N |
| S |
+---+
```

♠ A.K.Q.x.x.
♥ x.x.
♦ none.
♣ A.K.Q.x.x.x.

Three rounds of Hearts are led against you and you trump. Now if you draw trumps and they are 3–2 all is well on either of the normal Club divisions of 4–2 (most probable) or 3–3. But if trumps are 4–1 (a 28 per cent. chance) you can only make if Clubs now are 3–3. You should, of course, play a high Club at

171

trick two and then ruff a Club. Now with a 4–1 trump break you can afford the 4–2 break in Clubs.

Often the problem is much more complex, as in this slam hand. South played in Six Hearts doubled by East:

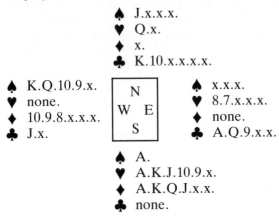

♠ J.x.x.x.
♥ Q.x.
♦ x.
♣ K.10.x.x.x.x.

♠ K.Q.10.9.x.
♥ none.
♦ 10.9.8.x.x.x.
♣ J.x.

♠ x.x.x.
♥ 8.7.x.x.x.
♦ none.
♣ A.Q.9.x.x.

♠ A.
♥ A.K.J.10.9.x.
♦ A.K.Q.J.x.x.
♣ none.

West led the King of Spades. It is fatal for South to draw even one round of trumps. Equally it is fatal to play a high Diamond although the play looks marked. The only way to make the contract is to play the small Diamond. The other losing Diamond can then be ruffed high. South was a good, even a very good, player, but this hand defeated him. And yet in a famous hand before the war in a match between Austria and Hungary, both declarers (Herr Frischauer and M. Alpar) found the safety play in a similar hand and made their contract.

Often an opportunity to ruff should be ignored particularly when to accept the force means relying on a 3–3 (36 per cent.) break. The standard example is:

♠ 10.x.x.
♥ x.x.
♦ x.x.x.
♣ A.K.J.x.x.

♠ A.K.Q.x.
♥ A.Q.x.x.
♦ x.x.
♣ Q.x.x.

If West leads three rounds of Diamonds against a contract of Four Spades, South must clearly put all his eggs in one basket, ruff and gamble on the even break in trumps. If this fails he will probably go at least two down. In Three Spades he should discard a Heart. A fourth Diamond can now be ruffed in dummy and the probable 4–2 break in trumps has no terrors. It is probably also necessary for South to duck the first round of trumps if a Diamond has to be ruffed in dummy. Now, when the lead is regained, trumps can be drawn.

THE CROSS RUFF

The beginner—even the average player—is far too ready to embark on a cross ruff. Often indeed they start on a line of play which simple addition should show them cannot yield enough tricks. When you do decide on a cross ruff play, remember these points:

(1) Cash your side winners at once.
(2) Trump the later rounds of a suit as high as you can afford.
(3) Watch the timing carefully.

As an illustration, study carefully this hand:

♠ A.x.x.x.x.
♥ K.
♦ A.10.x.
♣ x.x.x.x.

W E

♠ x.
♥ A.x.x.x.x.
♦ K.J.9.x.x.
♣ K.Q.

East played in Five Diamonds. Only a cross ruff offers a reasonable chance of success. If a Spade is led the club should be played at trick two. The tenace position in trumps makes a trump return unlikely and we will assume a second Club. The problem now, is to make seven of our trumps. A Heart is followed by a Club ruffed with a small Diamond. The Ace of Hearts, a Heart ruffed small, and a Spade ruffed small, leaves this position:

♠ x.x.
♥ none.
♦ A.10.
♣ x.

W E

♠ none.
♥ x.x.
♦ K.J.9.
♣ none.

This is the moment to play safe. A Heart is ruffed with the Ace (for if North over-ruffed and played a trump we would go down). Similarly a Spade is now ruffed with the King and when East's last Heart is ruffed with the ten only the Queen of trumps can be taken by the defenders. This sort of situation is very common, and very often a miserly reluctance to trump with high cards loses a lay-down contract.

There is one useful play which may be mentioned here: we might call it the pseudo cross-ruff. The defence to a cross-ruff if it can safely be done is for the defenders to lead trumps on every occasion. Sometimes you can use this to entice a trump lead:

♠ x.x.		♠ A.J.10.9.x
♥ A.x.x.x.x.	W E	♥ x.x.
♦ x.x.x.x.		♦ A.K.Q.10.
♣ J.x.		♣ A.x.

Against your Four-Spade contract South opens the King of Clubs. With only one entry in dummy your chances of only losing one trump trick are not good—unless the opponents lead trumps. Play back a Club at once and there must be a fair chance that South will switch to trumps.

REVERSE DUMMY PLAY

This sounds frightening, and is certainly unusual. It is not at all difficult. Try getting into the habit when a hand looks hopeless of taking a mental walk round the table and looking at the problem from dummy's point of view. Suppose you, as East, play Six Spades and South leads the King of Clubs. The hand looks impossible because of the two Club losers.

♠ K.Q.J.		♠ A.x.x.x.x.
♥ A.x.x.x.x.	W E	♥ x.
♦ A.x		♦ K.10.x.x.
♣ A.10.x.		♣ x.x.x.

You needn't give up. Look at it from Dummy's point of view. Now there is at least a chance. Duck the first Club and assume South continues the suit. Then start ruffing Hearts out. They are probably 4–3 (62 per cent.) and you can reach this position with West to lead.

♠ K.Q.		♠ A.x.
♥ x.x.	W E	♥ none.
♦ x.		♦ K.10.x
♣ 10.		♣ x.

Ruff a Heart with the Ace and draw trumps throwing the Club. Now if trumps were 3–2 and Hearts 4–3 your Heart is established. Play it and discard a Diamond. South may well be forced to unguard Diamonds or throw the master Club. True all this isn't likely to succeed, and you need a very favourable distribution of the minor suits. But you have nothing to lose by trying. Reverse dummy play nearly always consists in shortening the long trump hand, so that unwanted cards can be discarded on dummy's trumps.

LOSER ON LOSER

This group of attractive plays are usually linked with one of the end game manoeuvres and are treated more fully there. Two examples here will show the value and importance of the play:

♠ Q.J.x.x.		♠ A.
♥ x.x.x.	W E	♥ A.Q.x.
♦ A.Q.x.x.x.		♦ K.J.10.x.x.x.
♣ x.		♣ A.x.x.

East's Six-Diamond bid appears to depend on a Heart finesse or the Spade King being with North. Actually it is a certainty, wherever these cards lie. Trumps are drawn and the Spade Ace played off. Entering dummy, the Queen of Spades is led. If North plays small, declarer discards a Heart, and later the Queen of Hearts on the established Jack of Spades.

A more subtle example is shown:

♠ x.x.x.x.x.x.		♠ none.
♥ x.x.	W E	♥ A.x.x.
♦ A.x.		♦ K.Q.x.x.x.x.x.
♣ K.x.x.		♣ A.x.x.

South opens with a bid of Three Hearts and East–West reach Five Diamonds. South leads the King of Hearts and declarer ducks. South continues and East wins. To ruff the losing Heart with the Ace of Diamonds loses a trump trick if they are divided 3–1. The better chance is to play the Heart and discard a Club. Later—drawing one round of trumps in case South has a singleton—you try to ruff a Club with dummy's small trump. This can succeed even if trumps are 3–1, and even if South has only a singleton Club. The point of the play is not that you gain a trick, but that you transfer a dangerous Heart loser into a fairly safe Club one.

A PERFECT PLAN

From the Great Britain v. Norway match at Brighton in 1950, I take an illustration of superb technique:

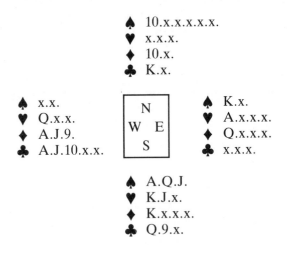

```
                    ♠ 10.x.x.x.x.x.
                    ♥ x.x.x.
                    ♦ 10.x.
                    ♣ K.x.

      ♠ x.x.                        ♠ K.x.
      ♥ Q.x.x.          N           ♥ A.x.x.x.
      ♦ A.J.9.       W     E        ♦ Q.x.x.x.
      ♣ A.J.10.x.x.     S           ♣ x.x.x.

                    ♠ A.Q.J.
                    ♥ K.J.x.
                    ♦ K.x.x.x.
                    ♣ Q.9.x.
```

Bidding:

W	N (Leslie Dodds)	E	S (Kenneth Konstam)
1♣	—	1♥	—
2♥	—	—	2♠ (!)
—	—	2NT	—
—	3♠	—	—

Konstam's Spade bid shows how anxious an expert is not to be shut out in partscore bidding. But the play's the thing. West

176

opened a Heart and East returned a Diamond. Konstam played low. West is now in difficulties and returned a Spade. Declarer won, led a Club and won with dummy's King. A Spade cleared the trumps. It is essential to keep East out of the lead and Konstam laid down the Queen of Clubs. West made a gallant effort to stave off the ending and played the Jack of Clubs. Konstam at once refused to trump and discarded dummy's Diamond. Whether West plays a Heart or a Diamond or a Club declarer now makes his contract. A gem of card-reading and play.

CHAPTER XVIII

DEFENSIVE PLAY

THERE is a bigger gap between the expert and the good player in this field of Bridge than in any other. I doubt if there are half a dozen defensive players of the highest class in this country. Their strength in defence perhaps more than anything else, makes Reese and Schapiro the best pair in this country. It is the foundation of much of the success of Leo Baron's small school of scientists. I'm afraid I cannot teach you to be a good defensive player, but perhaps I can make you a more efficient one than you are now. An expert needs knowledge and flair and toughness and above anything else, endless practice.

THE MECHANICS OF DEFENCE

I shall start by discussing in isolation, and without reference to the tactical situation in the hand, the accepted defensive plays. We have already given a chapter to the theory and practice of opening leads. Later rounds enable you to signal exact length and strength.

(a) If you have led the top card from 7.4.2. you should on the next round play the two.

(b) Holding three trumps you should make the peter as a routine play. Thus from 9.8.3. play the eight to the first round and the three to the second. The knowledge that you still have a potential ruffer left may be invaluable to your partner. It follows, of course, that if you do not peter you have either four or two, and partner can easily infer which it is.

(c) High-low is the recognised method of showing a doubleton. It is also usually encouraging and often shows a desire to ruff the third round. High-low from J.x. and 10.x. is correct, but NOT normally from Q.x.: the play of the Queen shows the Jack and partner can, if desirable, underlead on the next round.

(d) Returning partner's lead or clearing your own suit you should where possible play the fourth best to give partner a count on the hand. Watch carefully your play to the first trick and with A.x. against a No Trump contract overtake partner's lead of the Queen. Equally with Q.x. you should play the Queen on the Jack to avoid blocking the suit. Don't be too enthusiastic here though, or you may achieve the immortal coup (christened the "Fleet Street Coup") played by two well-known Bridge correspondents in a match before the war. Colin Harding and I had bid an appalling Three No Trumps with our combined Heart holding 10.x.x. and a singleton. When one of the journalists opened the King of Hearts our doom seemed sealed. Not a bit of it. The other after due thought overtook with the Ace and returned the Jack. Not to be outdone the other overtook the Jack with the Queen and played a small one. Colin's ten won the trick.

(e) The general rule for covering is that you should cover an unsupported honour, but wait till the next round if there are touching honours. For example, with K.x.x. cover the Queen led from Q.9.x. in dummy, but not from Q.J.9. In the second case you can probably establish your partner's ten by waiting to cover the Jack. Otherwise the ten would be caught by a finesse through dummy's J.9.

(f) Never hurry to take an Ace over a holding of two or three honours.

For example, if the suit falls:

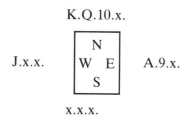

K.Q.10.x.

J.x.x.   A.9.x.

x.x.x.

and South leads small to the King, it is futile to win the trick because declarer is bound to finesse the ten on the next round. If you play small he may read you for J.9.x.

and go up with the Queen on the second round, establishing your partner's Jack.

(g) A different application of the same principle is when declarer leads a singleton from dummy (North) and you as East, hold the Ace. Usually it is best to duck. Declarer may have a K.J. holding and finesse to your partner's Queen. Even if he has K.Q. you have probably lost nothing. In Four Hearts for example, you have taken the first two tricks in Spades and a trump is led. Winning in dummy, South leads the singleton Diamond:

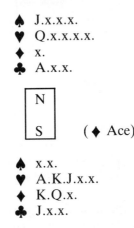

♠ J.x.x.x.
♥ Q.x.x.x.x.
♦ x.
♣ A.x.x.

```
┌───┐
│ N │
│   │
│ S │   (♦ Ace)
└───┘
```

♠ x.x.
♥ A.K.J.x.x.
♦ K.Q.x.
♣ J.x.x.

Study the position. If you play your Ace, two Clubs are discarded and the contract made. Give him the Diamond and he must still lose two tricks in Clubs to go down. Even in slam contracts unless you can see the sure defeat of the bid you should duck more often that not.

(h) On the other hand, there are occasions when the high card is correct play. The principal ones are:

(i) When you can block the suit:

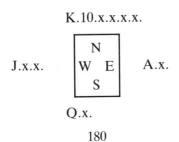

K.10.x.x.x.x.

```
            ┌───┐
            │ N │
J.x.x.      │W E│   A.x.
            │ S │
            └───┘
```

Q.x.

180

If declarer plays small from North, you should go in with the Ace and try to drive out North's entry (if any) at once. If you play small, South clears the suit easily. Nor does it cost you anything if South has in fact Q.x.x.

(ii) A whole range of entry destroying plays are available to the defence when their honours are divided. The standard example is:

A.J.10.x.x.

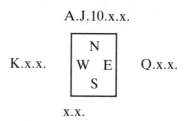

K.x.x.   Q.x.x.

x.x.

When South leads this suit West MUST play the King. Unless dummy has an entry the suit is shut out. The play is equally correct if West has K.10.x. and dummy a suit headed by A.J.9. There are numerous examples of this type of play.

(*i*) The defenders must be alert for declarer's efforts to snatch an early trick and must always be ready to protect partner's entry:

♠ A.K.
♥ A.Q.x.
♦ A.x.x.
♣ J.10.x.x.x.

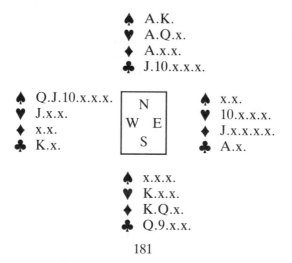

♠ Q.J.10.x.x.x.   ♠ x.x.
♥ J.x.x.   ♥ 10.x.x.x.
♦ x.x.   ♦ J.x.x.x.x.
♣ K.x.   ♣ A.x.

♠ x.x.x.
♥ K.x.x.
♦ K.Q.x.
♣ Q.9.x.x.

181

West leads the Queen of Spades against Three No Trumps. South now leads a Club. East can only beat the contract if he goes straight in with his Ace and clears Spades. This isn't a difficult play holding the Ace, but it is easier to miss, and just as important, if East has the King. He doesn't, of course, know that his King will win. He should know that he has nothing to lose by playing it.

(*j*) One of the few Bridge saws that are entirely misleading is the one, "never finesse against your partner". Indeed, you should do so much more often than not on the opening lead at least in No Trumps. If the cards fall:

Q.x.x.

4. led   K.*10*.x.

you should play the ten. The play is also sound with the nine or eight. To play the King cannot win. Assuming the lead of the four and a dummy holding of Q.x.x. the correct play for East is underlined, K.*10*.x., *J*.x.x., A.*J*.x., A.J.*10*., and with 10.x.x. in dummy you should play A.*Q*.x., *A*.x.x., *K*.J.x., and Q.*J*.x.

(*k*) When you can read your partner's opening lead as a doubleton and you hold the Ace, you should encourage him, but not win the first trick:

♠ Q.x.x.x.x.x.		N		♠ 10.x.x.
♥ x.x.x.				♥ J.x.x.x.x.
♦ 7.x.	W		E	♦ A.9.x.x.
♣ A.x.		S		♣ x.

You can only hope to defeat South's Five-Club contract by getting a ruff in Diamonds. To play the Ace on the first round is fatal. Drop the nine and if Diamonds stand up for three rounds you will defeat the bid.

(*l*) A similar ducking play should be routine for the defence in No Trump contracts when the long hand is short of entries. Usually the suit is divided A.x.x.x.x. and K.x.x. or equivalent combinations. There are, however, far more advanced uses for these plays. The following hand is taken from the 1950 England v. Scotland match:

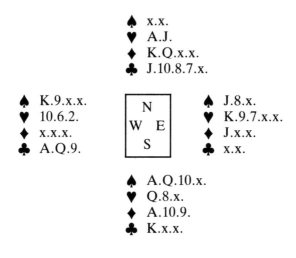

♠ x.x.
♥ A.J.
♦ K.Q.x.x.
♣ J.10.8.7.x.

♠ K.9.x.x.
♥ 10.6.2.
♦ x.x.x.
♣ A.Q.9.

N
W E
S

♠ J.8.x.
♥ K.9.7.x.x.
♦ J.x.x.
♣ x.x.

♠ A.Q.10.x.
♥ Q.8.x.
♦ A.10.9.
♣ K.x.x.

It is routine bidding to reach Three No Trumps. In one room West made the routine lead of x. Spades and R. Sharples made a routine Four No Trumps for England scoring 630. In the other room Harrison Gray found the devastating lead of the six of Hearts. The Jack was played and Marx (East) encouraged with the nine, but did not, of course, win the trick. Gray, in with his Club honours, cleared the suit and beat the contract for a swing to England of 730 points.

SUIT SIGNALS

It is common sense play to encourage partner to continue a suit by playing an unnecessarily high card, and discourage him with a low one. Apart from these accepted signals you should study and play what is called the "McKenney" suit preference signal. When a switch is indicated a high card calls for the higher ranking suit and a low card for the lower ranking. Normally—as it is often combined with ruffing play—the signals are in a suit contract, but they can also be used in No Trumps. If in a suit contract the trump suit is excluded from the calculation. An example makes it clear:

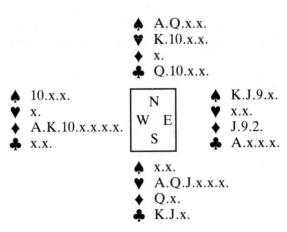

          ♠ A.Q.x.x.
          ♥ K.10.x.x.
          ♦ x.
          ♣ Q.10.x.x.

♠ 10.x.x.   ♠ K.J.9.x.
♥ x.   ♥ x.x.
♦ A.K.10.x.x.x.x.   N   ♦ J.9.2.
♣ x.x.   W   E   ♣ A.x.x.x.
                        S
          ♠ x.x.
          ♥ A.Q.J.x.x.x.
          ♦ Q.x.
          ♣ K.J.x.

North–South were forced up to Five Hearts by competitive bidding from East–West in Diamonds. The King of Diamonds was led. If West leads anything except a Spade at trick two the contract is made because dummy's fourth Club provides a discard for South's losing Spade. East must make a "McKenney" by throwing the Jack of Diamonds calling for a Spade switch.

There is a danger that a McKenney signal may be confused with the ordinary demand for the suit to be continued. West went wrong on this hand:

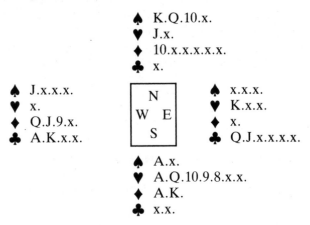

          ♠ K.Q.10.x.
          ♥ J.x.
          ♦ 10.x.x.x.x.x.
          ♣ x.

♠ J.x.x.x.   ♠ x.x.x.
♥ x.   N   ♥ K.x.x.
♦ Q.J.9.x.   W   E   ♦ x.
♣ A.K.x.x.   S   ♣ Q.J.x.x.x.x.

          ♠ A.x.
          ♥ A.Q.10.9.8.x.x.
          ♦ A.K.
          ♣ x.x.

Against Six Hearts West opened the King of Clubs and East played the Queen. Another round of Clubs defeats the contract for East must make a Heart trick. West, however, played a Spade and the slam was made. This is absurd play. If East has a

Spade trick it cannot run away for there is nothing on which South can throw his loser. A few moments thought will give you the real meaning of any signal that appears doubtful.

The other main use for the signal is indicating the best return for partner to make:

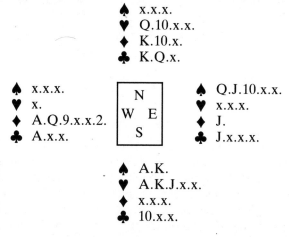

♠ x.x.x.
♥ Q.10.x.x.
♦ K.10.x.
♣ K.Q.x.

♠ x.x.x.
♥ x.
♦ A.Q.9.x.x.2.
♣ A.x.x.

N
W   E
S

♠ Q.J.10.x.x.
♥ x.x.x.
♦ J.
♣ J.x.x.x.

♠ A.K.
♥ A.K.J.x.x.
♦ x.x.x.
♣ 10.x.x.

Against Four Hearts West leads the Ace of Diamonds. To the second trick he leads the two of Diamonds. This tells East that his entry is in Clubs. Holding the Ace of Spades West would lead the nine to the second trick. Only in this way can the contract be defeated other than by guessing correctly.

Finally a McKenney in No Trumps—and in this case from play, at the first trick:

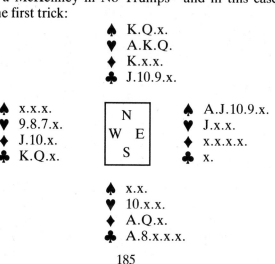

♠ K.Q.x.
♥ A.K.Q.
♦ K.x.x.
♣ J.10.9.x.

♠ x.x.x.
♥ 9.8.7.x.
♦ J.10.x.
♣ K.Q.x.

N
W   E
S

♠ A.J.10.9.x.
♥ J.x.x.
♦ x.x.x.x.
♣ x.

♠ x.x.
♥ 10.x.x.
♦ A.Q.x.
♣ A.8.x.x.x.

185

Against Three No Trumps West opened the nine of Hearts. East dropped the Jack. In view of dummy's holding this cannot be a signal for a Heart continuance. In with the Queen of Clubs West knows his partner wants a Spade lead, and the Spade switch defeats the contract.

TRUMP PROMOTION

Active co-operation between partners can promote quite a minor trump to winning rank:

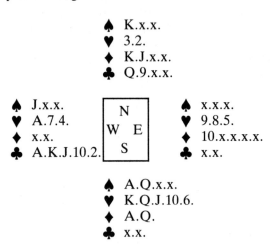

```
              ♠  K.x.x.
              ♥  3.2.
              ♦  K.J.x.x.
              ♣  Q.9.x.x.

   ♠  J.x.x.        N          ♠  x.x.x.
   ♥  A.7.4.                   ♥  9.8.5.
   ♦  x.x.       W     E       ♦  10.x.x.x.x.
   ♣  A.K.J.10.2.     S        ♣  x.x.

              ♠  A.Q.x.x.
              ♥  K.Q.J.10.6.
              ♦  A.Q.
              ♣  x.x.
```

Only one defence defeats Four Hearts. Two Clubs are cashed and a Club continued. East must ruff with the eight. South has to win and play a high trump. West wins at once and plays another Club. East ruffs again with the nine and West's seven must now win a trick—against one hundred honours. Notice two points. First, East must not ruff with the five, but with his highest trump. Secondly, West to the third trick should play the two of Clubs to force his partner to trump. If he leads the Jack, South may play the nine from dummy and East be too mean to trump his partner's "winner". Never give your partner—even an expert!—an extra chance to go wrong. Sometimes he'll take it.

There is, of course, another side to this question of trump promotion. In defence you can often secure an extra trick by refusing to over-ruff. The basic trump situation is:

186

<pre>
                         x.x.
         A.10.x.   x.x.
                     K.Q.J.x.x.x.
</pre>

If East now leads a suit of which you (West) and South are both void, you win an extra trick by refusing to take South's Jack. There are many variations of this play.

THE CREATION OF ENTRIES

Often you will know that partner has enough tricks to beat the contract, if he can get in. Earlier in this chapter we discussed the early play of a high card to protect partner's entry. Sometimes you have to create an entry for him.

A variation of the Deschapelles Coup (discussed in the next chapter) is one method of securing this:

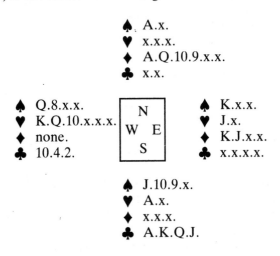

<pre>
                          ♠ , A.x.
                          ♥ x.x.x.
                          ♦ A.Q.10.9.x.x.
                          ♣ x.x.

      ♠ Q.8.x.x.   ┌─────────┐   ♠ K.x.x.
      ♥ K.Q.10.x.x.x.   │   N   │   ♥ J.x.
      ♦ none.   │ W   E │   ♦ K.J.x.x.
      ♣ 10.4.2.   │   S   │   ♣ x.x.x.x.
                          └─────────┘

                          ♠ J.10.9.x.
                          ♥ A.x.
                          ♦ x.x.x.
                          ♣ A.K.Q.J.
</pre>

South plays Three No Trumps against the opening lead of the King of Hearts. South is forced to win the second round and finesses a Diamond. On this lead West should play the two of Clubs to discourage East from attacking that suit. There is only one card East can play to defeat the contract and that is the King of Spades. West signals with his eight and whether South wins or not the contract is beaten. Here West's sacrifice of the King is not designed to shut out the Diamond suit, but to force an entry for West's Hearts.

These plays are not easy to spot. Sometimes an even more spectacular defence is called for:

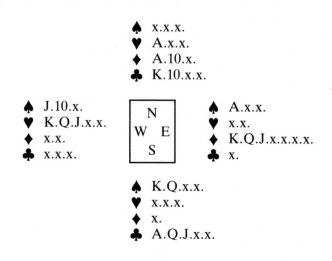

♠ x.x.x.
♥ A.x.x.
♦ A.10.x.
♣ K.10.x.x.

♠ J.10.x.
♥ K.Q.J.x.x.
♦ x.x.
♣ x.x.x.

♠ A.x.x.
♥ x.x.
♦ K.Q.J.x.x.x.x.
♣ x.

♠ K.Q.x.x.
♥ x.x.x.
♦ x.
♣ A.Q.J.x.x.

North–South reached Five Clubs after West had bid One Heart over South's opening bid of One Club, and East had bid and re-bid Diamonds. West opened the King of Hearts. South won the second round and drew trumps. On the second round of trumps East must throw his Ace of Spades to beat the contract. This looks like second sight, but in fact is a carefully reasoned play. West cannot have an entry except in Spades. If it be the King no harm is done. If he has the Queen he must also obtain the lead later. If he has only small Spades the hand is hopeless. But if he has the Jack you must seek to promote it. South, if he had foreseen this fine defence by East, could have made his contract by leading Spades at the third trick.

THE PRINCIPLES OF DEFENCE

I have explained in this chapter some, but not, of course, all, of the plays that a good defensive player must have at his command. The field is vast and largely uncharted. As with bidding it is far more important to understand the structure of defence than to attempt the hopeless task of learning a standard play for every situation. These I think, are the three principles that guide a good defensive player:

(1) *He takes his decisions in advance:*

As soon as dummy goes down, try and see what decisions you may have to take, and form at least a provisional opinion of what you are going to do. Decide that you will (or will not) duck when an honour is led from dummy, which suit you will discard, which line of defence you will pursue if you obtain the lead. When, then, the actual moment of decision comes at a later trick, you will be able to play naturally and without giving away information by indecision at the critical trick.

Example: You are East and North–South, vulnerable, bid as follows:

S	W	N	E
1♥	—	3♦	—
3♠	—	4♥	—
4NT	—	5NT	—
6♣	—	7♥	—
—	—	—	

Partner leads the Jack of Clubs and you can see:

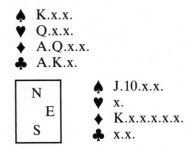

```
              ♠ K.x.x.
              ♥ Q.x.x.
              ♦ A.Q.x.x.
              ♣ A.K.x.
          ┌─────────┐
          │    N    │   ♠ J.10.x.x.
          │      E  │   ♥ x.
          │    S    │   ♦ K.x.x.x.x.x.
          └─────────┘   ♣ x.x.
```

Assuming South doesn't at once put his hand down, this is how you would reason. "If partner has a trump trick we need not worry. Otherwise our best chance is that South has five tricks in trumps, three in Clubs, three in Spades and one in Diamonds. Say:

```
              ♠ A.Q.x.x.
              ♥ A.K.J.10.x.
              ♦ x.x.
              ♣ Q.x.
```

189

If he has this holding he can, of course, make the contract by playing out his winners because I can't hang on both to Spades and Diamonds. The end game position may be:

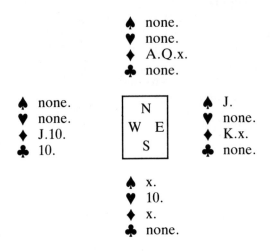

When South plays the Heart my partner will throw the Club and I must let my Diamond go. So I'll make up my mind now to that, I won't think when the time comes and when I toss away a small Diamond South will have to guess.

(2) *He saves his partner worry:*

Try and avoid the delicate dropping of threes and expecting partner to observe that the two is missing. You can bawl him out if he misses the inference, but that doesn't help. Throw the biggest card you can possibly spare if you want to encourage him. Show by your discards as soon as possible which suits you can take care of, and which you must leave to him. Throw not your lowest cards, but your useless ones, and seek always to keep declarer guessing.

Example: Partner (West) leads the Jack of Diamonds against Six No Trumps. South, as declarer, wins in dummy and plays a Club. West wins and continues with the ten of Diamonds. You can see:

♠ K.J.10.
♥ A.K.
♦ A.K.x.
♣ K.Q.J.10.9.

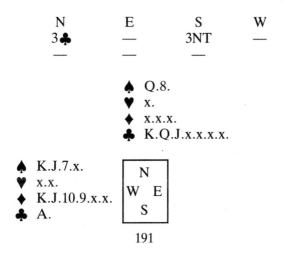

N	♠ x.x.x.x.
W E	♥ Q.10.x.x.
S	♦ x.x.x.
	♣ x.x.

Declarer has the Ace of Spades and the Queen of Dia-monds. He has not the Queen of Spades. If he has four Dia-monds (unlikely) there is nothing to be done. You must protect your partner's Queen of Spades by clinging on to three of your four useless ones even at the expense of Hearts.

(3) *His defence is hopeful and agressive:*
He never gives up trying till the hand is over. If his partner has to hold certain cards to defeat the contract, he assumes that he does in fact hold them and plays accordingly. He is on the alert for entry-protecting and entry-creating plays. He never plays a card that does not carry a message for his partner. He gives nothing away by despair or by hesitation or by inference. He is always full of confidence.
Example: You are West and have to lead against the bidding:

N	E	S	W
3♣	—	3NT	—
—	—	—	

♠ Q.8.
♥ x.
♦ x.x.x.
♣ K.Q.J.x.x.x.x.

♠ K.J.7.x.
♥ x.x.
♦ K.J.10.9.x.x.
♣ A.

	N	
W		E
	S	

Your opening lead of the King of Diamonds is taken by South's Ace, East playing the two. South leads a Club. Clearly South has nine tricks at least to make if he has the Ace of Spades. Partner's Hearts can hardly be good enough to win the next four tricks. So you assume partner has the Ace of Spades. Even so, if South has four to the ten he will win a trick if you play the small Spade. You must go further and assume the Spade suit is divided:

	Q.8.	
K.J.7.x.		A.9.x.
	10.x.x.x.	

Now you bang out the King. Partner (if he is awake) unblocks with the nine. You put him in with the Ace and a finesse picks up all four tricks.

CHAPTER XIX

SAFETY PLAYS AND DECEPTIVE PLAYS

INEVITABLY this chapter will be something of a catalogue. There seems little prospect of any dramatic new discoveries in play being made, and it is convenient to collect together the various coups, safety and deceptive plays, which have been discovered by countless players from the earliest days of Whist to modern Contract. This is, I think, the only chapter in the book which you should know by heart.

COUPS

(a) *The Bath Coup:* We have already mentioned this simple hold up play. The basic position is:

<u>K</u>.Q.x.x.x.   W

　　　　　　　　S
　　　　A.J.<u>x.</u>

(b) *The Deschapelles Coup:* Usually this coup consists in playing an unsupported honour in order to drive out dummy's entry and prevent the establishment of a long suit:

　　　　　♠ A.x.
　　　　　♥ J.x.
　　　　　♦ x.x.x.
　　　　　♣ K.J.10.x.x.x.

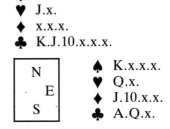

In Three No Trumps when East is in with the Queen of Clubs, he should play the King of Spades. Now—unless South has four Clubs—he cannot establish Clubs.

(*c*) *Grand Coup:* This was once supposed to be the most difficult and brilliant of all coups. Actually it is a simple exercise in trump reduction and the fact that you trump winners alone distinguishes it from its humbler cousin the trump coup. Here is a Double Grand Coup.

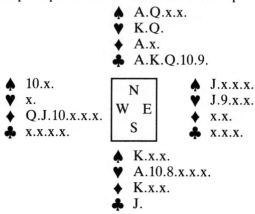

♠ A.Q.x.x.
♥ K.Q.
♦ A.x.
♣ A.K.Q.10.9.

♠ 10.x.
♥ x.
♦ Q.J.10.x.x.x.
♣ x.x.x.x.

♠ J.x.x.x.
♥ J.9.x.x.
♦ x.x.
♣ x.x.x.

♠ K.x.x.
♥ A.10.8.x.x.x.
♦ K.x.x.
♣ J.

South played in Seven Hearts against the opening lead of the Queen of Diamonds. South won in dummy and played the King and Queen of Trumps. When West showed out, declarer had to reduce his trumps. He took two top Clubs discarding a Diamond. Then he ruffed a Club, cashed his King of Diamonds and played a Spade. Another Club ruff and the two high Spades left this trump position with North to lead:

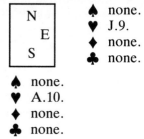

♠ none.
♥ J.9.
♦ none.
♣ none.

♠ none.
♥ A.10.
♦ none.
♣ none.

The hand, of course, is lucky to make and Seven No Trump, with the exact Club fit, is lay down. Because South has to trump two winning Clubs he has played a Double Grand Coup, but the play is mechanically exactly the same as if the Clubs had been losers.

(*d*) *Vienna Coup:* The Vienna Coup has two main variations.

In its simpler form it is an unblocking play as part of the preparation for a squeeze position. It consists in playing off a master card, so that a threat may be established to the card in the opponent's hand you have just promoted to master rank.

♠ A.x.
♥ A.Q.
♦ none.
♣ none.

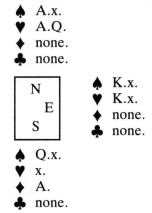

♠ K.x.
♥ K.x.
♦ none.
♣ none.

♠ Q.x.
♥ x.
♦ A.
♣ none.

Here when South plays his Ace of Diamonds, East is in no trouble and simply discards from the same suit as North picks. Suppose earlier South had played off the Spade Ace. This promotes East's King, but now the menace is behind him. South can now throw dummy's Spade on the Ace of Diamonds, but East is trapped.

The above play should be part of your routine manoeuvring for a squeeze position and you will find countless uses for the play. The second and more difficult variation is rarely of value in practical play, although it is a stand-by to the problem setters:

♠ x.x.x.
♥ x.x.x.x.
♦ A.10.x.
♣ A.Q.9.

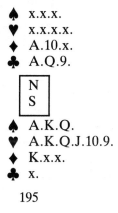

♠ A.K.Q.
♥ A.K.Q.J.10.9.
♦ K.x.x.
♣ x.

Let's assume a contract of Seven Hearts and the opening lead of the Jack of Clubs. If you are an experienced player, you can see three lines of play:

- (i) You finesse the Club at once. It's unlikely West would open away from the King against seven. Let's reject this.
- (ii) Simple squeeze against East (assumed to have the Club King) if he has five Diamonds.
- (iii) Simple squeeze against West (assumed to have the Club ten) if he has five Diamonds or any number of Diamonds including the Queen and Jack.

If our Club assumptions are correct (iii) is a better bet than (ii). At the second trick then you must play the Queen of Clubs. East covers and you ruff. Now you have transferred the Club menace to West and you make the contract if he has Q.J.x., Q.J.x.x. or any five-card Diamond suit.

(*e*) *Coup-en-Passant:* This is a pick-up play in the trump suit. Provided you recognise the position careful timing is all you need:

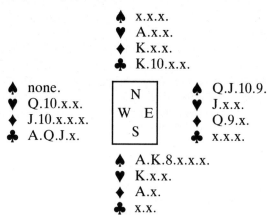

♠ x.x.x.
♥ A.x.x.
♦ K.x.x.
♣ K.10.x.x.

♠ none.
♥ Q.10.x.x.
♦ J.10.x.x.x.
♣ A.Q.J.x.

♠ Q.J.10.9.
♥ J.x.x.
♦ Q.9.x.
♣ x.x.x.

♠ A.K.8.x.x.x.
♥ K.x.x.
♦ A.x.
♣ x.x.

In Four Spades against the lead of the Ace of Clubs there seems no escape from going one down. Two trump tricks and a Heart trick must be lost. Careful play can amalgamate two of these losers. Suppose a Club continuation. Win with the King and— this pure technique of a very advanced sort—ruff a Club just in case. Then lay down the King of Spades. Now you know the trump situation and can pat yourself on the back for your Club play. Three rounds of Diamonds follow. Take the Ace of trumps and the King and Ace of Hearts. You have this position:

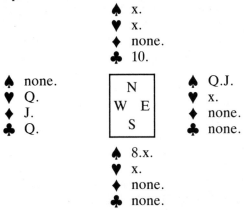

♠ x.
♥ x.
♦ none.
♣ 10.

♠ none.   ♠ Q.J.
♥ Q.   ♥ x.
♦ J.   ♦ none.
♣ Q.   ♣ none.

♠ 8.x.
♥ x.
♦ none.
♣ none.

Now you play the Club and you have the coup-en-passant position. Whatever East does you must make a trump trick. Go carefully back over the play and see how the contract is impossible, unless you ruff the Club trick at three. This play, of course, is not always a part of the coup-en-passant.

(f)   *Coup-without-a-name; (Scissors Coup):* This is the most delicate and imaginative of all coups. I believe Ely Culbertson first publicised it and called it the Coup-without-a-name. I call it the Scissors Coup which seems an accurate description of the quick snip of the opponents' communications which it involves:

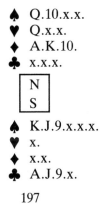

♠ Q.10.x.x.
♥ Q.x.x.
♦ A.K.10.
♣ x.x.x.

♠ K.J.9.x.x.x.
♥ x.
♦ x.x.
♣ A.J.9.x.

197

The following bidding takes you to Four Spades doubled:

E	S	W	N
1♣	1♠	1NT	Dble
2♣	2♠	—	4♠
—	—	Dble	—
—	—		

West opens the eight of Clubs and you win East's Queen. On the face of it the hand is hopeless for the opponents must take a Heart, a Club, a Club ruff, and the Ace of trumps. West is marked with the Ace of trumps and must have some slight red-card suit strength. If he has the Q.J. of Diamonds the coup-without-a-name enable you to cut their communications. Play off all three Diamonds and discard your Heart. Now if the hands are as shown West can never put his partner in to get a Club ruff, and you can play Clubs yourself later:

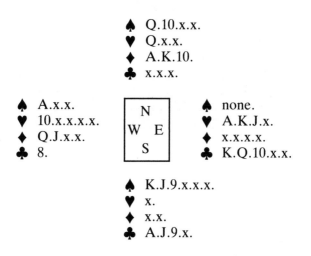

```
              ♠ Q.10.x.x.
              ♥ Q.x.x.
              ♦ A.K.10.
              ♣ x.x.x.

♠ A.x.x.        ┌─────┐        ♠ none.
♥ 10.x.x.x.x.   │  N  │        ♥ A.K.J.x.
♦ Q.J.x.x.      │ W E │        ♦ x.x.x.x.
♣ 8.            │  S  │        ♣ K.Q.10.x.x.
                └─────┘
              ♠ K.J.9.x.x.x.
              ♥ x.
              ♦ x.x.
              ♣ A.J.9.x.
```

(g) *The Devil's Coup:* When you have got two or one absolutely "certain" tricks in trumps, there is only one danger. The declarer may pull the Devil's Coup on you. If you have A.J.9. of trumps over K.10.x. you have two sure tricks. But look at this position:

198

Q.x.x.

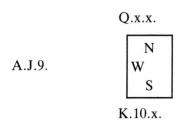

A.J.9.

K.10.x.

With the lead in North's hand at the eleventh trick he leads a small card and South puts the King on it. Where has your second trump trick gone to? Obviously this play (and its variations)rarely appear in practical play. Two forms of the Devil's Coup, however, are not such rare birds. The first consists in losing no Trump trick even when the opponents have split guarded honours. For example, you may be able to achieve this end game:

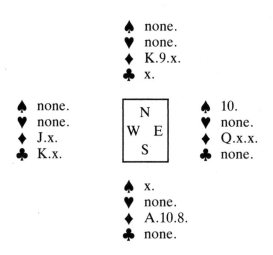

♠ none.
♥ none.
♦ K.9.x.
♣ x.

♠ none.
♥ none.
♦ J.x.
♣ K.x.

♠ 10.
♥ none.
♦ Q.x.x.
♣ none.

♠ x.
♥ none.
♦ A.10.8.
♣ none.

With Diamonds trumps and South to lead you play your Spade. West can only discard a Club and you ruff in dummy. Now the Club lead from North ensures the rest of the tricks whatever East does.

Finally, the original Devil's Coup (this is also known as smother play).

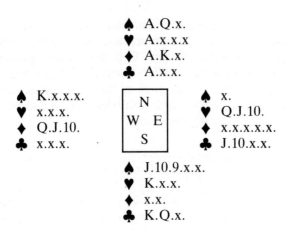

♠ A.Q.x.
♥ A.x.x.x
♦ A.K.x.
♣ A.x.x.

♠ K.x.x.x.   ♠ x.
♥ x.x.x.   ♥ Q.J.10.
♦ Q.J.10.   ♦ x.x.x.x.x.
♣ x.x.x.   ♣ J.10.x.x.

♠ J.10.9.x.x.
♥ K.x.x.
♦ x.x.
♣ K.Q.x.

Six Spades looks reasonable until East shows out on the second round of trumps. Yet the contract can still be made. Three rounds of Clubs, three more of Diamonds and finally two of Hearts leaves this position:

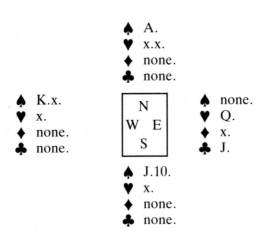

♠ A.
♥ x.x.
♦ none.
♣ none.

♠ K.x.   ♠ none.
♥ x.   ♥ Q.
♦ none.   ♦ x.
♣ none.   ♣ J.

♠ J.10.
♥ x.
♦ none.
♣ none.

The third Heart puts East in. Whatever he leads is trumped by South. West's trump "winner" disappears.

SAFETY PLAYS

In most of the difficult combinations there are two distinct ways of playing the cards. First the way to make the maximum number of tricks. Secondly—an insurance play—the way to make sure of a trick total less perhaps than the maximum, but sufficient to secure the contract. With this second approach, the safety plays, we are now mainly concerned. I list here all the important safety plays, but each of these has numerous variations. Considerations of time and entries may, of course, make a desirable safety play impracticable.

Q.x.x._x._
A.10.x.x.x.x.

Most books give the best safety play here (only to lose one trick) as small towards the Queen. This is wrong. Small towards the Ace loses no trick to the singleton King in East's hand. Of course if East plays a small card you play the ten.

_Q._x.x.x.
A.J.9.x.x.x.

The finesse is correct with ten cards. But you must play the Queen so that a later finesse can pick up K.10.x. with East.

A.J.x.x.
10.x.x._x._

To make three tricks here first finesse the Jack then play the Ace. If ony two tricks are required the 100% play is to play the Ace on the first round and then a small one.

_A._8.x.x.
K.Q.9.x.x.

Correct play is the Ace. Only if East has J.10.x.x. can you pick up all four trumps.

A.10.7.6.2.
K.9.x.x.

To make all four tricks play off the Ace and King relying on a 2–2 drop. In certain circumstances it may be wise, if an honour drops on the first round, to finesse on the second. If you can afford to lose a trick play small from either hand and put on the ten or nine as a protection against Q.J.x.x. in one hand. With:

K.x.x.
A.10.x.x.x.

first the King and then small to the ten in case East has Q.J.x.x.

A.Q.x.x.x.x.
x.x.x.

To win the maximum tricks finesse. To have the best chance of losing only one, play the Ace and then small towards the Queen. With a holding of eight cards:

A.Q.x.x.
x.x.x.x.

the Ace is correct in either case for at least one trick must be lost.

A.K.J.10.x.x.
x.x.

Correct play here is the first round finesse. Most players would play off the King first. This is correct with nine cards as protection against a lone Queen with East. In the example given you cannot pick up Q.x.x.x. with West unless you finesse on the first round and this distribution is more likely.

A similar situation is

A.K.4.3.2.
J.10.9.

You cannot afford to play a high honour first.

10.x.x.
A.K.9.x.x.

First round the King. Second round small to the ten in case East has Q.J.8.x. If West has this holding there is nothing to be done.

202

<u>A</u>.J.x.x.x.x.
Q.x.

Not small to the Queen which loses two tricks if West has a singleton King. Ace is correct. One trick anyway must be lost.

<u>K</u>.J.x.
A.9.x.x.x.

Play the King. Re-enter South and play small to the Jack. This copes with all 4–1 divisions. To make all five tricks you should play West for Q. to three and finesse.

K.9.x.
<u>A</u>.J.x.x.x.

A variant of the last hand. Ace first and then small to dummy finessing the nine if West plays a small one. To make five tricks play East for three to the Queen.

A.10.9.x.x.x.
J.<u>x.</u>

Most players play the Jack here. This gives away a trick if West has the King or Queen alone. If entries permit the small card is correct. Without the nine spot you should play small to the Jack hoping East has K.x. or Q.x.

A.9.8.x.
<u>Q</u>.10.7.x.

The best plan here eliminates the guess and takes two finesses. If the hands, however, have nine cards you should play the Ace first and then small to the Queen.

A.Q.10.x.
J.x.<u>x.</u>

You must, of course, finesse, but you should lead the small cards to dummy in case West has K.x. when, by covering the Jack if it was led he can establish his partner's 9.x.x.x.

K.J.x.x.
<u>A</u>.x.x.

If you can't lose a trick assume West has three to the Queen. If you can lose one bang out Ace and King (in case East has Q.x.) and lead small to the Jack.

Q.J.x.x.
<u>A</u>.x.x.

Ace and then small (twice if necessary) towards the Q.J. You cannot gain here by finessing and you lose if West has four to the King.

A.<u>10</u>.
K.9.x.x.<i>x</i>.

Small and finesse the ten. Doubleton honour with West or the 3–3 break wins four tricks.

K.9.x.
<u>A</u>.10.x.x.

To have the best chance of three tricks lead out the Ace and then the King. Now if the suit is 3–3 or if an honour has dropped on either of the first two rounds you are home.

Finally   A.
                            J.10.x.x.x.x.

Most players go wrong here. On the second round you should lead the small card not the ten which loses an extra trick if there is a doubleton honour. There are several variations of this play.

These plays are given here without clothing them with the flesh of actual hands. You will meet them all in play and, if you know them by heart, you will recognise them. Here and there they will cost you thirty points for an overtrick. They will also sometimes land you a game or a slam you would have missed. You can on some hands invent your own safety play. This one can't be original, but I have never seen it in any book. Playing six Hearts I eliminated trumps and the black suits, and with the lead in dummy, could afford to lose one trick:

♠ none.
♥ x.
♦ A.x.x.x.
♣ none.

```
┌───┐
│ N │
│ S │
└───┘
```

♠ none.
♥ Q.
♦ Q.J.9.x.
♣ none.

A small Diamond to my Jack won. I was just about to play back to the Ace when—luckily—I stopped to think. West was a very good player. Suppose he was fooling me? Suppose he had K.10.8. left? So I thought out the safety play—and led my Queen. West covered and I ducked. East showed out and West was trapped. Either he had to give me both Diamonds or a ruff and discard. Of course, if West shows out I duck again and East is similary trapped. The slam is a certainty, as long as the safety play is spotted.

THE PLAY FOR ENTRIES

Some plays combine a safety element with the necessity of securing entries. For example if you have no side entry in dummy and the following suit at No Trumps:

A.K.Q.x.x.x.x.
x.x.

you can normally take seven tricks. If six is all you need for your contract, you will be wise to duck the first round in case West has J.10.9.x.

Similarly if you have:

A.Q.x.x.x.
x.x.

and must make four tricks, you can only do this if you duck the first round, finesse on the second, and drop the suit 3–3 on the third.

Careful preservation of your small cards can often secure extra entries:

Q.8.5.3.

A.K.J.2.

If this suit breaks 3–2 an extra entry can be obtained in North's hand by overtaking the Jack with the Queen on the third round. A situation often mishandled is:

A.J.10.8.

9.4.3.

If you lead the nine instead of the three you must finally waste an extra entry to pick up Q.x.x.x. with West.

If entries are essential you may even have to take an unnecessary finesse. For example, if your only chance of entering dummy is in Hearts and you hold:

A.10.x.

K.Q.x.

you may have to finesse the ten, if two entries are needed. Sometimes if the defence spots what you are trying, they can foil you. In the last example, for instance, West ruins your plans if he plays the Jack when you lead the small Heart.

Another effective defence which, in essence, is an assault on timing consists in forcing the declarer to use his entries before he is ready. The commonest case is when dummy has a long solid side suit:

♠ A.x.
♥ x.x.
♦ A.K.J.10.x.x.
♣ x.x.x.

♠ K.Q.10.x.	N	♠ x.x.x.x.x.x.
♥ A.Q.x.	W E	♥ x.x.
♦ Q.x.	S	♦ x.x.x.
♣ x.x.x.x.		♣ Q.J.10.

♠ J.x.
♥ K.J.10.9.x.x.
♦ x.x.
♣ A.K.x.

Against Four Hearts you (West) open the King of Spades and at trick two are in with the Queen of trumps. You cash a Spade and now must attack Diamonds for clearly the suit will provide all the discards South needs. Declarer returns a trump but, winning with the Ace, you play another Diamond. South is forced to use his entries too soon and cannot rid himself of his losing Club. Watch carefully for this position. It is missed far too often.

DECEPTIVE PLAYS AND FALSE CARDING

Quite a number of plays in this group are more or less standard, although the brilliant improviser still has plenty of scope. In particular there are a number of situations in which a false card is obligatory. Some of these can be summed up in a phrase, "Play the card you are known to hold".

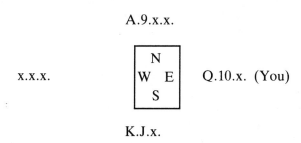

A.9.x.x.

x.x.x.   Q.10.x. (You)

K.J.x.

The first play is from dummy and the Jack is finessed. Then the King is played. Here you must play the card you are known to hold—the Queen. If you do, South may finesse the nine on the third round. If you do not, he cannot go wrong.

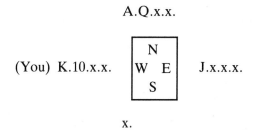

A.Q.x.x.

(You) K.10.x.x.   J.x.x.x.

x.

South finesses the Queen in this side suit and cashes the Ace.

207

You must drop the King. Till you do, South can trump small safely.

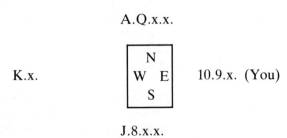

South leads small and finesses the Queen. Drop the nine (or the ten) and South must guess whether to lead the Jack or a small one next time. Play small and he must take all four tricks.

If your holding is K.10. the play of the King on the first round may create the impression of a singleton, and the ten wins subsequently on a finesse.

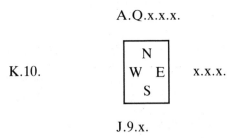

When South leads a small one, play your King.

DECLARER'S FALSE CARDS

Declarer has the great advantage that he has no partner to mislead. He can try and entice or stop a suit play at will. As long as his play is not obviously illogical he has a good chance of success. Oddly enough for these manoeuvres the deuce is the most important card: assuming, of course, that the opponents notice what cards are played. Terence Reese in his admirable *Reese on Play* lays down an excellent guide: "As declarer put out the same signals as you would if you were defending: play a high card if you want a suit to be led, a low one if you hope to stop it". He gives as an illustration:

208

A.K.J.

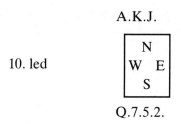

10. led

Q.7.5.2.

At No Trumps you are delighted if the opponents lead this suit. To play the Jack and win the trick gives everything away. Play the King and if East plays the three or four you play the five. West may think he has found a weakness in your holding.

Sometimes, if you can afford it, the winning of a trick with the King rather than the Jack from an A.K.J. holding may put the opponents off a more likely scent. Or again, West may miscount your holding for A.Q. alone if you win the opening lead "twice" with the ten and the Queen from:

J.10.x.
A.Q.9.

For the rest it's enough to sum up the remaining plays with our old advice for bidding and play—"make them guess".

The first time I ever saw this theft brought off was by Howard Schenken when he and Gottlieb first came over here in 1934:

K.x.x.

A.Q.9.x. 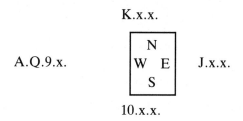 J.x.x.

10.x.x.

Schenken led the Queen and South, of course, ducked "in dummy" intending to cover the Jack on the next round. But Schenken now played low and so did South. East-West took all four tricks.

When you are up against our old friend the two-way finesse:

A.10.x.
K.J.9.

it's usually a good idea to play the Jack even if you don't intend to run it. West may cover and probably will, if he's a weak player. Sometimes, then, if West is a good player you can get one through the slips (when you think he has the Queen) by playing the Jack from this position:

A.9.x.

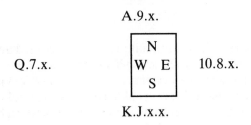

Q.7.x. 10.8.x.

K.J.x.x.

By the way, in the absence of any other information, the Acol team always used to play for Queens being over Jacks. The main merit of this is consistency, but there is also some slight theoretical advantage in that Queen's tend to cover Jacks and the imperfect shuffle leaves them undisturbed.

Often the defenders are trapped in a prepared end play. Even here there is usually a chance. In a Heart contract, South was able to strip the hand and West had to lead:

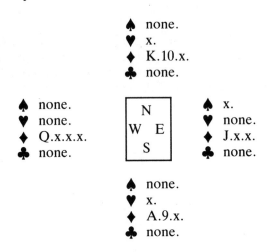

♠ none.
♥ x.
♦ K.10.x.
♣ none.

♠ none.   ♠ x.
♥ none.   ♥ none.
♦ Q.x.x.x.   ♦ J.x.x.
♣ none.   ♣ none.

♠ none.
♥ x.
♦ A.9.x.
♣ none.

If West plays a small Diamond he might as well throw his hand in. The play of the Queen is the only chance hoping South will play him for Q.J.x. Again, if the side suit is:

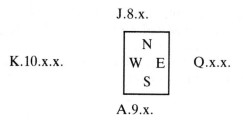

West has no chance if he plays small. He must play the King and South may guess wrong by assuming West has K.Q.

Finally there are dozens of variations on the "make 'em guess" theme at the disposal of declarer. Most of them depend on the nervousness of the defenders about the pattern and high card strength of the closed declarer's hand. I remember once making all the tricks in a suit distributed:

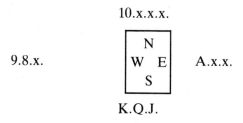

West led the nine and East ducked. I won with the Queen. Going into dummy I discarded the King on a side-winner and led the suit again. East ducked again and my Jack won! Later I ruffed the suit and established the ten. Things don't always go so well, but you can always try.

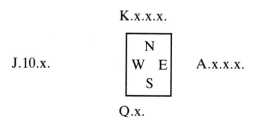

If you win the first trick with the Queen and decide East has the Ace try leading again from dummy. East must guess and you may have started with Q., Q.J., or Q.x.

In a slam contract smooth play to the first and second trick of the Ace (throwing the Jack) and a small one gives East a horrible headache.

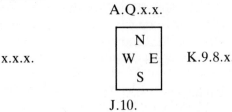

A.Q.x.x.

x.x.x.   K.9.8.x.

J.10.

Actually, if he studies West's opening lead carefully, East can probably solve the riddle.

There is even a chance when the Ace and King are against you that they may fall together. With:

Q.x.x.
J.10.x.x.x.x.x.

you should lead the Queen from dummy. With either A.x. or K.x. a thoughtless East may cover.

ONE MORE CHANCE

This hand from rubber Bridge is a pleasant memory. I cut Kenneth Konstam and we reached Five Diamonds doubled by East and re-doubled. West was a good player and East was not:

♠ Q.9.x.x.
♥ x.x.x.
♦ A.K.10.x.x.
♣ x.

♠ K.8.x.
♥ A.
♦ Q.J.9.x.x.x.
♣ K.9.x.

The Queen of Hearts was led. Clearly the only chance is to lose only one trick in Spades. In other words, either to get the opponents to lead Spades and hope the Jack and ten are divided, or find an opponent with A.x. The Club finesse is pointless, because East wasn't good enough to duck even if he had the Ace. So I played a trump, West showing out. Then a Heart ruff, another trump, and another Heart ruff. Now I played the King of Clubs from my own hand and West, who won, has a chance to go wrong. My play looks as if I have the Queen of Clubs, but West guessed correctly and returned the Club. I ruffed and led a Spade. East played the ten and my King won. Obviously East started in Spades either with A.10. alone or A.J.10. In the first case I cannot lose. In the second, I cannot win. Yet there is still a chance, against a weak defender. I ruffed a Club and played a Spade away from the Queen tossing my eight on it. East won with the Jack and began to think. He thought as far as concluding that my Spade eight was genuine, and if he played his Ace he would set up dummy. The secondary conclusion that if I had a Club left I could put my hand down never occurred to him. He led the Queen of Clubs!

ONE THROUGH THE SLIPS

The perfect illustration of this comes from the so-called World's Champion Team-of-Four event in Chicago a couple of years back. Johnny Crawford (North) and Margaret Wager (South) reached a near-hopeless contract of Seven Spades.

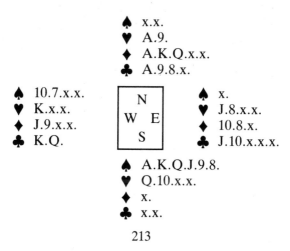

Margaret Wager won the opening Club lead and drew four rounds of trumps. Then she blandly led the Queen of Hearts. East ducked and the Queen won the trick. Switching to Diamonds declarer made her contract. Certainly South's play is admirable, but the sympathy extended to West is misplaced. He should have thought this out when dummy went down. You cannot construct a hand for South (having six trumps which you know, and the Jack of Hearts which your play of the Queen of Hearts assumes) on which she will play Hearts before testing Diamonds. And so she is putting one over. She was, and she did.

CHAPTER XX

THE END GAME

THE PLAY of an expert flourishes most in the small contracts. There, where the choice of method is wider, the percentage for skill is greater. And yet Bridge writing tends to concentrate on the end game. There is some excuse for this. It is true you can learn all the theory you need about the end game—from this chapter for example. But after that you must practise till it becomes wearisome, and play till your skill becomes automatic. It is in the end game that most of the big fish are finally landed, it is around the end game that all problems are woven, and it is in the end game that you can best exploit the coups and plays we looked at in the last chapter.

THROW-IN PLAY

This is the basis of most end game positions where there is a trick to be lost:

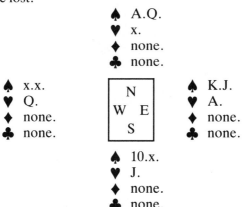

♠ A.Q.
♥ x.
♦ none.
♣ none.

♠ x.x.   ♠ K.J.
♥ Q.   ♥ A.
♦ none.   ♦ none.
♣ none.   ♣ none.

♠ 10.x.
♥ J.
♦ none.
♣ none.

The Spade finesse fails to gather two tricks out of three. The throw-in with the Heart succeeds. There is more to be learnt from this simple example than might appear at first sight. First of all the need for careful timing, and the elimination of all irrelevant cards. For example, if each hand had one extra small Heart there is no way for South to make two tricks. Secondly, the need for the defence to foresee this position: and in this example, for East to have played, or discarded, his Heart Ace on an earlier round. Thirdly, the importance of exit cards—the struggle for tempos and entries in reverse. South wins because he can throw the lead away. East loses because he cannot:

♠ x.x.x.
♥ K.J.x.x.x.
♦ A.x.x.
♣ x.x.

♠ Q. led

♠ A.K.x.
♥ A.Q.10.x.x.x.
♦ K.x.
♣ A.Q.

South plays six Hearts against the lead of the Queen of Spades. The contract appears to depend on the King of Clubs. Throw-in play greatly increases your chances. You draw trumps and eliminate Diamonds. Then play the King and another Spade. The position is:

♠ none.
♥ K.J.x.
♦ none.
♣ x.x.

♠ none.
♥ A.10.x.
♦ none.
♣ A.Q.

Now if West has either five Spades or some holding like Q.J.10.9. he has to lead and your contract is sure. Even if East wins you still have the even-money Club finesse. West then must strive to hold an exit card and if his original Spade holding was Q.J.10.4. he must throw the ten on your King and hope East wins the third round with the nine.

Sometimes the declarer, if the cards lie favourably, can bring off a partial elimination and then throw an opponent in.

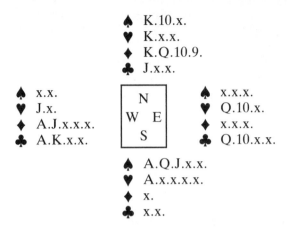

♠ K.10.x.
♥ K.x.x.
♦ K.Q.10.9.
♣ J.x.x.

♠ x.x.
♥ J.x.
♦ A.J.x.x.x.
♣ A.K.x.x.

♠ x.x.x.
♥ Q.10.x.
♦ x.x.x.
♣ Q.10.x.x.

♠ A.Q.J.x.x.
♥ A.x.x.x.x.
♦ x.
♣ x.x.

South was playing four Spades after West had opened with one Diamond. The defence was the A.K. and another Club. The contract looks hopeless, for it looks impossible to prevent the loss of a trick in both Hearts and Diamonds. South saw just one chance. If Spades and Hearts were each divided 3–2, the long card with East, and if West had A.J. of Diamonds, it could be done. He took two rounds only of trumps and the Ace, King of Hearts. Then he led a Diamond. West had to win with this Ace and this was the position:

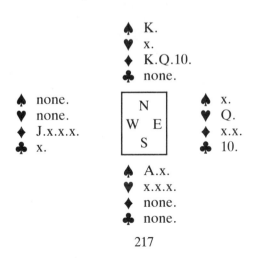

♠ K.
♥ x.
♦ K.Q.10.
♣ none.

♠ none.
♥ none.
♦ J.x.x.x.
♣ x.

♠ x.
♥ Q.
♦ x.x.
♣ 10.

♠ A.x.
♥ x.x.x.
♦ none.
♣ none.

217

If West plays a Club, North ruffs throwing a Heart in South's hand and plays two high Diamonds. If West plays a Diamond, North finesses the ten and draws East's trump. Here a complete elimination could not be achieved in either suit, but the effect was the same.

Sometimes a perfect end game position can be seen as soon as dummy's hand goes down. Terence Reese, for example, had this hand in the 1949 final of the Harrogate Congress Teams-of-Four. He played as West in Six Spades against a Heart lead:

♠ K.Q.J.x.x.	W E	♠ A.9.8.x.
♥ A.K.		♥ x.x.x.
♦ J.9.x.		♦ A.10.x.
♣ K.10.x.		♣ A.Q.x.

He won the first lead and the opponents both follow to a round of trumps. Terence put his hand down. "I draw trumps, eliminate the hand and concede a Diamond". This would be the end position:

♠ x.	W E	♠ x.
♥ none.		♥ none.
♦ J.9.x.		♦ A.10.x.
♣ none.		♣ none.

West leads the Jack of Diamonds and, wherever the honours lie, can only lose one trick. There are a number of combined holdings which you should seek to avoid playing yourself. Study these and you will see how much better your prospects are if the opponents can be forced to lead them:

A.10.x	J.x.x.	A.J.10.	A.10.x.	A.x.	K.10.x.
J.x.x.	K.x.x.	K.x.x.	K.9.x.	Q.x.	Q.9.x.
		J.x.x.	Q.10.x.		
		Q.x.x.	A.x.		

and dozens of other combinations.

There are also a few combinations similar to the one in the last hand given (J.9.x.

A.10.x.) which ensure (at trump contracts) a definite number of tricks in the suit, provided the side suits can be eliminated and a trump retained in each hand. For example with Hearts trumps you are sure to make two tricks out of the last four if South leads in this position:

♠ none.
♥ x.
♦ K.10.x.
♣ none.

```
┌───┐
│ S │
│ N │
└───┘
```

♠ none.
♥ x.
♦ x.x.x.
♣ none.

You play a Diamond and cover the card West plays. Other sure combinations to pick up one trick in the suit under such circumstances are Q.J.x.   K.9.x.
           x.x.x.   J.x.x.
and to pick up two tricks:
A.Q.9.   A.J.10.
x.x.x.   x.x.x.
Such holdings as: K.Q.10.x.x.x. are not, however, sure for two tricks as East holding A.J.x. can duck.

LOSER-ON-LOSER

We discussed this group of plays in an earlier chapter. Sometimes they can be used in preference to an odds-on elimination play because they offer a certainty:

♠ A.Q.8.
♥ x.
♦ A.x.x.x.x.
♣ x.x.x.x.

♠ x.x.x.
♥ A.x.
♦ K.Q.10.x.x.x.x.
♣ x.

In Five Diamonds West starts off with two rounds of Clubs.

South obviously will seek to draw trumps, eliminate Hearts and Clubs, and lead a Spade to dummy's holding. This is not a certainty (as West by playing the nine or ten can force a finesse) but it is a very good chance. If, however, on the third Club West discards, the hand becomes a certainty. Dummy is re-entered with a trump and the Club is played, South discarding a Spade. East has to lead in this position:

♠ A.Q.8.
♥ none.
♦ x.
♣ none.

♠ x.x.
♥ none.
♦ K.x.
♣ none.

South makes the rest and his contract.

When one finesse is thought to be wrong, the refusal to take it often gives declarer a much better play:

♠ x.x.x.x.
♥ K.x.x.x.
♦ A.Q.x.
♣ x.x.

♠ K.x.
♥ Q.J.10.9.x.x.
♦ K.x.x.
♣ A.Q.

West opens a Club and doubles South's bid of Four Hearts. He opens the Diamond Jack. As long as West has Ace of Hearts and the King of Clubs the contract is safe. Trumps are drawn, Diamonds played and then the Ace followed by the Queen of Clubs.

The loser-on-loser technique can play a part in all the end game positions and coups. Sometimes it is an end in itself, sometimes only the means to an end as in this last example:

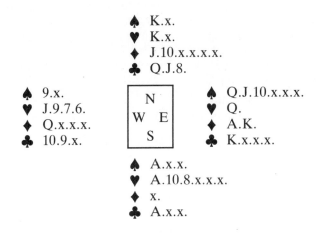

                    ♠ K.x.
                    ♥ K.x.
                    ♦ J.10.x.x.x.x.
                    ♣ Q.J.8.

♠ 9.x.   ┌─────────┐   ♠ Q.J.10.x.x.x.
♥ J.9.7.6.   │   N   │   ♥ Q.
♦ Q.x.x.x.   │ W   E │   ♦ A.K.
♣ 10.9.x.   │   S   │   ♣ K.x.x.x.
                    └─────────┘
                    ♠ A.x.x.
                    ♥ A.10.8.x.x.x.
                    ♦ x.
                    ♣ A.x.x.

South played in Four Hearts after East had opened with One
Spade. The opening Spade lead was won by dummy. South now
played a Diamond. This is a variation of the coup-without-a-
name (scissors). It has the double effect of cutting communica-
tions between the defending hands, and preparing for a trump
reduction and coup against West. A Spade was continued and
South played a third Spade. If West ruffs declarer discards a
Club—loser-on-loser. If West—correctly discards a Diamond
—South ruffs and, by ruffing Diamonds twice and taking the
Club finesse, reaches this position:

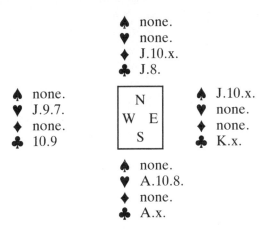

                    ♠ none.
                    ♥ none.
                    ♦ J.10.x.
                    ♣ J.8.

♠ none.   ┌─────────┐   ♠ J.10.x.
♥ J.9.7.   │   N   │   ♥ none.
♦ none.   │ W   E │   ♦ none.
♣ 10.9   │   S   │   ♣ K.x.
                    └─────────┘
                    ♠ none.
                    ♥ A.10.8.
                    ♦ none.
                    ♣ A.x.

East is thrown in with the Club and West forced to lead trumps
at the twelfth trick.

We have talked a good deal about the battle for tempos. Squeeze play is the best example of this conflict. Master first the basic position in the simple squeeze:

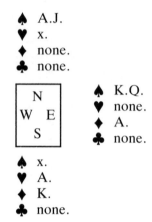

♠ A.J.
♥ x.
♦ none.
♣ none.

♠ K.Q.
♥ none.
♦ A.
♣ none.

♠ x.
♥ A.
♦ K.
♣ none.

South has to lead and needs all three tricks. There is one in Spades and one in Hearts. Time and position provide him with the third. South plays the Heart. East cannot now cope with the war on two flanks and has to throw either a winning Diamond or the guard to his King of Spades. Notice as in the trump coups how all irrelevant cards must be stripped away. It is because East has no useless card to discard that the squeeze operates.

Because we will be using the terms later, let us describe more accurately the six cards in North and South's hands which make up the basic position:

(1) *Squeeze Card:* In the diagram this is Ace of Hearts. Any Club would do just as well. In this position the squeeze card is any winner to which the opponent being squeezed has no safe discard.

(2) *Menaces:* The Jack of Spades (called a "two-card menace" because the Ace is in the same hand) and the King of Diamonds ("one card") are the twin menaces that threaten East.

(3) *Entry:* The Ace of Spades provides the essential entry to the two-card menace, and the small Spade in South's hand enables him to cross to dummy.

(4) *Discard:* Finally the small Heart in dummy (a small card in any other suit is just as good) gives declarer a discard on the squeeze card. Otherwise he will be squeezed himself.

So every card is doing a job of work. There are three points to notice. First that, as the menaces are in different hands, either opponent can be squeezed. If they are in the same hand, only the opponent playing before the hand with the menaces is vulnerable. For example:

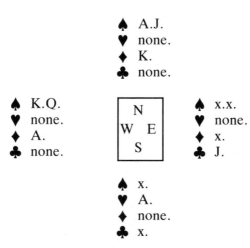

```
              ♠ A.J.
              ♥ none.
              ♦ K.
              ♣ none.

♠ K.Q.       ┌───────┐      ♠ x.x.
♥ none.      │   N   │      ♥ none.
♦ A.         │ W   E │      ♦ x.
♣ none.      │   S   │      ♣ J.
             └───────┘
              ♠ x.
              ♥ A.
              ♦ none.
              ♣ x.
```

West is now squeezed, but nothing can be done if the East and West cards are reversed for North must discard first. The second point is that the squeeze card must be in the hand opposite the two-card menace. Obviously if they are in the same hand in a three-card ending, there cannot also be an entry to the dummy. The third point is that in nearly all normal squeeze positions you must be able to take all the remaining tricks except one.

Unless squeeze play is already almost tediously familiar to you, I hope you'll stop now, go back and read again, and again, and again, what I have written about the fundamentals of the simple squeeze. From sure knowledge now the rest is not difficult. You must also practise looking at hands, which can only be made on a squeeze, until you can see the bones. Take this position where Clubs are trumps and you cannot afford to lose another trick:

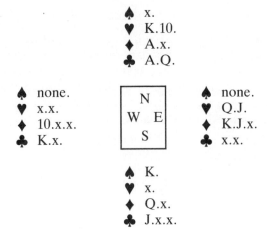

```
                    ♠ x.
                    ♥ K.10.
                    ♦ A.x.
                    ♣ A.Q.

  ♠ none.          ┌─────────┐        ♠ none.
  ♥ x.x.           │    N    │        ♥ Q.J.
  ♦ 10.x.x.        │  W   E  │        ♦ K.J.x.
  ♣ K.x.           │    S    │        ♣ x.x.
                   └─────────┘
                    ♠ K.
                    ♥ x.
                    ♦ Q.x.
                    ♣ J.x.x.
```

You must assume K.x. of Clubs on your left. If so, you can make three Clubs, one Diamond, one Heart and one Spade. Six tricks or one short of the remainder and a squeeze may be on. Look then for your squeeze card. It is, of course, the third Club. Look for your menaces. The Queen of Diamonds can be the one card and the K.10. of Hearts the two-card menace. Anything else? Yes, we must strip everything we don't need and that includes the Ace of Diamonds (Vienna Coup). So we end with the following position and the lead of the last Club squeezes East:

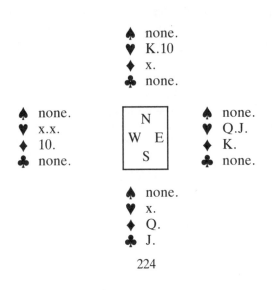

```
                    ♠ none.
                    ♥ K.10
                    ♦ x.
                    ♣ none.

  ♠ none.          ┌─────────┐        ♠ none.
  ♥ x.x.           │    N    │        ♥ Q.J.
  ♦ 10.            │  W   E  │        ♦ K.
  ♣ none.          │    S    │        ♣ none.
                   └─────────┘
                    ♠ none.
                    ♥ x.
                    ♦ Q.
                    ♣ J.
```

We now go a step further, but if you are sure of the first, the second is easy. When both opponents hold the two-card menace you can still bring off a squeeze against them if you can find an extra one-card menace, and if both the one-card menaces sit over (to the left of) the player you threaten. Let's dig up our original example, and vary it slightly:

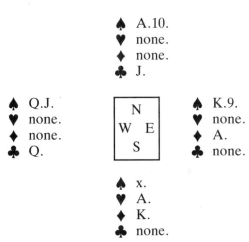

♠ A.10.
♥ none.
♦ none.
♣ J.

♠ Q.J.   ♠ K.9.
♥ none.   ♥ none.
♦ none.   ♦ A.
♣ Q.   ♣ none.

♠ x.
♥ A.
♦ K.
♣ none.

The new features are the fact that West now holds Spades as well as East, and that two Club honours have appeared. The two-card menace as before is in Spades. The one-card menaces (King of Diamonds and Jack of Clubs) lie over their opponents. All is set and once more the squeeze card (Ace of Hearts) starts what is this time a double agony. West cannot throw his Club or else North's Jack is established. So he must throw a Spade. Declarer throws dummy Jack of Clubs—his task is done—and East in turn is squeezed. The double squeeze then is simply two single squeezes at the same trick. Careful placing of the menaces and an eye for the basic position is all you need.

A slight variation shows what is called the "split double menace" in a four-card ending:

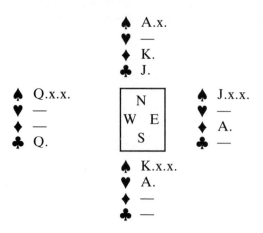

Again the Ace of Hearts starts the double squeeze.

Here is a beautiful double squeeze from the 1947 final of the Crockford's Cup won by Leo Baron's team:

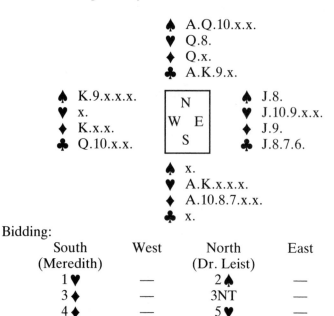

Bidding:

South (Meredith)	West	North (Dr. Leist)	East
1 ♥	—	2 ♠	—
3 ♦	—	3NT	—
4 ♦	—	5 ♥	—
6 ♦	—	—	—

The lead was the singleton Heart. Adam Meredith won in his own hand and led a small Diamond. He has no need to take the Spade finesse for if that is right the double squeeze also works, with a Heart menace against East. This was the end position:

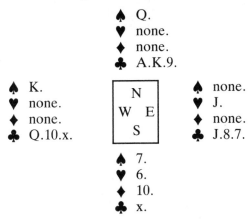

```
                    ♠ Q.
                    ♥ none.
                    ♦ none.
                    ♣ A.K.9.
♠ K.                              ♠ none.
♥ none.          N                ♥ J.
♦ none.        W   E              ♦ none.
♣ Q.10.x.        S                ♣ J.8.7.
                    ♠ 7.
                    ♥ 6.
                    ♦ 10.
                    ♣ x.
```

Neither opponent can hold Clubs as the last trump starts the double squeeze.

REPEATED SQUEEZE

In this variation the same opponent is squeezed on consecutive leads:

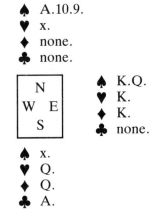

```
                    ♠ A.10.9.
                    ♥ x.
                    ♦ none.
                    ♣ none.
                                  ♠ K.Q.
                 N                ♥ K.
               W   E              ♦ K.
                 S                ♣ none.
                    ♠ x.
                    ♥ Q.
                    ♦ Q.
                    ♣ A.
```

This position, although not a practical one, shows the position most clearly. When the Ace of Clubs is played East cannot discard a Spade or dummy is high. He must throw a red King. South, of course, then merely plays whichever red Queen has

227

been established and a further (simple) squeeze follows. Note that when this squeeze begins to operate South is two tricks, not one, short of making the rest. The extra winner is provided by the first squeeze. The real value of the repeated squeeze then lies when you know—perhaps as an inference from the bidding—that one opponent has the guards in all three side suits, and you have suitably placed menaces.

The ruffing element introduces the variation here. The end game is usually more complicated:

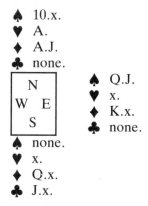

```
            ♠  10.x.
            ♥  A.
            ♦  A.J.
            ♣  none.
   ┌─────────┐      ♠  Q.J.
   │    N    │      ♥  x.
   │  W   E  │      ♦  K.x.
   │    S    │      ♣  none.
   └─────────┘
            ♠  none.
            ♥  x.
            ♦  Q.x.
            ♣  J.x.
```

Clubs are trumps and you have the usual four tricks on top. When you play a Club you can discard the Jack of Diamonds. East cannot throw a Spade because one ruff establishes North's Spades, nor can he throw a Diamond for his King would then fall to the Ace and the Queen still be a winner. So he throws a Heart. Now again when you play a Heart he has nothing left to throw that does not yield the last trick. To establish the trump squeeze position you need as the diagram shows, an extra entry in dummy's hand plus a secondary threat (the Spade suit) which a trump can convert into a winner if the opponents only hold the suit once.

Rectifying (Heaven knows why) is the usual jargon. It is an essential part of the squeeze play technique and very easy—as long as you remember. We agreed that to get a squeeze position you had to strip the hand to its essentials. Apart from the repeated squeeze you have to be able to take all the tricks except one. Suppose you can't? Easy. You lose a trick on purpose. And that's all there is to it. Indeed, often you lose it on the opening lead:

♠ A.x.x.
♥ K.Q.x.x.
♦ x.x.x.
♣ K.x.x.

```
┌─────┐
│  N  │
│     │
│  S  │
└─────┘
```

♠ x.x.x.
♥ A.x.
♦ A.K.Q.J.10.
♣ A.10.x.

You play in Six No Trumps against the lead of the King of Spades. Count your tricks. Eleven on top and no smell of the twelfth. So we try a squeeze. Against whom? I don't know. Maybe a double squeeze. Maybe against West if he has four Hearts and five Spades. Or if he has four Hearts and the Q.J. of Clubs. Or if he has five Clubs and the fourth Heart or the fifth Spade. Or....There are at least ten possibilities. I cannot have any idea which to pick on the first trick and I needn't guess till I've seen some discards. But one thing is clear. I cannot get a squeeze against West or East till I can win all the tricks bar one. And that's impossible till the opponents take theirs. And so you must duck to the first trick. There is no other hope for the hand.

Sometimes you have the chance of correcting the count—as in this case—given to you. Sometimes you have to find the opportunity yourself for giving up a trick. Keep an eye cocked for this. Provided you count your winners, it is simple enough.

SUICIDE SQUEEZE

You may be able to correct the count or even bring off a squeeze because the opponents cash, or are forced to take their winning tricks. If one opponent squeezes his partner it is called the suicide squeeze. Ewart Kempson, a fine player of the cards, pulled off this pleasant example of the play:

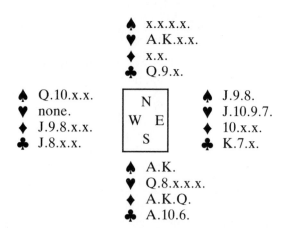

```
              ♠ x.x.x.x.
              ♥ A.K.x.x.
              ♦ x.x.
              ♣ Q.9.x.

♠ Q.10.x.x.        N        ♠ J.9.8.
♥ none.                     ♥ J.10.9.7.
♦ J.9.8.x.x.    W     E     ♦ 10.x.x.
♣ J.8.x.x.         S        ♣ K.7.x.

              ♠ A.K.
              ♥ Q.8.x.x.x.
              ♦ A.K.Q.
              ♣ A.10.6.
```

The bidding, Two Hearts—Four Hearts—Six Hearts was brisk and brusque. The opening lead was a Diamond, and a round of trumps disclosed the bad break Spades were cashed and a Spade ruffed, the extra entry to dummy being obtained by a Grand Coup (ruffing the winning Diamond). All this led to this end game:

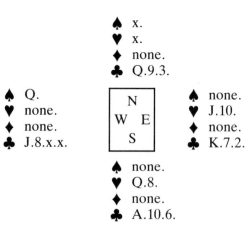

```
              ♠ x.
              ♥ x.
              ♦ none.
              ♣ Q.9.3.

♠ Q.               N        ♠ none.
♥ none.                     ♥ J.10.
♦ none.         W     E     ♦ none.
♣ J.8.x.x.         S        ♣ K.7.2.

              ♠ none.
              ♥ Q.8.
              ♦ none.
              ♣ A.10.6.
```

The Queen of Hearts was led and West could throw a Club. But on the next trick the small trump squeezed West who had to throw a second Club. North discarded a Spade (no longer needed) and now South must make all three Club tricks. The Club and Spade distribution is, of course, fortunate: on the other hand, only the 4-0 trump break puts the contract in jeopardy. A fine example of how expert technique can pull a hand, that looks lost, from the fire.

This is the last of the main variations on the squeeze theme. The added factor is that an opponent may have to keep cards to protect his partner from a finesse, and this necessity may be embarrassing if he has to find discards. If a suit falls:

A.9.x.x.

J.x.   Q.x.x.

K.10.x.x.

West cannot discard the small card for then the play of the Ace establishes a finesse through East.

The Guard squeeze is not at all well known and is difficult to recognise. It is, in fact, more difficult to diagnose than execute. These are the points to look for:

(1) A double menace which can develop into a finessing position (as in the diagram above).

(2) A one-card menace controlled (this is distinctive from other squeezes) by both opponents.

It is this last feature, of course, that starts the pressure on the West hand and forces it to yield the protective guard, or submit his partner to a simple squeeze.

A complete end position looks like this:

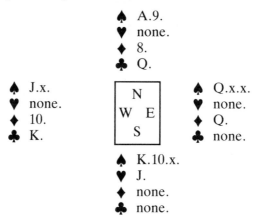

On South's lead of the Heart, West cannot discard a Spade without setting up a finesse against East. Nor can he throw the Club. So he must throw the ten of Diamonds, and when dummy discards the Club, East is caught in a simple squeeze.

We have so far discussed genuine squeezes. Many contracts are made not because the opponents are squeezed, but because they think they are. We saw earlier that an incomplete elimination might still obtain the desired result. Much the same is true of the pseudo-squeeze and although careful counting and discarding should always defeat you, it is surprising how many contracts can be stolen in this way. Be careful to prepare the hand exactly as if the squeeze was genuine:

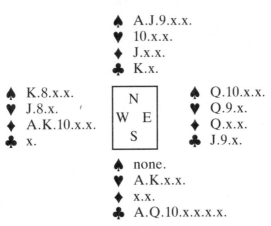

♠ A.J.9.x.x.
♥ 10.x.x.
♦ J.x.x.
♣ K.x.

♠ K.8.x.x.   ♠ Q.10.x.x.
♥ J.8.x.   ♥ Q.9.x.
♦ A.K.10.x.x. ♦ Q.x.x.
♣ x.   ♣ J.9.x.

♠ none.
♥ A.K.x.x.
♦ x.x.
♣ A.Q.10.x.x.x.x.

Three rounds of Diamonds were led against South's Five Club bid. Clearly the hand is impossible. One Heart can be thrown on the Spade Ace, but the opponents must know then that you have only Hearts left and you must go down. You have a much better chance if you ignore the Spade Ace and conceal your void. Draw trumps and cash the Ace of Hearts—a sort of pseudo Vienna Coup to set up the ten as a menace! Then run your trumps. The end game may be:

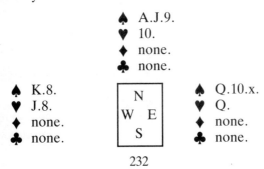

♠ A.J.9.
♥ 10.
♦ none.
♣ none.

♠ K.8.   ♠ Q.10.x.
♥ J.8.   ♥ Q.
♦ none.   ♦ none.
♣ none.   ♣ none.

Unless they are very wide awake your opponents may throw their Hearts and cling to the Spades. There is at least nothing to be lost by trying.

DEFENCE IN THE END GAME

The principles of defensive play already discussed hold good. In the end game, because the field of manoeuvre is smaller, the play, both in attack and defence, must be more accurate. A very high proportion of end plays could be defeated by early and intelligent defence.

The key to successful defence is anticipation. It is fairly easy to see what end game the declarer is striving for. When you know that he plans to throw you in, try and keep a safe exit card, and remember to unblock suit combinations so that your partner can if need be hold the trick. When he plans a trump reduction you can often defeat him simply by refusing to lead the suit that he wants to ruff, or by forcing him to use entries before he is ready. When, in either a genuine or a pseudo squeeze, declarer starts to reel off his trumps or an established suit, tell your partner at once, by your discards, which suits you can protect.

All this is negative defence, and, as you will rarely be in the lead, most defence in the end game is negative. Positive defence should take the form of an assault on declarer's entries and menace cards. A simple example follows:

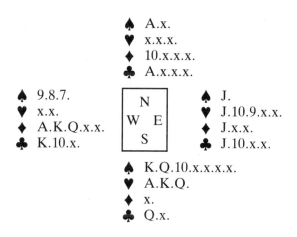

♠ A.x.
♥ x.x.x.
♦ 10.x.x.x.
♣ A.x.x.x.

♠ 9.8.7.   ♠ J.
♥ x.x.   ♥ J.10.9.x.x.
♦ A.K.Q.x.x.   ♦ J.x.x.
♣ K.10.x.   ♣ J.10.x.x.

♠ K.Q.10.x.x.x.x.
♥ A.K.Q.
♦ x.
♣ Q.x.

Against Six Spades West leads the King of Diamonds. A second

233

Diamond would be fatal because declarer by ruffing a third Diamond, could reach this simple squeeze position:

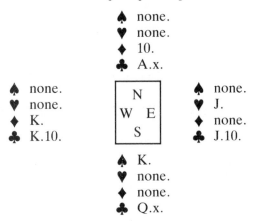

♠ none.
♥ none.
♦ 10.
♣ A.x.

♠ none.   ♠ none.
♥ none.   ♥ J.
♦ K.   ♦ none.
♣ K.10.   ♣ J.10.

♠ K.
♥ none.
♦ none.
♣ Q.x.

All West has to do at the second trick is to play a trump or a Heart and declarer's timing is upset. He cannot eliminate East's Diamonds and there can be no squeeze. This negative defence indirectly attacks the Diamond menace by interfering with the timing of the play.

Alter the hands slightly, and West must attack the entry directly:

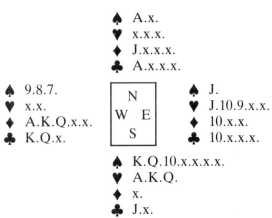

♠ A.x.
♥ x.x.x.
♦ J.x.x.x.
♣ A.x.x.x.

♠ 9.8.7.   ♠ J.
♥ x.x.   ♥ J.10.9.x.x.
♦ A.K.Q.x.x.   ♦ 10.x.x.
♣ K.Q.x.   ♣ 10.x.x.x.

♠ K.Q.10.x.x.x.x.
♥ A.K.Q.
♦ x.
♣ J.x.

Now it is essential at the second trick for West to make a direct assault on the entry by leading the King of Clubs. If he does not a squeeze at the eleventh trick is inevitable and this time East cannot come to his rescue in Diamonds.

CHAPTER XXI

IN CONCLUSION—YOUR PARTNER, *ET AL.*

YOUR partner is the most important factor in your Bridge development and success! Without the co-operation and understanding of your partner, you'll never win—or even do well. So, as soon as you've mastered the principles of the game, and you feel fairly confident and competent in play, turn your attention to your partner's thoughts. Try to work out the significance of his bids and signals. I've occasionally heard suggestions of cheating made against married couples who, being individually quite average players, get uncannily accurate results when playing together. More likely, this is the evidence of partnership understanding which you might expect between people who spend their lives together. Mental rapport is conducive to, although not essential for good understanding with your Bridge partner. The important thing is that you must both recognise that your bidding and play is for the benefit of partner; so each bid and each play you make must be with your partner in mind. Inevitably, you're going to say "That's all very well, but how do I know what partner will understand?" The simple answer is that you must learn the same language and use the same methods. I always try to put my mind into partner's head, sometimes with disastrous results, but usually with a lot of fun.

Here are a few tips for new partnerships in which there's a significant difference in age, experience and/or ability. When your partner is much older, more experienced or better than you—tell him/her what and how you play—don't be persuaded to play anything with which you're not familiar, assume that his bids and signals are as you've requested, and respond accordingly—concentrate on avoiding being wrong—don't be nervous. If you can achieve these, even in part, you're guaranteed to improve your game. When your partner is much younger, less experienced, or less competent than you—ask

235

how he/she'd like to play and adapt to that style—don't ask him to play any conventions with which he's not familiar, and might forget (unless you're specifically giving tuition)—don't make bids or signals which might be misunderstood (if in doubt, err on the side of caution)—don't expect too much of him/her—compliment him when he does well, (chastise him if he does something silly).

With a partner of similar experience and ability, you first establish the common ground in your styles and preferences, and then negotiate a compromise in any remaining areas of difference. Avoid at all costs a mixture of all your pet conventions and gimmicks with those of your partner; this almost inevitably results in complete mayhem, with each of you doing your own thing. The more artificial bits and pieces which you have in your system, the more scope there is for misunderstanding with partner.

Players wonder why the best session they have with a partner is often the first one. The reasons are simple, and psychological. Each partner is well-disciplined and ultra-attentive to what the other is doing. He's concentrating more on making the textbook bids he knows he should make, rather than allowing his imagination to run riot! But as a partnership becomes more familiar and relaxed, there's a tendency for at least one member to start reverting to his customary bad habits and idiosyncrasies, which are part of his own natural individual style. This usually leads to disaster, as partner hasn't been forewarned and is caught unawares. More significantly, the partnership starts to add numerous conventions to its bidding system, because that's popularly perceived as a sign of improvement—the converse is usually the case, for conventions are generally abused by players, who, for some reason have an urge to make artificial bids at every opportunity.

Rubber Bridge players don't suffer from this problem to any great extent, for the game has traditionally been confined mainly to the use of totally natural methods, and one is able to concentrate on the skills of card play.

However, tournament Bridge has created a new breed of player, who has become "gadget" crazy. Not content with the versatility which Acol offers in its natural form, the true "gadgeteer" will want to give an artificial meaning to as many bids as possible. Such exotic names as Multi-Coloured Two Diamonds,

Tartan Twos, Sputnik, Ripstra, Gladiator, Fishbein, and a host of others have become commonplace on the tournament player's convention card. The balance of artificiality often far outweighs the element of naturality about the system, so perhaps it's time to have a Government health warning printed on convention cards "Artificiality can damage your game"! Conventions are used either to give, or ask for specific information; they don't have the same flexibility as do the natural Acol system bids, and therefore can only be used in a very limited number of situations. Every convention which you adopt means that you're converting the natural meaning of bids into artificial. As the same bids can't be used in the dual role of both natural and artificial, you have to decide in which context it has most value. There are a few 'spare' bids in Acol, which can be harmlessly assigned to conventional use; the most obvious of these is the jump response to the four-level in a minor suit after partner has opened in a major suit at the one-level. Clearly, there's no logic in wasting two rounds of bidding space—and by-passing Three No Trumps—to show a minor suit naturally, however good the suit might be. Therefore, the bids of Four Clubs and Four Diamonds over One Spade or One Heart are generally used conventionally to agree the major suit as trumps and show controls. This is known as the Swiss Convention and there are several variations of it according to what values you want to ascribe to each bid. Most conventions have variations, so, with a strange partner, you certainly don't want to introduce anything into your system which isn't well-understood by both you and partner.

The message to all new partnerships is clear—keep it simple, and as natural as possible; try to avoid being wrong, and study partner's style.

If, after your first outing with a new partner, you feel there's an empathy and compatibility of approaches to the game, you should play a few more times together. Your chances of improving are much greater with the same partner, than with a variety of 'strangers'—provided you treat each session constructively. Bridge players are usually interested in talking about their successes and their partner's mistakes for hours after the event, so you should have no problem in finding a partner who'll be happy to spend time discussing the things you each get wrong. At social rubber Bridge this can often be done between the deals, but at duplicate, it's best to make a note on your score card of the hands to be looked at and go through them quickly at the end. If you're both inexperienced, and can't remember the hands, or what went wrong, there's always a willing "expert" nearby to offer guidance and demonstrate his wisdom. "Post-mortems" are very helpful in the improvement of your game, so long as they're constructive, and not recriminatory. Looking at your cards again some time after you've played them is an excellent way of developing your card memory, and it's also easier to examine bids and plays which the partnership got wrong. Situations do repeat themselves in Bridge, and progressively you'll find that you start to recognise them, and, from recalling the previous post-mortem, you'll do the right thing next time round. This process of discussion and analysis will inevitably lead to a growth of confidence with partner, and a partnership style will start to emerge. More especially, you'll be able to practise the skills which aren't generally taught in Bridge class: card signalling in defence, protective bidding, and penalty/competitive doubles.

Note that I've excluded mention of conventions from the practice list deliberately, for the use of conventions isn't a skill; more often than not, it's an obstacle to skill's development. You'll find that conventions have a nasty habit of creeping unobtrusively into your system, and you must suppress the temptation to adopt more than the basic ones, before you've understood how they can help you.

If, while still a relative beginner, you get lured into playing competitions prematurely, you'll be confronted by a convention card, which requires completion to describe your basic method of bidding and play. Leave this as blank as possible—ideally, state only that you play Acol and give the point range of your No Trump bids, possibly adding the two simple conventions of Stayman and Blackwood. Recently I came across a young pair who'd been playing Bridge for less than two years, yet their convention card was smothered with every conceivable piece of gadgetry. When asked why they were being so foolhardy, they replied that this intimidated the opponents, who didn't know how to compete against their artificial bidding, and often did the wrong thing, giving them good results. It's hard to blame them for this attitude when they see international teams using similar tactics.

However, I'm unreserved in condemning any bidding methods

which aren't comprehensible to the opponents, and for which the opponents haven't had adequate opportunity to plan a defence. Not only is this practice unethical but it's now illegal in tournament play. Success by foul means is certainly a hollow and immoral victory.

The full enjoyment of Bridge comes from the satisfaction of being able to communicate successfully with your partner. If you can't communicate with a partner, you're virtually playing against three people—and you'll never win at this game on your own. Bridge partnerships are rather like marriages—you have to work at them, but the rewards are very worthwhile. Good luck!

SUMMARY OF THE ACOL SYSTEM

GENERAL

THE Acol System has two main objectives:

1. To make bidding easy for your partners.
2. To make bidding difficult for your opponents.

It is based on Approach Forcing, but with several system bids peculiar to itself. It believes in light opening bids, light informatory doubles and in natural bidding whenever possible. It treats all big hands as separate problems and—if necessary—improvises a bidding sequence to interpret them. The Milton Work count (Ace–4, King–3, Queen–2, Jack–1) is used. In No Trumps a ten may be counted as ½ point.

OPENING BIDS OF ONE OF A SUIT

If there is a probable game even if partner cannot reply to a bid of one, then you must open with a stronger bid. The lower limit, except for freak holdings, is covered by these general requirements:

1. Always bid with fourteen points.
2. Always bid with thirteen points unless your shape is 4–3–3–3 and you are vulnerable. A pass here is optional.
3. Always bid on twelve points with a fair five-card suit.
4. Always bid on eleven, and usually on ten, if you have one six-card or two five-card suits.

Below ten points only freak holdings qualify. *When in doubt—bid.*

Open: 1NT Weak 12–14 or 13-15.
                1NT Strong 15–17 or 16–18.
                2NT at all scores 20–22.
                3NT at all scores? (7–8 playing tricks).
                4NT at all scores? (Conventional demand for
                    Aces.)

Raise: 1NT Weak to 2NT 11–12.
                1NT Weak to 3NT 13–15.
                1NT Strong to 2NT 8.
                1NT Strong to 3NT 10.
                2NT to 3NT 4–5.

Rebid: Opener raises Weak 2NT raise to 3NT on 14.
                Opener raises Strong 2NT raise to 3NT on 17.

Slam Zone: The small Slam zone is around 34. Grand Slam 38.

RESPONDING TO A BID OF ONE OF A SUIT

Range for a One No Trump response is 5½–9½. If the opening bid was One Club the response shows 8–9½. One-over-one response normally not more than 16 and may be as low as 5 or even less. Two No Trump response 11–12½, and Three No Trump 13–15.

LIMIT BIDS

All raises of partner's suit, to whatever level, are limit bids and are non-forcing, i.e. One Heart—Two Hearts, One Spade—Three Spades etc. Similarly, all rebids of the suit opened are non-forcing, i.e. One Diamond—One Heart—Two Diamonds, One Heart—One Spade—Four Hearts.

All No Trump bids are limit bids.

REVERSE BIDS

A rebid in a second suit, which forces partner to bid a level higher in order to give preference to the first bid suit, is forcing for one round, i.e. One Diamond—One Spade—Two Hearts, or One Heart—Two Diamonds—Three Clubs.

NO TRUMP REBIDS

Rebid to Two No Trump after one-over-one suit response or response of One No Trump shows 17-18½.

Rebid to Three No Trump after one-over-one suit response or response of One No Trump shows 19.

If the response to your opening bid is at the two-level these point counts can be shaded by about 1½ points.

TRIAL BIDS

Once the suit is agreed all other suit bids are forcing for one round.

TWO CLUB OPENING

Game forcing except for the sequence:

2♣	—	2♦	—
2NT	—	—	—

which shows 22½–24. Partner raises on three points.

Two Club opening shows five high card tricks. Negative response is Two Diamonds unless partner holds:

An Ace and a King, or
K.Q. and two Kings, or
Two K.Q.s, or
Four Kings, or
One K.Q. and one King if either heads a six or a strong five-card suit.

With no biddable suit, but one of these holdings, respond Two No Trumps.

JUMP REBID

A jump rebid whenever a forcing situation exists shows a solid suit.

ACOL TWO BID

The Bid of Two of a suit (except Clubs) is forcing for one round. The negative response is Two No Trump. The opening bid shows eight playing tricks and the responses are at partner's discretion. As a rule you should make the same response at the appropriate level that you would have made to a bid of one (i.e. if you would have bid One Spade over One Heart, then bid Two Spades over Two Hearts). The response of Three No Trumps is a slam try, and the double raise shows a good hand, but without first round controls.

BLACKWOOD CONVENTION

Four No Trumps, bid after the trump suit has been agreed, asks for Aces on the following scale:

0 or 4—5 ♣
1   —5 ♦
2   —5 ♥
3   —5 ♠

Five No Trumps after Four No Trumps asks for Kings on the same scale, except that with all four Kings, the response is Six No Trumps, NOT Six Clubs.

If responder to Four No Trumps holds a 'working' void, he shows aces at the six-level.

4/5 NO TRUMP CONVENTION

Acol used this convention in preference to Blackwood, in the early days of the system, but it is now only rarely used by established partnerships, despite its considerable merit.

Conventional bid of Four No Trumps shows: Three Aces or Two Aces and the King of a bid suit.

Conventional bid of Five No Trumps (preceded by Four No Trumps) shows: Four Aces between the two hands.

Conventional bid of Five No Trumps (not preceded by Four No Trumps) shows: Three Aces and the King of a bid suit.

Five No Trumps response shows: Two Aces or One Ace and ALL the Kings of suits bid.

If not holding one of these requirements, responder may either:

(*a*) Sign off in lowest suit bid, or

(*b*) Cue bid an Ace or a void, or

(*c*) Encourage by bidding a suit (not the sign off suit) at the five level, or

(*d*) Bid a direct slam.

THE ODDS IN PLAY

TABLE I

Distribution Odds

You and Dummy hold in any suit	Division of Remainder	Percentage Frequency
Five Cards	5–3	47
	4–4	33
	6–2	17
	7–1	3
	8–0	2
Six Cards	4–3	62
	5–2	31
	6–1	7
	7–0	5
Seven Cards	4–2	48
	3–3	36
	5–1	15
	6–0	1
Eight Cards	3–2	68
	4–1	28
	5–0	4
Nine Cards	3–1	50
	2–2	40
	4–0	10
Ten Cards	2–1	78
	3–0	22
Eleven Cards	1–1	52
	2–0	48

TABLE II

Hand Patterns

There are thirty-nine hand patterns. These are the commonest.

				per cent
1.	4–4–3–2	...	...	22
2.	5–3–3–2	...	...	16
3.	5–4–3–1	...	...	13
4.	5–4–2–2	...	...	11
5.	4–3–3–3	...	...	10
6.	6–3–2–2	...	...	6
7.	6–4–2–1	...	...	5
8.	4–4–4–1	...	...	3
9.	5–5–2–1	...	...	3
10.	6–3–3–1	...	...	3
11.	7–3–2–1	...	...	2
12.	5–4–4–0	...	...	1
13.	5–5–3–0	...	...	1
14.	6–4–3–0	...	...	1

All others total 3 per cent.